P9-CNB-795

STREET
WITH
NO
NAME

STREET WITH NO NAME

A History of the Classic American Film Noir

Andrew Dickos

THE UNIVERSITY PRESS OF KENTUCKY

791. 43655 D561s
Dickos, Andrew, 1952-
Street with no name : a
history of the classic

Publication of this volume was made possible in part
by a grant from the National Endowment for the Humanities.

Copyright © 2002 by The University Press of Kentucky

Scholarly publisher for the Commonwealth,
serving Bellarmine University, Berea College, Centre
College of Kentucky, Eastern Kentucky University,
The Filson Historical Society, Georgetown College,
Kentucky Historical Society, Kentucky State University,
Morehead State University, Murray State University,
Northern Kentucky University, Transylvania University,
University of Kentucky, University of Louisville,
and Western Kentucky University.
All rights reserved.

Editorial and Sales Offices: The University Press of Kentucky
663 South Limestone Street, Lexington, Kentucky 40508-4008

06 05 04 03 02   5 4 3 2 1

Frontispiece: *Force of Evil* (1948).
Joe Morse (John Garfield): a fugitive from himself.

Library of Congress Cataloging-in-Publication Data

Dickos, Andrew, 1952-
    Street with no name : a history of the classic American film noir /
Andrew Dickos.
      p. cm.
    Includes bibliographical references and index.
    ISBN 0-8131-2243-0 (alk. paper)
    1. Film noir--United States--History and criticism.
    I. Title.
    PN1995.9.F54 D53 2002
    791.43'655--dc   212001007224

This book is printed on acid-free recycled paper meeting
the requirements of the American National Standard
for Permanence in Paper for Printed Library Materials.

♾ ⊛

Manufactured in the United States of America.

3 4015 06846 3098

To JoAnn
and to my sister, Anne
who must surely remember the times
we got ready for bed by preparing to watch
His Girl Friday on the late show

CONTENTS

PREFACE

Attempting to write a history of the film noir provokes two questions. First, what does one mean by chronicling a loose number of films considered films noirs; that is, What is the film noir? What makes a film noir? And which films best serve to illustrate film noir? Second, how can one offer a historical perspective, and of what kind, to such an amorphous "cycle" of films. It is hardly a neat package for historical organization, and therein lies the folly of undertaking an account of such movies that have had a significant and compelling influence on postwar cinema. Consequently, this history of a number of films considered on many counts to be noir is digressive in form, free-ranging in scope, and, through the combination of these strategies, specific and illuminating, I hope, in reaching an essential understanding of the film noir.

I discuss the subject in terms of its roots in the classical German cinema of the period following World War I, its genesis in the French cinema preceding World War II, and its flourishing in the American cinema since. The discussion touches upon film history in terms of nations and national artists, film industry developments, and sociopolitical changes. It also envelops the noir in philosophical and aesthetic concerns and their connections to film as it reflects the changing world perceived by its audiences. I also seek to discern the distinctiveness of the film noir and its motifs through the styles of its key artists in the first four decades of its existence in this country. It has been argued that, like other kinds of films, the film noir has certain narrative and structural requirements and a distinctive iconography. This is truest to the extent that these merge with the filmmaker's personal vision of the noir's bleak world.

In this historical framework, the film noir is viewed for the potent force it has become in the evolution of cinematic style. But what, then, is it? Is it a style? The expression through which a mood or temperament is revealed? And what of generic conventions? What makes the noir such argumentative fodder for those wishing to define or distress it as a genre proper? Here some basic definitions and descriptions are necessary in order to discuss the film noir in a comprehensible historical context.

The film noir as I have approached it is a group or collection of films that were first made in about 1940 (1938 in France) and continue to be produced in the present. (The hesitation in calling these films a cycle lies in the implication of ending, of finality, of the cycle's having been "exhausted.") The year 1940 serves as an index for a climate of change in the tone of many melodrama films in America because of the sociocultural changes in American and European society, the ominous politico-historical wind of the time, and the formal developments in film present at the advent of World War II. Although the innovations of Orson Welles's *Citizen Kane* were not yet marveled over, the gradual if not particularly anticipated change in the perception of what narrative Hollywood cinema could offer in its depiction of human problems, their ambiguities, and the social landscape from which they emanated nonetheless provided trail markers of what was to follow. The Carné-Prévert *Quai des brumes* (1938) and *Le Jour se lève* (1939) and Carné's *Hôtel du Nord* (1939), for example, were potent enough indications on the international film scene to parallel, for another example, Raoul Walsh's 1941 *High Sierra*. That film was scripted by John Huston and starred Humphrey Bogart in a decidedly more complex variation of the gangster film, where the ambiguous tone lies in contradistinction to Walsh's own *Roaring Twenties,* made two years earlier.

The year 1940, fraught with anxiety despite an isolationist policy, was a ferment of artistic change in Hollywood that would see a fine rupture develop into a chasm between what industry entertainment had offered before and what it would soon offer in the future. Those who joined the émigré movement, which was nurtured on the disillusionment of a crumbling European society, left the tyranny replacing an Old World they knew but never created and came to Hollywood. As products, too, of the artistic developments of the interwar years (modernism, in its broadest appeal), particularly the expressionist movement in Germany, German and Viennese filmmakers such as Fritz Lang, Robert Siodmak, Otto Preminger, Billy Wilder, Edgar G. Ulmer, and William Dieterle brought to a new environment lifetimes of cultural experience. To the coast of southern California they carried a philosophical worldview, ironic and bleak with the possibility both of a redemptive universe and of a place where people succumb to their weaknesses and passions; they contributed to the American screen in the guise of popular entertainment a necessary maturity, the next phase of its growth.

When Welles made *Citizen Kane* and John Huston made *The Maltese Falcon* in 1941, the American cinema could no longer ignore the schism that had been created. Screen melodrama would now, however unconsciously and unperturbingly, evoke elements of unexpectedness and intrigue that it had not aroused in the past. Characters were insinuatingly more complex, mirroring a society not always just despite the story's happy ending. What Charles Foster Kane and private eye Sam Spade have in common above all is that they are not happy men and that knowledge of the world ensures not harmony but elusiveness and uncertainty. Kane dies without the satisfaction of a precise meaning for his life, and Spade turns over a duplicitous Brigid O'Shaughnessy to the cops despite his feeling for her because it enforces his code of honor. But he does not forget that there are other Miss O'Shaughnessys out there. Throughout the 1940s and 1950s, the American screen was riddled with this dark alter-side of American life. Random movie titles evoke countless variations of a despairing and haunted universe, often of fatalistic design: *Where the Sidewalk Ends*; *The Asphalt Jungle*; *The Street with No Name*; *The Big Heat*; *The Big Sleep*; *Act of Violence*; *Force of Evil*; *Touch of Evil*; *Desperate*; *Detour*; *Caught*; *Railroaded!*; *The Set-Up*; *Kiss Me Deadly*; *Murder, My Sweet*; *Fallen Angel*; *On Dangerous Ground*; and *In a Lonely Place*.[1] The directors of these films and their literary counterparts—Dashiell Hammett, Raymond Chandler, Cornell Woolrich, James M. Cain, and Jim Thompson, among others—fashioned this noir landscape in the city and peopled it with troubled and desperate characters whose passions and obsessions drive them to upset a precarious moral ground. It is fitting, then, to begin a definition of the film noir by recognizing the city.

Urban America, as a panorama of the anonymous, emerges as a moody set piece of human anxiety. Most often depicted at night and often in the rain, the city is where human motivations find action, where people betray, lie to, and hurt others, where their passions are activated. Films noirs have been set outside the city, but they invariably require an urban influence either through refugees that attempt, unsuccessfully, to find solace in the country (Anthony Mann's *Desperate*, Nicholas Ray's *They Live by Night*) or in the damaged lives that have gone there to be nourished by rural peacefulness (Ray's *On Dangerous Ground*). Of course, a small town can function as well as a city, but it must have those social and legal-political institutions that urban civilization has bequeathed us, for it is in the encounter with these corrupted institutions in one's pursuit of a derailed American Dream that the film noir displays its greatest vigor. The happiness promised in the daylight normality of home and wholly integrated personal and social relationships runs awry in the face of human weakness and desire. The institutions of the law, the sanctity of marriage and family founding, and the zeal to overcome personal economic distress through ingenuity and hard work fail. The psychic variables of the human condition intrude all too often in the noir world to make these features of American life little more than a cruel deceit. It is, then, a characteristic of the film noir that life is seen through the eyes of the city and its shrewd and often broken denizens.

Who are these people, though, and what has shaped them? Who best represents them? In the American noirs (and to some extent in the French, too), the characters most clearly illustrating the influences of this urban landscape are involved with crime and the law, usually law enforcement. The private detective and the police detective have acquired the stature of phlegmatic heroes because of their ability to move in all circles of urban society: institutional and criminal, "respectable" (of seemingly unimpeachable wealth and social status) and disreputable (often by implication, as through nightclubs and casinos, the numbers racket, horse racing, organized crime in various forms, and other illicit personal enterprises). The symbiosis between them and their adversaries and sometime alter egos—the racketeers, club owners, grifters, and extortionists—contains the basic dramatic tensions in greed, intimidation, submission and betrayal, fear and violence. And the supporting types include petty chiselers, cops on the take, boxing promoters, lounge singers, stoolies, gunsels, molls, and an assortment of down-and-outers. The detective's mobility exposes him to such characters, and it has hardened his vision in the cynical, all-too-knowing sense that he accepts how little human behavior can be trusted, how easily betrayal occurs, and how illusory the truth is.

All this indeed sounds enrapt in the romantic nihilism that the patina of time has given the noir. It is perhaps its most compelling legacy that the movies in their magical connection to our lives have shown these features of the human condition with a seductive, modern allure, a tawdry glamour at once mesmerizing and disturbing. The handiest representatives of the noir hunters and hunted—Bogart, Robert Mitchum, John Garfield, Barbara Stanwyck, Robert Ryan, Gloria Grahame, Burt Lancaster, Richard Conte, Claire Trevor, Kirk Douglas, Richard Widmark, Joan Crawford, Dick Powell, Lizabeth Scott, Dan Duryea, Ida Lupino, and Sterling Hayden, among so many others—all invested their roles with the existential idiom of the noir city.

Equally important are the passionate natures so often igniting criminal acts by the characters of noir drama: Stanwyck and Fred MacMurray in *Double Indemnity*; Mitchum, Douglas, and Jane Greer in *Out of the Past*; Farley Granger and Cathy O'Donnell in *They Live by Night* and *Side Street*; John Dall and Peggy Cummins in *Gun Crazy*; and Joan Crawford and Ann Blyth in *Mildred Pierce*. Their crimes result from sexual and love drives too single-minded or selfish to satisfy socially sanctioned prescriptions for shared happiness; in their desperation these characters go too far and pay a price for it. Such men and women caught in their obsessions acquire a rebelliousness and individualism of spirit in a doomful atmosphere. For the men, breaking the law or getting caught in the injustices of it often provokes the psychotic appearance of running. Running away from danger, from entrapment by the authorities or one's own enemies, brings the noir man into the even greater entrapment of a dark moral tangle from which the only escape is often suicide before the otherwise inevitable end of being killed. "I did something wrong, once," answers a doomed Ole in Robert Siodmak's *Killers*. For this vague but unforgivable transgression we know he must die. Bowie must pay an equally harsh price for his criminal complicity in *They Live by Night*. Dix Handley cannot have his gentle horses but instead must die in the grass at their feet in John Huston's *Asphalt Jungle*. And John Garfield's Nick Robey "runs all the way" to his death in the gutter—a bit of grim poetry in this, Garfield's last film (*He Ran All the Way*). This rebellion marks the impossible division between freedom and entrapment as it reminds us that one cannot truly be defined without the other and that each is the incomplete part of the existential equation befitting the noir world.

The noir women, in contrast, have often been doomed to live because of their intelligence and individualism. Barbara Stanwyck wants money, sex, and quite possibly love, but she has given Fred MacMurray little apparent reason to trust her style in *Double Indemnity*; nor can Wendell Corey trust her in *The File on Thelma Jordon*, nor Robert Ryan in *Clash by Night*. If misogyny appears the order of the day in the treatment of many noir women, then it is also true that the ordinarily available option of hearth and home unavailable to so many of them exacts a price in sacrifice and madness. The noir woman is rarely a bedrock of domestic virtue, but the alternative role as *femme fatale* has also been overemphasized. The Joan Crawfords, Gloria Grahames, Rita Hayworths, and, above all, Barbara Stanwycks have joined the ranks of women with the psychic force of Hedda Gabler, striking out against the fate of their conventional social roles. In a notably cruel irony of this, Joan Crawford, who sacrifices all for her daughters in *Mildred Pierce* and for her husband in *Flamingo Road*, is not punished for her efforts so much as for the direct *manner* of their execution. The tragic consequence can also come in the *femme fatale*'s penitent conversion. It is not enough to be disfigured with scaldingly hot coffee; Gloria Grahame's Debbie Marsh must also take the bullet for Glenn Ford in Fritz Lang's *Big Heat*. As he cradles her in his arms, the mink-coated vestige of her past gently soothes her burned, scarred face. It is the poetry of stark violence, one that can be mitigated only by her death.

In the end the lives of these people come to represent that exciting and often fearful image of the darker recesses of human nature unleashed and unappeased in definition of an American culture at odds with its most optimistic illusions. The two confront each other to produce the anxiety we often face in modern life and see displayed in noir cinema. "[N]ow trembling and creative, now panicky and destructive," wrote the philosopher-critic William Barrett, "always it is as inseparable from ourselves as our own breathing because anxiety is our existence itself in its radical insecurity."[2]

This writing project would have been immensely more difficult had it not been for the help of several kind and generous friends. I am grateful to Robert Kalish, Ira Hozinsky, and the late William Everson for making so many films materialize for my viewing needs. Damien Bona has been a friend in the many kindnesses he extended me, and George Robinson has my gratitude for sharing his library of books and films and the erudition of his conversation. I also thank Marva Nabili and Thomas Fucci for their encouragement over the years; Hannah Low, who indulged my peculiar errors in French conversation over as many years while graciously correcting them with good humor; and Geraldine Youcha, who always inquired with interest and sympathy about the progress of the manuscript. JoAnn Crawford, whose support and perspective saw this writer through some of the more difficult moments of this project, has my particular gratitude and affection.

I am indebted to Charles Silver of the Film Studies Center at the Museum of Modern Art for providing its facilities and his service in the projection of several films. I am also indebted to Mary Corliss and Terry Geeskin of the Film Stills Archive at MOMA, to the staffs of the Cinémathèque Française in Paris and the Cinémathèque Royale de Bruxelles for their research assistance, and, not least of all, to the staff of the Billy Rose Theatre Collection of the New York Public Library for the Performing Arts, Astor, Lenox, and Tilden Foundations, for their constant availability and help.

All film stills used are with the permission of the Film Stills Archive/Museum of Modern Art in New York City.

I must acknowledge the thoughtful and accommodating treatment I received from Lois Crum, my copy editor, and Kenneth Cherry, who, as director of the University Press, displayed the equipoise of an astute businessman and of a publisher that never relinquished his taste or his sensitivity to the writer's voice. May he paint many beautiful paintings in his retirement.

This book is by no means complete; most of the films discussed here are, above all, those that fueled my imagination of a noir world over the years and that resonated beyond their running times to hold me in thrall of a cinema whose vibrancy still excites. These films, and many others, still speak to us in the manner of passionate replies to the dark nature they exhibit. If this book does nothing more than provoke a consideration of them, and of those omitted, then their legacy remains vital, trapped, as it were, in that pocket of consciousness that perpetually connects movies to our lives.

INTRODUCTION

To Name the Thing—Film Noir as Style, as Genre

The persistent questions in most theoretical discussions of the film noir are what makes a film a film noir and whether such films can be considered to constitute a genre, an entity that possesses a language of iconography and conventions, or whether they instead merely display a certain cinematic style, intergeneric and substantially the product of film technique that augments screen narrative. To answer these questions, perhaps consideration of what a screen genre is and is perceived to be will help; it may illuminate not only the fundamental recognitions we make of genres but also the cultural meaning we attach to their identifications and conventions.

Thomas Sobchack observed that "the subject matter of a genre film is a story. It is not something that matters outside the film, even if it inadvertently tells us something about the time and place of its creation. Its sole justification for existence is to make concrete and perceivable the configuration inherent in its ideal form. That the various genres have changed, gone through cycles of popularity, does not alter the fact that the basic underlying coordinates of a genre are maintained time after time."[1] With this classical, literary definition, the film noir may be challenged as a group of films that, though identifiable in *look* (lighting, nighttime urban settings) and *iconography* (seedy hotels, cars, lounges, cigarette lighters, smartly dressed *femmes fatales,* etc.), resists the appeal "to make concrete and perceivable the configuration inherent in its ideal form," for there is no ideal form upheld in this modern group of commercial films. There are stories analogous to the myths of classical Greek drama, but this is not peculiar to the noir; comedies and westerns have appealed to this dramatic heritage—so often, as a matter of course, that an Oedipal, Medean, or Hamlet-like protagonist or story scarcely redefines its recognizable genre associations. Sobchack further notes: "There is little room in the genre film for ambiguity anywhere—in characters, plots, or iconography. But even when seeming ambiguities arise in the course of a film, they must be either de-emphasized or taken care of by the end of the film" (199). By this continued definition, the film noir can hardly qualify as a genre, since, at its finest and with recognizable characters and iconography, it is rarely without ambiguity.

I bring Sobchack's definition of a screen genre to the forefront of my discussion of genre and its application to the film noir because it is an important touchstone for any critical evaluation of and divergence from the issues raised in its wake. In response to such a definition, film critics have described the film noir as a deflection from genre or, more interestingly, as an emanation from it. Raymond Durgnat wrote: "*Film noir* is sometimes called a genre, but it's a moot point whether it's normally used for a perennial mood (a gloomy cynicism), or restricted to a particular historical epoch (around the Forties); whether it's a certain kind of thriller, or whether it includes Westerns, domestic dramas, and normally unclassified films (*Citizen Kane*). Thus *noir* could signify an attitude, or a cycle, or a subgenre, or a tonality."[2] John Whitney concluded that the subject matter of the noir "took the private detective film, the gangster film, the police film, middle class melodramas, and films about boxing and prisons, all of which were established genres in their own rights, and absorbed large portions of them."[3] And Alfred Appel contended that "because the *film noir* is not a genre, its properties cannot be defined as readily or exactly as those of, say, the Western. It is a kind of Hollywood film peculiar to the Forties and early Fifties, a genus in the gangster film/thriller family. The taxonomic tag first introduced by French *cinéastes* of the Fifties is appropriately imprecise—*film noir* is a matter of manner, of mood, tone, and style—though its cultural attitudes are concrete enough, its psychological appeal quite direct."[4]

What Durgnat and Appel speak of is a kind of film recognizable from types of screen stories, those belonging in various genres and subgenres, peculiar in style and standing apart from, although perhaps alongside, familiar genre narratives. Whitney simply acknowledges that film noir is a generic amalgam of established independent genres. These partial descriptions have one common point of departure: each recognizes the film noir *in relation or juxtaposition to* other kinds of film stories. The point is worth noting because it highlights the dilemma of how film noir is perceived: not as a subset of any given genre, the noir here becomes a screen entity of parasitic definition, dependent upon those very taxonomic standards that may seek to subsume its expression but cannot quite do so. It is that problematic space between "kind" of film recognized and the constituent qualities of structural style that make this particular film recognizable as something other, or more, than its "kind." Robert Porfirio clarifies the issue when he observes that "much of the trouble plaguing scholars attempting to deal with the *film noir* as a genre stems from the fact that it stands somewhere between a historical and a theoretical genre."[5]

Tzvetan Todorov noted that genres as entities "can be described from two different viewpoints, that of empirical observation and that of abstract analysis. In a given society, the recurrence of certain discursive properties is institutionalized, and individual texts are produced and perceived in relation to the norm constituted by that codification. A genre, whether literary or not, is nothing other than the codification of discursive properties."[6] Because the film noir speaks to us in certain patterns of visual narration and, through them, establishes a bleak mood that defines the melodramatic conventions of story and character in peculiar recurrence to their time (mostly, the 1940s and 1950s) and place (Hollywood's representation of modern urban America), we come to recognize such a cinema as a discrete area of investigation. René Wellek and Austin Warren conceived of genres as having both "outer form (specific metre or structure) and . . . inner form (attitude, tone, purpose—more crudely, subject and audience)" and saw the critical project in finding the two.[7] The task is similar to Todorov's necessity to combine the constituent "historical reality" (the trend, movement, school, of a body of work) with the constituent "discursive reality" (modes, registers, forms, manners, styles).[8] And in discussing literary studies—which for our purposes crosses over into the narrative concerns of genre cinema—he concludes, "Genres are the meeting place between general poetics and event-based literary history; as such, they constitute a privileged object that may well deserve to be the principal figure in literary studies" (pp. 19–20).

But film noir as a staple of postwar commercial American cinema developed according to aesthetic and financial influences that often compromised each other with the kind of overtness rarely recognized in the production of genre pieces in the other arts. "Genres communicate indi-

rectly with the society where they are operative through their institu-
tionalization," Todorov continued. This applies well to the culture of
Hollywood as well as to American society as a whole. And, "like any
other institution, genres bring to light the constitutive features of the
society to which they belong."[9] Hence, in this sense and as a product of
commercial American filmmaking, screen genres emerge as "sets of
cultural conventions" that, according to Andrew Tudor, "seem best immediately employed in the analysis of the relation between groups of
films, the cultures in which they are made, and the cultures in which
they are exhibited."[10]

Because of the film noir's palpably felt and expressed philosophical dimensions and the discursive methods that give them narrative shape,
what emerges is the fusion of myth—a very modern myth of alienation
and obsession—with an essential style inextricable from its representation. The dilemma of how noir cinema should best be categorized has
most often hedged toward its being named, however unspokenly, a genre.
But it has been the ineffability of its psycho-philosophical stance as a
modern experience, with the corresponding formal depiction of bleak
mood; the hardened and nihilistic attitudes of its characters, with their
often obsessive drives; and an aura of hopelessness and doom that enve-
lopes their lives, that has given hesitation here. (Classical literary and
other film genres hardly serve to illustrate this dilemma well.) Yet one
has always known which films are significantly noir, albeit not without
occasional qualification: the popular references have rarely been de-
bated. What the film noir has done is to structure this stance as the peculiar and defining structure of its otherwise traditional melodrama (or, in
rare cases, tragedy) storytelling. The question that emerges then is, Why
must we resist recognizing the development of a *kind* of film during
World War II that later increasingly embodied in its narrative concerns
the disruptive, dark forces that drive and deplete modern urban man?
The growth of such a cinema cannot be regarded only as a historical
development, although it surely is that. Rather, it must be seen as a specific aesthetic response to the way we have come to see our human condition, shaped by the world and the movies expressing it.

Therefore, in considering the film noir to be a body of work conforming
to generic standards, we may apply the historical dimension to its creation. Porfirio recognized four stages in its development, from its "early
period of 'experimentation' (1940–43)," to "the 'studio-bound' period

of the 'private eye' (1944–47)," to "the 'location' period of the semi-documentary and social problem film (1947–52)" and on to its "final period of fragmentation and decay (1952–60)."[11] Porfirio here recognizes the noir as a movement. However, in a different perception of the film noir—as a genre—and with much qualification, this course of progression is still largely, but by no means completely, correct, and it serves to recognize some of the historical influences that shaped the film noir in wartime and postwar America. The first recognition of a noir cinema must inevitably be the stylistic distinctiveness that transformed the conventions of the crime and private eye dramas into those peculiar to the noir. Raymond Borde and Étienne Chaumeton saw this back in 1955 when they wrote in their landmark book on the American film noir: "In its most typical works, the *film noir* tried to give rise to a 'new thrill,' indivisible and inimitable. It juxtaposed certain themes within the framework of a particular technique: unusual plots, eroticism, violence, psychological ambivalence within criminal parties. It is the convergence of these dramatic particulars, some of which are not new, that created a style."[12] This is, of course, largely the case, but it is only partly true in that Borde and Chaumeton did not fully recognize the ramifications of a technique that finally transformed a style into a new narrative expression.

The visual style of noir cinema is the first and most obvious point of departure toward that end, since the influence of the Golden Age of German cinema in the 1920s and early 1930s crossed the Atlantic in the directorial sensibility of several of its émigré practitioners (Lang, Siodmak, Dieterle, etc.). As in the German expressionist and *kammerspiele* cinema, low-key lighting, with the effective contrast of chiaroscuro to delineate the shadows of people, buildings, and cityscapes, predominates.[13] In such exterior settings, the lighting design often shows distorted, outsized shadows, menacing and paranoiac in the mind of those sought or hunted. Oblique and vertical lines capture buildings, lampposts, and alleyways in similar distortion. The lighting of interiors shows the same scaled-down pattern, but revealing entrapment over pursuit. Venetian blind slats, hallway and other room lights left on in the dark, and shafts of light shooting inside windows from blinking or partially broken neon signs form a looming and palpable geometric design of psychic imprisonment and terror. Low-angle and, to a lesser extent, high-angle shots in this context are more common in the film noir than in any other genre except the science fiction film. As Paul Schrader noted, "the typical *film noir* would rather move the scene cinematographically around the actor than have the actor control the scene by physical action."[14] In the most evocative films noirs, nothing could be truer.

The visual style of noir narrative structure is a recurrent theme throughout the development of the genre and in the particular expressiveness it attains in the hands of notable noir filmmakers, usually in collaboration with their cameramen. (One thinks here of Otto Preminger and Joseph La Shelle, Anthony Mann and John Alton, Robert Siodmak and Woody Bredell, and Robert Aldrich and Joseph Biroc, among others.) Accordingly, this style is discussed throughout the book. The other structural elements of noir narrative that are considered in this book and that established its genre status include

- An urban setting or at least an urban influence. This setting, according to noir convention, is captured mostly at night and often just after rain.
- A modern, twentieth-century setting, from the Great Depression on, and usually of the 1940s, 1950s, or early 1960s, with latitude permitting its extension to the present day.
- A lack of comic structure, although the film noir may have comic elements (Dassin's *Rififi*) and often has humor (*The Big Sleep*). There can be no true noir comedy as there is a western comedy or a war comedy. (Frank Capra's *Arsenic and Old Lace*, George Marshall's *Murder, He Says*, and Preston Sturges's wonderful *comédie noire, Unfaithfully Yours*, function as black comedies, a distinct variation of comedy.) Two directors often considered to have made films noirs, Alfred Hitchcock (*Shadow of a Doubt, Strangers on a Train, I Confess, The Wrong Man*, and perhaps *Rear Window*) and Billy Wilder (*Double Indemnity, Sunset Boulevard, Ace in the Hole*) are problematic cases because their visions are steeped in cruel and corrosive humor, distinctive in its own right and in its ability to function apart from the noir universe. One senses that both of these artists, especially Hitchcock, would have expressed their personalities unallied with any particular genre. The one notable exception is Wilder's *Double Indemnity*. Any film that is based on James M. Cain, is scripted by Raymond Chandler, stars Barbara Stanwyck, and

contains every stylistic convention of the film noir, insists upon recognition of that kind.

- A denial by its main characters of conventional social and domestic happiness through unattainability or refusal.
- An assertion of individuality as defined by the killing (although not necessarily murder) of someone (including oneself) in defiance of modern social mores and the law.
- The iconic representation of the above-mentioned features by a definitive star of the screen or through a striking performance by a less recognized screen star or actor.

The conventions of the film noir ensconced in its narrative structure, which make it distinctive yet are not exclusive to the noir, include the following:

- The *femme fatale* or her counterpart, the *homme fatal.*
- The active/sexual and passive/nonsexual characters.
- The voice-over narration and the flashback. Both are usually from the male protagonist's point of view.
- Frequent portraits (*Laura, The Woman in the Window, Scarlet Street*).
- Telephones—ringing, answered, or dialed—that portend bad and often incriminating news. (*Sorry, Wrong Number* is the obvious case. In *Detour* the telephone is literally an instrument of manslaughter, and in *Double Indemnity* a Dictaphone functions as a confessional.)
- Temporary amnesia, often suffered by noir characters and often diagnosed in tandem with the increasingly popular use of Freudian psychology in postwar American cinema (*Phantom Lady, My Name Is Julia Ross, Black Angel, Somewhere in the Night, The Dark Past*). Psychology itself can acquire a sinister, manipulative function in noir films (*Nightmare Alley, The Accused, Hollow Triumph* [*The Scar*]). Nightmares or daydreams function as disturbing symptoms of hidden fears or desires (*The Woman in the Window, Scarlet Street, The Chase, Crack-Up, Fear in the Night*).
- Cars as indispensable devices of escape, from crime or a criminal past, one's pursuers, the law, or marital and domestic unpleasantness.

- Apartments or bungalows as the dwellings of most characters in films noirs.
- Art and its collection—paintings, antiques, rare acquisitions, objets d'art—suggesting corruption, effeteness, and a European sensibility held in general contempt by the common American (*The Maltese Falcon, Laura, The Dark Corner, Crack-Up*).
- The inclusion of nightclubs and lounges, neon signs, cigarette lighters, trench coats, hotel rooms both cheap and elegant, pool halls, boxing rings, gyms, guns, and smart fashion in the iconography of the film noir.

The very characteristics of narration, convention, and iconography defining the noir communicated a disturbed vision to a spectator already complacent about the activity of moviegoing and about what kind of film this was. What did it speak to? The compulsion to subvert our screen's imagery—in beautiful chiaroscuro cinematography, no less—of those myths encoded to prescribe harmony for a world troubled with psychic dislocations stems from the convergence of film history, and cultural history generally, with the historical realities of American life at the onset of World War II. The worldwide depression and the state of the Western world at that time expressed little hope for the redemption of mankind from the tragedy of his self-destruction. The fallout from what was supposed to be the Great War had left the human distress of adjusting to a changed modern world. And the task of responding to it had to be a somber assignment to the artists, writers, and philosophers who had seen too much to deny an essential dark force in man's relationship with himself and others.

This seems indeed a broad stroke taken in locating a screen genre in the course of modern events. Outsized perhaps, but perhaps not so much so. For if genres exist historically as well as aesthetically, then might they not allow us to investigate the impulse that gave rise to their creation? In the criminal doings, rapacious desires, passions, and weaknesses of those who navigate the noir world, we find our own rejection of a society constructed in denial of such disruptive motivations. "Disequilibrium is the product of a style characterized by unbalanced and disturbing frame compositions, strong contrasts of light and dark, the prevalence of shadows and areas of darkness within the frame, the visual tension created by curious camera angles and so forth," wrote Sylvia

Harvey in her essay on women and the family in the film noir. Her description continues into one of the best definitions of the film noir: "[I]n *film noir* these strained compositions and angles are not merely embellishments or rhetorical flourishes, but form the semantic substance of the film. The visual dissonances that are characteristic of these films are the mark of those ideological contradictions that form the historical context out of which the films are produced."[15] It is from this vantage point, almost sixty years after the first films noirs appeared, that our investigation yields a remarkable unity—a unity in exactly such dissonances, of image and voice—in a kind of cinema that speaks, often with sadness, to the implacable animus within us. Cast here in its distinctive light, that animus is nonetheless the very dilemma that troubled the ancients, who first illuminated it.

GERMAN EXPRESSIONISM AND THE ROOTS OF THE FILM NOIR

The language common in describing the film noir invokes the stylization of painterly and theatrical expressionism. We casually associate the chiaroscuro and melodrama of the work of the German émigré filmmakers of the forties studio noirs with their backgrounds and youthful inspirations in Wilhelmine and Weimar Germany. The connection, a handy one, also misleads and requires clarification, and the differences between influence and practice are perhaps best delineated by recognizing the affinities between them. Many films noirs, particularly in America, were made by a number of German and Viennese filmmakers and stage directors (Lang, Siodmak, Dieterle, Douglas Sirk, Preminger, Max Ophüls, even Wilder) who participated at least marginally in the Golden Age of German filmmaking—from roughly 1919 to 1933. They were inspired by the innovative staging and lighting techniques of producer and director Max Reinhardt as much as by any imprecise quasi-literary and artistic movement called expressionism.[16] With that in mind, we can identify the following two stylistics, first emphasized in the German silent film, as influences in the noir cinema that we have seen on the American screen since 1940.

First, the chiaroscuro lighting—frontal lighting, low-key lighting (sometimes) contrasted with high-key lighting, and close shots—was a staple of film language by the early twenties. The German filmmakers, aided by the expressionist stylistics affecting all their arts, stylized these technical effects to make melodramas of spiritual isolation, anxiety, and fear. They created the *stimmung* (the aura or shimmer of mood resonating from an object filmed) and the *umwelt* (the uniting and protective rays of light generating a recognition of objects and characters clustered in their discretely intimate environment, apart from the unknown and feared, apart from what is "out there").[17] One need only think of a street lamp providing the shelter of light to the mysterious silhouettes conspiring in fugitive schemes of escape to envision an Edward Hopper painting or a forties film noir. Lang, Friedrich Murnau, G.W. Pabst, and Paul Leni incorporated light and dark to express, primarily through the sets and in the facial gestures of their screen characters, sensational and often irrational feelings that illustrated the specific context of German society during its sudden change after the collapse of the Wilhelmine empire and Germany's defeat in World War I. As seen in the film noir, rarely is the phantasmic quality present; but in its debt to the German silent film, the modified and more refined use of chiaroscuro lighting in noir cinema sought to express the anxieties felt in a wartime (this time, World War II) and postwar society—anxieties that, widely considered, conveyed the feelings of modern man alienated from himself and others and having fallen prey to his obsessions and weaknesses. The fatalism of noir cinema stems from this anxiety and loss of self in the modern world, and the parallel runs steady along the social and psychological dislocations of a demoralized Germany twenty years earlier.

Second, the stylization of expressionism—denying that nature was the all-inclusive answer to human truth and identifying it instead as the object to be interpreted for its hidden forces—evolved into the noir city, artificial and with an iconography understood by its denizens. The city in German silent film, however, was excavated in a manner not yet fully appreciated by its audiences. To be sure, urban poverty and slums had been shown on screen before, as had city high life, but most often as set pieces to the rather generic melodrama narratives presented. In German film, Murnau showed Emil Jannings's hotel porter in *Der Letze Mann* (*The Last Laugh,* 1924) against the backdrop of a metropolitan tableau at once callous and exciting but, in any case, vibrant. G.W. Pabst showed postwar Vienna in *Die Freudlose Gasse* (*The Joyless Street,* 1925)— albeit through creaky sets—as a specific urban trap of poverty, despair, and corruption. The city became a world of vice and pleasure, of ignominy and anonymity. Its dynamics represented a moral conundrum; all that is humanly possible existed in a state of constant contradiction. The German silent film further specialized in recognizing the city through its "street" films, which rendered urban life by focusing on episodes of it emanating from the street: the street became a metaphor for the urban drama unfolding in its many manifestations. The street films of Karl Grune (*Die Strasse* [*The Street*], 1923), Bruno Rahn (*Dirnentragödie* [*Tragedy of the Street*], 1927), Joe May (*Asphalt*, 1928), Murnau, and Pabst are microcosms of the city's excitements and hardships experienced during the Weimar years. From the nighttime sidewalks to the nightclubs, to the apartment buildings, to the neon signs, only the transplantation to urban America two decades later would be needed to suggest a noir story. However, these elements in themselves would not have been adaptable from UFA-Berlin to Hollywood USA if the irony and subversive temperament of the German émigrés had not found at least a tolerant home in the American movie industry. This, in the end, is the vital connection between the stylistics seen as expressionistic and the cinema recognized as noir.

A brief account of the development of the early German cinema reflects a society traumatized and dislocated by the collapse and defeat of the old monarchy, the humiliating loss of a war that Germany itself encouraged through imperial vanity, and the subsequent workers' revolution that left the nation in a state of anarchy. The social landscape in 1919 was chaotic, and it is unsurprising to read in Siegfried Kracauer's landmark critical study of the German cinema, *From Caligari to Hitler*, that "no social whole existed in Germany. The middle-class strata were in a state of political immaturity against which they dreaded to struggle lest they further endanger their already insecure social condition. This retrogressive conduct provoked a psychological stagnation. Their habit of nurturing the intimately associated sensations of inferiority and isolation was as juvenile as their inclination to revel in dreams of the future."[18] From 1919 into 1924, rampant inflation and unemployment, political assassinations, civil violence, and various foreign interventions left Germany as battered as at any time in its history as a nation-state. In this environment Universum Film Aktiengesellschaft (UFA) and the German cinema of the period were born. UFA was the preeminent production company to emerge out of the ruins of World War I in November 1917 under the combined auspices of prominent businessmen and financiers and the Reich command, which owned roughly a third of the enterprise. Its purpose was to revitalize the German film industry and promote a favorable image of German culture abroad. In addition to

UFA, the studios Decla and Bioscop were formed and joined and then, in 1920, merged with UFA under the decisive influence of one of the great film producers in history—to call him an impresario of the screen would be no exaggeration—Erich Pommer. "At the end of World War I, the Hollywood industry moved toward world supremacy," recalled Pommer many years later. "Germany was defeated; how could she make films that would compete with others? It would have been impossible to try and imitate Hollywood and the French. So we tried something new: the expressionist or stylized films. This was possible because Germany had an overflow of good artists and writers, a strong literary tradition, and a great tradition of theatre."[19]

Expressionism as a movement is an extreme expression of romanticism subsumed by the despairing and alienated anxiety (the fear, the *lebensangst*) of the soul longing for the ecstasy of spiritual knowledge. Renouncing the aesthetics of naturalism and impressionism as too near the surface of the objective world, expressionism offered "more vital emotions . . . more dynamic powers of description were extolled, a creation from within, an intense subjectivity which had no reluctance in destroying the conventional picture of reality in order that the expression be more powerful. . . . And if distortion and aggressive expression of emotion were found in earlier works of art, then these works were extolled as forerunners of the new outlook."[20] Expressionism, like the mood in the best films noirs, reflected a pervasive fear of the ineffable and unknown through imagery and metaphor—the metaphor that, as Walter Sokel put it, "serves to objectify an intensely subjective content without losing its subjectivism, but, on the contrary, deepening and clarifying it."[21]

The expressionism of the pre–World War I period was taken from the label invented by Antonín Matějček, a Budapest art history student who, in 1910, published an essay in Prague that defined a recent current in art antithetical to impressionism in French art.[22] Wilhelm Worringer was among its first and most prominent theoreticians, and he held that expressionism was that "form of spiritual activity that sought, through a process of visionary abstraction, to penetrate appearance and reveal reality."[23] Such an abstract style, the critic Roger Cardinal noted, could be located "in [expressionism's] frenzied quest for principles of pattern within a world of collapsing spiritual and psychological certainties."[24] The grotesqueries of film sets with their backdrops of distorted building facades and their unending stairways; the extravagant gestures of actors declaiming brief but potent words of passion, love, or impending catastrophe; and the sharp chiaroscuro of painted shadows and light made expressionist and expressionist-inspired cinema a cultural tableau of the contemporary anxieties expressed, as they also were, in drama and painting. Of the cinema of that period, Jean Mitry wrote: "It was no longer a matter of conveying things by a sign but of making them part of an organic whole symbolized by its forms or structures, reduced to their essentials, all possible forms of abstractions; to ensure that the things themselves, without ceasing to be what they are, become a sign or a symbol. In short, the meaningful qualities of cinematic expressionism can be understood as a plastic symbolism, an architronic symbolism or a realistic symbolism according to the meaning of their appearance."[25]

When we think of German expressionist cinema, *Das Kabinett des Dr. Caligari* (*The Cabinet of Dr. Caligari*), made in 1919, often comes to mind as the first expressionist film. Raymond Durgnat, among other film historians, has pointed out that it was not the screen's first expressionist film but that Robert Wiene's film "initiated the screen's first concerted attempt to emotionalize architecture, along principles derived from Max Reinhardt's stage décor and the theories of [Kasimir] Edschmidt," a leading expositor of the expressionist goal.[26] The seeming contradiction of influences here—Reinhardt having rejected any affinity for the expressionist movement—becomes much less contradictory and more tenable when we see that the influence of Reinhardt in the work of Murnau, Pabst, and Lang suggests a confluence of the creative ferment in Weimar Germany, where "the city of Berlin came more and more to amaze and horrify several of the young German Expressionist poets, with its size and fearful indifference to suffering."[27]

> The German soul instinctively prefers twilight to daylight.
> —Lotte Eisner, *The Haunted Screen*

The nighttime hours so predominant in the film noir, along with their intrusions of neon lights, nightclubs, automobile headlights, and other such iconography, constitute an amorphous yet ubiquitous presence in the narrative. Eerie alleys, menacing corridors, stairways climbed to inevitable doom, guns fired—by whom?—all accrue in a repository of fatalistic images. Just as the settings in noir cinema animate the mood in advance of much of the action of the characters, the link to German silent film lies in the stylistic anthropomorphizing of set and hence at-

Das Kabinett des Dr. Caligari (1919). Early screen images of chiaroscuro set design.

mosphere. Indeed, the expressionist sets of Hermann Warm, Walther Reimann, and Walther Röhrig in *The Cabinet of Dr. Caligari*, the shtetl houses and the golem in Paul Wegener and Carl Boese's 1920 *Der Golem*, the dark side streets in Lang's *Dr. Mabuse, der Spieler* (*Dr. Mabuse, the Gambler*), and the underground factory-city with its false Maria in Lang's

Dr. Mabuse, der Spieler (1922). The chiaroscuro subterranean world of vice.

Metropolis are but the most prominent examples of this impulse. "In the normal syntax of the German language objects have a complete active life," explained Lotte Eisner. "They are spoken of with the same adjectives and verbs used to speak of human beings, they are endowed with the same qualities as people, they act in the same way.... When couched in expressionist phraseology the personification is amplified; the metaphor expands and embraces people and objects in similar terms."[28] Hence the hallucinogenic quality of distorted winding streets, slanted buildings with pitched roofs hovering overhead, grimacing faces with demented glaring eyeballs, and rigid fists unfolding and extending accusing fingers—all form a visual lexicon of expressionism on screen. The influence of these on noir iconography becomes, out of necessity because of the contemporary realism of the Hollywood narrative tradition, subdued, much less emphatic, and most often translated into the lighting and urban setting of 1940s and 1950s America. The transformation is derivative, for the German cinema sought to transform nature, the objective force, into the product of the mind, an imagined world, and the film noir has taken this cue in transforming its milieu into the paranoia of its characters, perceiving, as they do, their entrapment in a threatening world obscured of clarity.

The film noir in America found its inspiration in the German style through just this obscurantism of its characters' mental activity, not only their paranoia but also their amnesia and their disorientation in the perception of the world around them. Cesare, the somnambulist, in *Caligari* predetermines Martin Blair's blackouts in Roy William Neill's 1946 *Black Angel* and Chuck Scott's amnesia in Arthur Ripley's 1946 *The Chase*— and indeed, the amnesia, hallucinations, and strange otherworldly perception of reality found in almost every Cornell Woolrich character adapted for the American screen. Dr. Mabuse and Moloch have the hypnotic and destructive power over their subjects that parallels Jack Marlow's muted psychosis in Robert Siodmak's *Phantom Lady*. The grandiose and stylized gesturing of characters that prevailed in the German expressionist cinema seems in retrospect the product of an often turgid acting style of the silent screen in general, only compounded by a stereotyped shorthand of movement and gesticulation. In the American noir cinema of twenty years later, the context is not the ecstatic gyrations of its madmen but rather the thwarted desires and active fears of its protagonists (Who am I? What am I doing here?). Hence, Martin Blair and Jean Courtland in *Night Has a Thousand Eyes* (John Farrow, 1948) and Al Walker in *The Dark Past* (Rudolph Maté, 1948), for instance, are all framed within the reality of a modern world seen through their derangements yet elucidating the conflict born out of dis-ease over—even terror of—the unknown and the actions it provokes.

The *stimmung*, or visually generated mood through light, not only accorded subject-objects an emotional connection to the story dilemma, heartbreak, or suspense but also helped define the emotional resonance of the "new city" as an exciting place to both body and mind. If the "street" films did little else, they brought into the moviegoer's consciousness the idea that a milieu could be the subject of a film as much as the characters shaped by it. In this case, the chiaroscuro of the street, alleyway, or deserted corner, often displaying the *umwelt* of two or several people congregating, for example, under a well-lighted street lamp, brought to life the sensation of urban anxiety. In *The Street, The Last Laugh, The Joyless Street*, and *Tragedy of the Street*, the city and the street—and the "street," after all, meant the street of the city, not of the small town and not a country road—projected an image of urban decay

Die Freudlose Gasse (1925). The street as a microcosm of the human experience.

Die Strasse (1923). The street as a world of temptation and danger.

at odds with the original intention of these films. The street films were originally meant to serve the German film industry as examples of the *aufklärungsfilme*, ostensibly "educational" films about sexuality, venereal disease, and personal hygiene made to advance "sexual enlightenment" in moviegoers.[29] In reality simply a commercial exploitation of sex fantasies and taboo subjects, the street films defined a certain "call of Destiny," according to Eisner, who saw in them all the urban enticements decried by bourgeois convention.[30] Paul Monaco observed that the street of the German films of the period was portrayed as "dark, gloomy, and dangerous . . . the site of crimes, where low life flourishes. More specifically, the street is the place in which order breaks down unless a figure of authority maintains it." He also noted that the French films of the same period displayed the street normally well lighted, as a pleasant place full of life.[31]

The street films incorporate the expressionist influence within the *kammerspiele*—or intimate drama—tradition and throw into the blend a tentative smattering of documentary aspiration (often clumsily realized). *The Joyless Street* is the perfect example of the "new objectivity" (*Neue Sachlichkeit*) of the mid-1920s, which followed the miserable years immediately after the thwarted Communist revolt of November 1919, a period when the street and its drama offered audiences a portrait of the hardships still prevalent among the forgotten and classless many. *The Last Laugh* illustrates the fragility of this class-structured existence, personified by the pathetic demise of Emil Jannings when he loses his doorman's position at the Hotel Atlantic and the all-too-important uniform that symbolized his self-respect. However, it is the passions of these street films' stories that constitute a more compelling ancestry to the film noir. In *The Street*, the notion of the street is as a force "out there," out of the protective womb of family routine, and as an enticement through the images of desire that our bourgeois everyman sees of a flirtatious couple across the street silhouetted on his living room ceiling. The play of shadows lures him to explore the nighttime excitements of the street. We see him, once outside his apartment, against a series of expressionistic settings: the stairway leading down to the landing of his apartment building, the street lamps outside casting light on the prostitutes and the pedestrians, and the restaurants and dance halls that provide a panoramic fusion of expressionism and *kammerspiele*. The eyes of the optician's store sign follow the man's tentative excursion through the darkened and slightly menacing side street, and the art gallery portraiture displayed in the window very much suggests images from Fritz Lang's *Woman in the Window* and *Scarlet Street* more than twenty years later. When he meets a gang of con artists at the dance hall and is enticed by their attractive female cohort, the man sees the history and fidelity of his marriage pass before him in images framed by the wedding band he takes off, enlarged and holds between his two fingers. The technique replicates the flashback device of the film noir and serves to exhort the man to consider his actions before he takes a wrong step. In the man's apartment building resides a blind grandfather who ventures out in search of his little runaway granddaughter. He loses his cane, falls to the ground, and shakily tries to pick himself up, pleading for help to uncaring pedestrians that step around him. As in *Joyless Street*, we see images of a ratlike self-preservation and callousness, as people scurry away, noticing the pathetic man not with compassion but with disdain. The connecting stories of the pitfalls of the street suggest Schnitzler in concept, with the narrative bringing together the grandfather, the con artists, the prostitute, and the bourgeois umbrella-swinging man with the perils of city life.

However, the connection to noir cinema can be seen in the atmosphere of portending doom permeating this and the other street films—a feature as much the product of the expressionist project as it was a reflection of urban Germany at the time. These films echo in the film noir cinematography of John Alton (*T-Men*, *Side Street*), Franz Planer (*Criss Cross*, *99 River Street*), Nicholas Musuraca (*Deadline at Dawn*), Milton Krasner (*The Set-Up*), Lloyd Ahern (*Cry of the City*), Harold Rosson (*The Asphalt Jungle*), and even James Wong Howe (*He Ran All the Way*, *Sweet Smell of Success*) by revealing the street, the neighborhood, and the city as the philosophical summation of their characters' existence.

FRITZ LANG (1890–1976)

Dr. Mabuse, der Spieler (1922)
M (1931)
Das Testament des Dr. Mabuse (1933)
You Only Live Once (1937)
The Woman in the Window (1944)
Scarlet Street (1945)
Secret beyond the Door . . . (1948)
The Big Heat (1953)
The Blue Gardenia (1953)
While the City Sleeps (1956)
Beyond a Reasonable Doubt (1956)

Fritz Lang may well be considered the absolute moralist of noir cinema: what Cotton Mather is to American literature, Lang became to the film noir. His direct link to the German cinema of the twenties confirms the roots of his noir style and thematic concerns; and in this it should be remembered that Lang worked in three national cinemas during three significant eras of film history (the silent, Hollywood sound, and widescreen color film periods) and that he was the only future Hollywood director solicited by Josef Goebbels on behalf of Adolf Hitler (who purportedly admired *Metropolis*) to run the Nazi film industry. He fled, of course, to Paris and then to Los Angeles, where in 1936 he made his first

M (1931). Franz Becker (Peter Lorre) and the pathos of psychopathology.

American film, *Fury*, about the injustice of mob tyranny. The following year he made *You Only Live Once*, the prototype of the persecuted-and-pursued-by-the-law-and-society films that were to find varied expression in Ray's *They Live by Night* (1949), Lewis's *Gun Crazy* (1950), and Penn's *Bonnie and Clyde* (1967). The theme of persecution and pursuit is central to Lang's vision of injustice in the world and, more specifically, of the cruelty and paranoia spawned in such persecution and infecting the Langian man with fear in expectation of doom, the only certain condition of life. The architecture of fear—in lighting and sets, in the sudden violence of his characters and their nemeses, and in the arbitrary twists of fate that destroy them—expresses an intransigent view unmitigated by any hope of human salvation. The personification of such fear is found in Franz Becker, in *M*, as he is hunted by others and haunted by himself, a child murderer who cannot help his own actions and for whom, Lang instructs us, mercy must be shown. This fear, which all too often walks hand-in-hand with the very darkness of the human soul unleashed in Lang's world, makes Franz Becker the most fitting prophet of noir cinema.

Lang made four films that presaged his films noirs—*Dr. Mabuse, der Spieler*; *M*; *Das Testament des Dr. Mabuse*; and *You Only Live Once*—and then, from 1944 to 1956, made seven films noirs, of which *The Big Heat* towers as a model of noir cinema. His German films displayed the quasi-expressionistic, mostly dark style he would adapt to his noirs and explored the theme that preoccupied his career: the malevolence and destructiveness of the human will and the fear they foster. Lang understood as a matter of psychic principle that there is a Mabuse in each of us, provoked to the surface under the right circumstances. The sinister and menacing figure came under scrutiny both as the symbol of an interwar Germany, vanquished and directionless after World War I and foundering after an aborted Communist attempt in 1920 to gain control of its government, and as a ghostly character in *Das Testament des Dr. Mabuse*, portending the ominous future of a totalitarian state. Mabuse represents the easy submission to the weaknesses and corruption in Weimar urban society (*Dr. Mabuse, der Spieler*) as much as the nihilistic ruler whose power over criminal minions bears a disturbing correlation to the rise of Adolf Hitler in the chancellery just months before *Das Testament* was released. The moments that suggest the future noir world of Lang, however, come in two scenes with and about the women in *Dr. Mabuse, der Spieler*, and through Inspector Lohmann's gradually becoming consumed in unraveling the mystery of his disappeared informant, Hofmeister, in *Das Testament*. In the latter instance, Lohmann must admit the inadequacy of his crime-fighting pursuit when the asylum director, Dr. Baum, possessed by the evil spirit of his now-vacant, zombielike patient, Mabuse, emerges as the apparent villain. There, next to the cell where the ghostly Mabuse shreds the pages of his diabolical journal, Baum is apprehended and carted away as Lohmann remarks to Kent, "Come on, this is no longer a police job." His closing line on the Mabuse case reveals the mission's failure to subdue the self-generating animus of a society approaching self-destruction. It is the same pessimism that informs the audience of the hopeless prospect for defeating corruption in a world whose constructs for meting out justice prove inadequate to the realities of human nature and circumstance, true enough in *You Only Live Once* and, more strikingly, in *The Big Heat* sixteen years later.

In *Dr. Mabuse, der Spieler*, Lang shows the climate of emptiness and boredom in Weimar society that allows Countess Told to search for "unusual excitements and sensations" in the secret gambling clubs of Berlin. The rich gamble in smoke-filled after-hours clubs where vice is their diversion. "Cocaine or cards" become the options of pleasure, and the loss of all one's money merely a momentary frantic spectacle among other distractions. In this heady and distorted atmosphere, expressionistic decor and lighting come alive, and Cara Carozza's seductive phallic dance—where two outsized noselike creatures converge on her—arouses the club patrons to frenzied abandon as the delighted madman Mabuse looks on. "There is no such thing as love—there is only desire—and the will to possess what you most desire," he says. His abduction of Countess Told is perhaps the flip side of the same impulse that fuels Cara's devotion and desire to be loved by him. The jaded ennui of the countess and the blind yearning of Cara, two variants of the *femme fatale* (whose behaviors here are rendered in distinctive silent-screen gesticulations and with Cara's makeup particularly classic), would certainly find their way to the noir cinema of Lang twenty-three years later in Kitty March, in *Scarlet Street*.

M, Lang's German masterpiece and first sound film, compares well with one of his last films, the 1956 RKO *While the City Sleeps*. The stories of the murders of little girls and young women and the manhunts for their killers are shot in a visual style of subdued dramatic effect, with violence not graphic but seen as a statement of civil anarchy and its gruesome consequences. In *M*, little Elsie Beckmann is approached by the looming shadow of M; we then see the ball she was playing with rolling across the ground on the screen; next is a shot of the balloon M bought her, tangled in the telephone wires above. We know she was his latest victim. In *While the City Sleeps*, the killer enters his victim's apartment as she prepares her bath; the next scene shows us her apartment wall scrawled with "Ask Mother" in lipstick. We know what happened. Unlike some of his other noirs—*The Woman in the Window, Scarlet Street,* and *Secret beyond the Door . . .*—where violence accompanies oneirism and its visual furniture to show fear, trembling, and paranoia, the greater realism of modern urban life here translates horrible acts of violence into cautionary tales, quandaries about human behavior and corruption, where considering evil is a screen-time activity just as such evil occurs off screen. The most striking instance of this is in *The Big Heat* when Dave Bannion's automobile explodes off camera, killing its unintended victim, his wife, as she turns on the ignition.

Lang is least effective in his social dramas and films noirs when he appeals to action sequences. In fact, fast action sequences are rare in Lang, and compared with Joseph H. Lewis's handling of Bart Tare and Annie Starr's frenzied getaways in *Gun Crazy*, Eddie and Joan's flight in *You Only Live Once* is comparatively intimate, mostly shown by a frontal two-shot of them as Eddie drives. In *While the City Sleeps*, however, Ernest Laszlo shot an attempted escape by the "lipstick killer" in a darkened New York City subway tunnel worthy of the best expressionist-inspired moments in Lang's career. With streaks of light piercing his pursuers among passing subway trains, the tension heightens until the killer flees through a manhole cover to the light of afternoon and awaiting police. The scene reminds us of *M*, where the network of beggars, scouring the storage rooms of an office building, finally trap the meek and frightened Becker. The two pursuits accentuate similar motives. In *M*, Inspector Lohmann (who made his first appearance here) and his detectives pursue Becker simultaneously with the underworld, whose criminal activities have come under undue police scrutiny in search of this child killer. Public, official, and criminal motives propel the urgency of his capture. In *While the City Sleeps*, metropolitan New York is offered the sensationalism of the media, as one of their new moguls, Walter Kyne Jr., decides to make the lipstick killer's capture a contest for a senior editorial position coveted by his three top editors. Both narratives show the diluted, compromised motives of greed and reputation, as well as justice, in the pursuit of an anarchic force. In *M*, not only social good suffers, but vice as well suffers; in *While the City Sleeps*, the lurid urban pulse promoted by big-city communications is exploited in the name of public interest, albeit with selfish gain.

It is this compromised moral condition of urban institutions and their machinery, which Lang recognized in *While the City Sleeps* and saw ever so clearly in *The Big Heat,* that gives further definition to his noir vision. The moment signifying the conflicting anxieties in *While the City Sleeps* occurs in a scene set with the evocation of an Edward Hopper painting. A high-angle chiaroscuro shot of the towering Kyne building in the rain-glistening nighttime, precise and two-dimensional, tracks back to show the neon-lighted basement bar next door, a reporters' hangout. Lang then cuts to the face of the young murderer peering through the window at Ed Mobley, the reporter who televised a ridiculing profile of him and whose fiancée the psychopath is targeting next.

The Woman in the Window, Scarlet Street, Secret beyond the Door . . ., and, to a lesser extent, *The Blue Gardenia* are Lang's most

The Woman in the Window (1944). Death and seduction: Richard Wanley (Edward G. Robinson) helps Alice Reed (Joan Bennett) dispose of her lover's body.

schematic films noirs, together a fairly comprehensive array of noir conventions. *The Woman in the Window* and *Scarlet Street*, both starring Edward G. Robinson, Joan Bennett, and Dan Duryea, can be seen in retrospect as films of temptation sublimated (*Woman*) and temptation fulfilled (*Scarlet Street*). Both are parables of one wrong step first taken, and both show the dreadful price paid by those submitting to desire in a universe bound by laws of moral absolutism. Because Professor Wanley is much smarter about this equation than Christopher Cross, he understands that whatever implicating evidence remains after such a killing as his, it must be scrupulously disposed of. What he will never know—since his narrative is, after all, shown to be a conceit, a dream, a fantasy—is what Chris Cross discovers: that fate can turn a man blinded by love and desire into a tortured, guilt-ridden murderer.

Lang's lucid accounts in these films on what "the web of circumstances" can mean, and the moments of fear and entrapment that result, go to the core of his noir sensibility. Wanley scours Alice Reed's apartment for any incriminating evidence after he kills her lover in self-defense. He then carefully arranges to dispose of the body. In the process, Lang teases us with suspenseful interruptions that threaten to expose Wanley: a policeman stops him for having a broken headlight while Mazard's corpse is hidden in the car; Wanley discovers his fountain pen missing, apparently left in Alice's apartment; and his friend, an assistant district attorney, pieces together the killing with remarkable accuracy and invites the professor's observations in the process. Alice, a selfish but not necessarily reckless seductress, is an unreliable accomplice in a plan of concealment. Lang reveals this plan in a tight narrative development of de-dramatized motive.

Psychology is not a tool for character development here or in *Scarlet Street*, and Wanley and Lalor's intellectual discussions of criminal profiles and motive become instead a thesis, or proof, that Lang works out, illustrates. Medium shots of interiors with monochromatic or dull lighting counterpoint nighttime shots in the rain—here, when Wanley transports Mazard's corpse, and in *Scarlet Street* when Chris Cross interrupts Johnny's assault of Kitty—but there is little starkly contrasted low-key lighting in these films, no heady musical score, and no intriguing dialogue. Lang develops the improbable narrative line of *Scarlet Street* without regard to the nuances of passion or deception. We are shown simply that Kitty is cemented in an abusive relationship with Johnny, to whom she is perversely loyal, and she deceives Chris with stated repul-

Scarlet Street (1945). The allure of a plastic raincoat: Christopher Cross (Edward G. Robinson) meets Kitty March (Joan Bennett).

sion and no remorse. It is her rejection of Chris, activating the Langian passion and his impulse to stab her, that illustrates the infection of an obsession built up by willing blindness.

The point here is that these films are designed to show, but not necessarily explore, the implications of noir narrative as a structure in which fantasy (or wish fulfillment), obsession, guilt, and entrapment may be visually stated and in that statement validated as actions with moral gravity. The doppelgänger of Richard Wanley (his dream-professor counterpart), Christopher Cross (a clandestine famous painter), and Kitty March (a prostitute posing as an artist), each shown in the same plausible light as their "real selves," distance the viewer from the emotional involvement solicited by more psychologically torn characters. (One need only compare Joan Bennett's Alice Reed or Kitty March with infinitely more emotional Lang women—Sylvia Sydney's Joan Graham in *You Only Live Once*, Barbara Stanwyck's Mae Doyle in *Clash by*

Night, or Gloria Grahame's Debbie Marsh in *The Big Heat*—to feel the difference.) In this, Lang's project becomes one of harsh admonition, sermonic in its narrative design, as we see these characters prepare themselves for the fall. "The pathos of *The Woman in the Window* is predicated on the definitive self-knowledge supplied by Wanley's nightmare," observed Alfred Appel. "Viewed as the logical culmination of a myriad of effects, as the exit from the labyrinth, the dream-ending should seem considerably less blatant."[32] As indeed it does, especially in comparison to the grim reality of Christopher Cross's descent into madness, unimaginable at the beginning of *Scarlet Street*.

The last sequence of this film is virtuoso Lang. In the mind's eye of Chris Cross, Lang shoots imagined moments of Johnny Prince's murder trial and guilty verdict and of Johnny being sentenced to death. Johnny's cries of innocence haunt Chris, as do the voices, in two-part harmony, that seductively greet Kitty—"Lazylegs"—and elicit her reply in total erotic submission—"Jeepers, I love you Johnny!" The scene is set in a dingy hotel room, evoking those transient hotels where lost souls are the forgotten lives of any city, and the neon sign outside blinks on and off, a visual parallel to the lovers' refrain tormenting Chris. He tries to hang himself but fails. The dark of this scene eclipses visual design to become a vacuum of all-consuming guilt. The sequence moves to Central Park, where Chris is rousted from his derelict's slumber by a cop, jostling him to move on and remarking to his partner how nutty this man is to suffer such self-condemnation for two imagined murders. But Chris is, in fact, responsible for two deaths, and as he walks past the gallery where his painting of Kitty has just been sold, the destructiveness of this triangle achieves a formal completion. For it was not merely a plan of deception—not of Chris and Kitty's, nor of Johnny and Kitty's—but the collapse of romanticism in the throes of its subsumption within the larger design of a cruel fate that leaves Chris haunted, alone, and with nothing.

Oneirism also becomes a visual motif in *Secret beyond the Door . . .* and *The Blue Gardenia* to reveal the fear and paranoia enshrouding Lang's women. Celia Lamphere's feelings about her brother's death and her lonely life are communicated in voice-over throughout *Secret beyond the Door*, and her fear of marrying a stranger in Mark are expressed so as well. It is one of the most extensive voice-over narrations used for self-rumination in noir cinema, highlighting Celia's doubts about why she married this enigmatic man and explaining her commitment to help him overcome the guilt that torments him over a suspected murderous past. Lang fuses this voice-over narration with a dream motif in which even the realism of the Lamphere mansion, photographed by Stanley Cortez in a turgid, low-key chiaroscuro style, achieves an otherworldly quality. In contrast to *Woman in the Window* or *Scarlet Street*, oneirism here becomes an active device in Celia's search for answers and meaning in a married life increasingly mysterious and incomplete. Equally revealing is her fascination with violence and blood lust. She first encounters Mark on a Mexican vacation; she is immediately attracted to him across the town square from her hotel bar's veranda as both observe two young men in a knife fight over a peasant girl. "How proud she must be!" Celia wonders of the girl's power to command the affections of these rivals. At this moment we begin to recognize her dangerous attraction to Mark and eventually to understand her acceptance of his morbid indulgence, a collection of "murder" rooms—rooms meticulously furnished as they were when they served as settings for infamous murders.

Mark Lamphere is himself tortured by such blood lust, as his manner suggests guilt in the death of his first wife. (His teenage son by her accuses him of as much.) The fact that the mystery surrounding her death is revealed and exonerates him (no doubt a studio requirement at the time) does not mitigate the power of the dream sequence where, crazed, he prosecutes, defends, and sits in judgment on himself—the kind of nightmare in guilt that Lang showed with Christopher Cross and would suggest with Norah Larkin's behavior in *The Blue Gardenia*.

Unlike Lang's other films noirs, *The Blue Gardenia* presents the torment of guilt seen through, and in, the eyes of a woman. Norah Larkin not only had reason to kill Harry Prebble, but she also assumes she did strike him dead with a poker, drunk one night after they dined together and he tried to assault her. When his body is found, the story rides every assumption about the *kind* of woman who would be with and kill a leech like Prebble, as Norah, unconscious of the murder, is terrified over the image constructed of the presumably female killer, an image at odds with the one we see of her and she sees of herself. Norah is a victim of someone else's murder, but much more, of the media and law enforcement's distortion of her very identity as a woman. The female perspective here holds in contempt the easy assumptions—of jealousy, promiscuity, and an implicit prostitution—made about the killer by the predominantly masculine world of the noir and conceived in terms of the most common image of the noir woman: the *femme fatale*. For Norah is not the fatal woman nor the ancillary suffering woman of a victimized noir man. Attractive and sympathetic, she is simply an ordinary woman who represents a postwar generation of single women, working and quite visible in American society. Norah's trap in *The Blue Gardenia* is typically Langian and appeals to the questions of truth and the appearance of guilt expressed in two of his other films, *You Only Live Once* and *Beyond a Reasonable Doubt*. Her blackout on the night of Prebble's murder masks the truth, leaving Norah to wrestle with the fear and guilt that alter her personality. She begins to "act guilty," and she functions similar to the way writer Tom Garrett does in *Beyond a Reasonable Doubt* when he schemes to incriminate himself in a recent murder for an exposé on the misbegotten penalty of capital punishment.

In *The Blue Gardenia*, as in *Beyond a Reasonable Doubt* and *You Only Live Once*, truth becomes not merely elusive but also manipulated—an "honest lie" of sorts—and the dilemma is how to best capture it from its elusion. Tom Garrett fabricates his guilt in murder only to find his sole witness, his future father-in-law, suddenly struck dead in an auto accident. Hence he appears truly guilty. His scheme is finally exposed by the deceased publisher's attorney. But then he betrays a detail of knowledge about the murdered dancer that reveals to his fiancée that he truly *is* the murderer. Unlike Eddie Taylor, who is cornered by fear to kill without murder in his heart and is victimized by a society that inflates his notoriety, Garrett turns the appearance of certain guilt ("beyond a reasonable doubt") into a shadow game of distraction from the inevitable truth of his calculated murder. Norah Larkin finds her place between these two, and in far more Langian fashion: her living nightmare is indeed based on a rational fear of what appears to be true.

The living nightmare in Lang's noirs is a visualization of dread, of the trap seen in the victim's mind and by us to take shape as a total universe. In the interwar Mabuse films, such oneirism has an apparitional quality; in *M*, it is seen written on the face of Franz Becker; in *Woman in the Window* and *Scarlet Street*, it swings from daydream to nightmare; and in his urban noirs, *The Big Heat* and *While the City Sleeps*, the nightmare achieves the verisimilitude of daily reality in the city. With *The Big Heat*, Fritz Lang returned to the theme that preoccupied his Mabuse films and *You Only Live Once*: the social structures that predestine tragedy. Cast in the noir vision of modern urban America, it is his most seamless fusion of personal torment generated by actions taken in battle with corrupt society, seen here through the organized

The Big Heat (1953). A disfigured Debbie Marsh (Gloria Grahame) insists on retribution.

criminal activity of the Mafia-like mobster Lagana. The *big heat,* an appropriately urban term for intensive police action taken against organized crime, comes during a time in the 1950s when the scope of such criminal activity was being recognized as a sophisticated network whose pernicious undermining of civil institutions posed a domestic threat. Lang succeeded in transforming such topicality into a morality play, a noir myth, about the personal toll exacted in violence, pain, and death by those who confront such evil. In *The Big Heat*, an uncompromising, scrupulously composed, and elegant film, each scene follows with a logic and dramatic rigor that increases the story's emotional power as it reinforces its moral vision.

The film opens with a close-up of a gun, the gun to be used by Records Sergeant Tom Duncan to commit suicide. From this act forward, the chain of events complicating the narrative hinges on violent incidents, each one—from the torture and murder of Duncan's mistress, Lucy Chapman (which we never see, but the horrible account of which is described), to the car explosion killing Dave Bannion's wife (again, occurring off screen), to Debbie Marsh's death—escalating toward a crescendo of dramatic consequence. It is interesting that the only violent act we see before Debbie's disfigurement is Vince Stone burning a cigarette into a barfly's hand—a silencing act of cruelty, even today—and the implication is twofold. Modern organized crime has shown a victory, no less, in the discreet and obliterating exercise of murder, methodical and clean. An angry Lagana reprimands the hit man responsible for disposing of Lucy Chapman's body so clumsily and thus opening the way for further police inquiry, and he talks about the election-year implications of further killings. Secondly, Lang prepares us for the sting of the violence he does show, that which attends Debbie when Stone throws a pot of boiling hot coffee in her face. The more gruesome and lethal violence that Lucy and Bannion's wife suffer unseen is eclipsed by this brutal act of mutilation and pain, justifiably repeated, in Lang's view, when Debbie flings a pot of coffee in Stone's face before being shot by him. The moment of pain and suffering is central to the Langian design and often, as in *The Big Heat*, comes as a direct consequence of one's actions. "Do you think there are many people in our audience today who believe in punishment after death?" Lang asked. "No. So what are they afraid of? Only one thing—pain. For example, torture in a Nazi camp; not so much death on a battlefield as being hurt, being mutilated. At this moment violence becomes an absolutely legitimate dramatic element, in order to make the audience a collaborator, to make them feel."[33] It is a caveat for the extreme consequences of human actions that Lang insists we dare not ignore.

Lang's film reveals much more than the institutional corruption of society; it countenances the good act. It is the crippled woman who, unobtrusively and with good conscience, furnishes the testimony that leads Bannion to his wife's killer. It is Lucy Chapman, a B-girl of dubious reputation but decent character, who attempts out of love to rescue Tom Duncan's name. And if ever murder had a justification, then Debbie Marsh's shooting of Bertha Duncan may be seen as the pivotal act that exposes the depth of evil in the story. It is, in fact, the women in *The Big Heat* that propel the narrative and make up the composite female image rarely seen in Lang's work; their influence is central from the first scene in the film, when Bertha Duncan telephones Lagana to shrewdly convey the implications of her husband's suicide. If she is the venal blackmailer, then Debbie, resurrected from pain cleansed, is the avenging Maria who will destroy her and restore justice. There is more implied in Debbie's description of them as "sisters under the mink" than their complicity in corruption: they share the indistinguishable image of greed and luxury, evil and power, the disreputable and the respectable, and the mark of the imminent fall.

The image of happiness visualized in Bannion's marriage offers the first indication that the possibility for order cannot be accepted blindly. The domestic moments of Dave and Katie Bannion are warm ones of mutual sharing. She smokes his cigarette, sips from his can of beer, and eats off his plate; he helps her prepare dinner. They talk about their future responsibilities as parents and laugh good-naturedly about the financial sacrifices they will have to make for their daughter. Indeed, our introduction to Mike Lagana, in his home giving his daughter a cheerful coming-out party, bespeaks a similar pleasing family life. However, these interludes only counterpoint the destabilizing incidents that fracture the illusion of sustained happiness in Bannion's household, just as they underscore the hypocrisy and payoff of public appearance in Lagana's.

The Big Heat is photographed in a subtle spectrum of black-and-white lighting, from bright shots both evoking the domestic bliss of the Bannnions and revealing the lie behind Lagana and Bertha Duncan's respectability, to the low-key nighttime lighting outside the apartment building where Bannion's little daughter is guarded by her aunt and uncle as Bannion, suspended from the force, searches for his wife's murderer. But *The Big Heat* "demonstrates that a *film noir* doesn't have to be dark," noted Tom Flinn, "proving that there is more to creating the corrosive mood of the genre than just duplicating the trappings of its style."[34] For Bannion undertakes his search with the hardened clarity and relentlessness that only a transformed *soul* bent on revenge in the name of justice can have acquired; he is visibly not the same man now, and his quest is "no longer a police job." Moreover, when justice is achieved, it is only a temporary victory. Bannion returns to work to find his world essentially unchanged. This bitter vision of life that Lang portrayed throughout his career found particular accommodation here, in an unkind noir world, a place where people battle the demonic forces within themselves as often as they do those around them.

ROBERT SIODMAK (1900–1973)

Phantom Lady (1944)
Christmas Holiday (1944)
The Killers (1946)
Cry of the City (1948)
Criss Cross (1949)
The File on Thelma Jordon (1950)

Few images of the American film noir that stream through the popular imagination rival those from the noirs of Robert Siodmak. If only one filmmaker were chosen for having created a body of work emblematic of a genre, Siodmak, within a five-year period—from 1944 to 1949—would have to be the one to sum up the essence of the American studio noir in its peak moment and into its transition period incorporating documentary shooting. The line extending from his German silent film career (*Menschen am Sonntag* [1928], *Abschied* [1930], *Voruntersuchung* [1931]) to his emigration to Hollywood and rapid immersion in noir filmmaking makes him the most decisive example of the German expressionist-inspired film artist to find work in the American film industry. Murnau, Lang, even Otto Preminger and Billy Wilder, provide solid examples, but only Siodmak provides an elegant one. The expressionism of his visual design emerges as a vision of fear, obsession, entrapment, resignation, and finally release, in such a concentration of work as to make his name synonymous with the genre. Indeed, Siodmak was the first Hollywood filmmaker to present us with noir protagonists resigned to the endgame of prison or death before their stories are told.

Both Scott Henderson in *Phantom Lady* and Swede Anderson in *The Killers* resign themselves to an unjust fate, and those who attempt to give it meaning are caught in a labyrinth of deceit and half-understood, dark motives. Psychology is used to explain much of the disorder visited upon Siodmak's characters here: both Jack Marlow in *Phantom Lady* and Robert Mannette in *Christmas Holiday* have exceptional egotistical sensibilities; both men are detached from the world of reality and incapable of functioning in it. This, in turn, fuels the internal anguish of the sculptor Marlow just as it arouses the paranoia of Mannette against his devoted wife Abigail. Unlike the oneiric moments in Lang, signifying entrapment stemming from his characters' submission to weakness and paranoia and symbolized by an appropriate visual geometry, Siodmak's world is a *living* nightmare of fragmentation and imbalance. *Phantom Lady*, *Christmas Holiday*, and *The Killers* are stunning examples of the tension inherent in the clash between the geography of lighting and the palpable fear it expresses. Carol "Kansas" Richman enters a world of inchoate menace in *Phantom Lady* (very much in keeping with Cornell Woolrich's novel), where shafts of light dart from nowhere to illuminate a rainy, deserted pavement as she tracks down clues to the phantom lady who can exonerate her boss. Chiaroscuro flashbacks come from every character's perspective in *The Killers*, for example, as we attempt to understand Swede's willing submission to his executioners from the perspective of the hotel housekeeper who inherits his life insurance, of his childhood friend Lubinsky, and of Lubinsky's wife, who was previously in love with Ole.

Images that come to mind instantly in any discussion of the film noir are those of Humphrey Bogart, perhaps of Bogart and assorted character actors or with Lauren Bacall, Fred MacMurray and Barbara Stanwyck in *Double Indemnity*, Gene Tierney in *Laura*, possibly a trench-coated Robert Mitchum in a blurry amalgam of postwar noirs, and undoubtedly the opening sequence of Siodmak's *Killers*. The cinematographic code of light and dark; the menace, the violence, and an unknown past from which one can no longer escape; and the sense of inevitable doom are all written in the first twelve minutes of this film, from its opening credits to the murder of Ole "Swede" Anderson. "The Hemingway original [short story] has only eighteen pages which were used only for the opening," Siodmak said in 1959. "The amazing thing about *The Killers* is that it is the only film of a Hemingway story that Hemingway actually likes! (We gave him a print of the film and I know that he has run it over 200 times.)"[35] Few openings of films noirs have quite this resonance, and few films up to that time had opened on such a grim note.[36] Here, in a small-town New Jersey diner, two silhouetted hit men (soon revealed, and beautifully played by William Conrad and Charles McGraw) arrive one night. The shafts of light just outside the diner as they walk toward it portend trouble. The scene in the diner is a slow buildup of menace by these two men. After terrorizing and tying up the owner and his only customer, they leave for the Swede's rooming house. Meanwhile, Ole lies in bed, lost in thought. When his coworker, Nick Adams, runs ahead of them to warn him of their arrival, Ole tells him not to worry, that he knows they are coming. After Nick leaves, the light from under the doorway of his darkened room reveals that there is someone standing just outside the door. Shots are fired, and then we see only the Swede's hand releasing its grasp from the bedpost. It is a poetic moment in American noir cinema, one that expresses all the existential elements of death and finality that would be discussed in every future discussion of the genre.

Siodmak was the first noir filmmaker to appreciate the complementary value of a sympathetic cinematographer. Elwood—Woody—Bredell lighted *Phantom Lady*, *Christmas Holiday*, and *The Killers* and almost single-handedly blueprinted the noir "look" in the early studio years. Quite apart from this signature sequence, the Siodmak-Bredell chiaroscuro in *Phantom Lady* highlighted the evocative grinding sound of menacing footsteps following on a rain-glistened nighttime pavement—in an exquisite rendering of the Woolrich source material—as well as the eroticism represented in a daring jazz scene, where Cliff March (Elisha Cook Jr.) takes Kansas to a secluded after-hours spot for a jam session and beats his drum with increasing frenzy in order to impress her. Cliff, in a full frontal shot, becomes increasingly aroused and exhausted almost to the point of collapse, as the camera shows the various shades of light falling on his perspiring face. The scene comes as close as anything that could be filmed at the time (*Phantom Lady* was shot in 1943) to representing the sexual energy contained in noir culture.

Cry of the City is Siodmak's attempt to integrate the documentary technique popularized in 1947 into his studio filmmaking, with the result that the film, a familiar tale of two childhood friends who take opposite paths in life—one criminal and one committed to law enforcement—seamlessly draws from the most evocative elements of both. *Cry of the City* is another emblematic noir by the filmmaker, easily recognized and referred to by the Alfred Newman street scene score that opens the film. By limiting his use to a few judiciously chosen exterior shots when Rose Given drives Martin Rome to the subway locker where the jewels are kept, Siodmak emphasized the unity of his largely expressionistic style. The chiaroscuro cinematography of Siodmak's richly patterned shots—the close-ups of Martin Rome's face before his surgery and after his meeting with the crooked lawyer Niles; the scenes when Brenda (marvelously played by a young Shelley Winters) rescues Martin and takes him to a doctor against the backdrop of a neon-lighted and rainy city; the neighborhood street outside the Romes' apartment building; and Rose

Given's walk down the entranceway of her massage parlor to admit Rome—all achieve a narrative significance unequaled in the work of most of the other noir filmmakers. For the intricate and dramatic chiaroscuro in Siodmak's world, unlike that in other studio-period noirs, seeks not to draw the sharp distinctions between good and evil, although it may certainly do so correspondingly, but to restate over and over again— from *Phantom Lady* and *Christmas Holiday* to *The Killers* to *Criss Cross*, and even in his noirlike psychological drama, *The Dark Mirror* (1946), and his gothic melodrama, *The Spiral Staircase* (1946)—the extremes of paranoia and terror and the obsessiveness tormenting his characters. Sculptor Jack Marlow is tormented by his impulse to strangle. Hands that can do good can also do evil, he remarks to Carol. Franchot Tone's Marlow has a beautiful, spare, Bauhaus-inspired modern apartment. Obviously a man of aesthetic taste, he, like Clifton Webb's characters in *Laura* and *The Dark Corner*, is malevolent. The studio film noir luxuriates in the behavior of such characters, so representative of the unsettling modern world that opposes the illusion of comfort and familiarity, because they subvert our complacency about a sociable, integrated humanity. Marlow stands apart from others, and his paranoid psychosis is the ostensible reason. "[T]he people! They hate me because I'm different from them," he says about living in New York. In the background of his apartment, we see a copy of Van Gogh's self-portrait.

Such paranoia, often breeding obsessiveness, continues in its various manifestations throughout Siodmak's noirs. Abigail Mannette knows that her husband is unstable and senses that he is disturbingly attached to his mother, but she is devoted to him—"as if you could stop loving because it's shameful to love," she tells Lieutenant Mason. In *Christmas Holiday*, Siodmak explores this obsessive love as a continuum of the past into the present, not as a point-counterpoint between the past and the present. Hence, like Jackie Lamont, now working as a prostitute at Valerie de Merode's house outside New Orleans after her husband's arrest, Abigail still yearns for Robert, unable to forsake her soul at the expense of her body. Deanna Durbin's portrayal of Abigail-cum-Jackie is a truly extraordinary transformation of the former Universal child star into a sultry, rueful creation exuding a strange, detached eroticism. When Durbin sings Irving Berlin's "Always," she elicits a melancholy longing that does not end when Robert is jailed for his bookie's murder. And when he escapes from jail only to confront her with his disgust over what she has become, she is still in his thrall.

Christmas Holiday (1944). The dual character of love and guilt: Abigail Mannette (Deanna Durbin) attends Christmas Eve mass with Lieutenant Mason (Dean Harens).

There is a dark, sinister undertone throughout *Christmas Holiday*, suggesting that devotion has been perverted in these relationships, throwing them into imbalance for the sake of placating Robert's volatile nature, and that this disequilibrium is soon to end in some violent way. Siodmak's fluid, graceful tracking, particularly throughout the Mannette home and patio and at the beer garden where Robert has his first date with Abigail, creates a visual paradox of harmony masking some unknown destabilizing animus. When Abigail as Jackie is introduced to the lieutenant, who offers to escort her home, she asks him to take her to Christmas Eve mass first. Siodmak's camera weaves through the cathedral and pulls back to generate a truly moving moment of all the despair that cannot be spoken, a moment of intoxicating spiritual appeal soon punctuated only by Abigail's uncontrollable weeping.

In the final analysis, Siodmak's chiaroscuro emphasizes the ambivalence—the joy and torture—of romantic desire taken to the extreme and poisoned by possessiveness. This is what abuses Abigail Mannette and destroys Ole Anderson in *The Killers* and Steve Thompson in *Criss Cross*. Unlike *Christmas Holiday*, where Abigail's masochistic love for Robert is eventually exorcised, in *The Killers* and *Criss Cross* obsession ends in death. When Ole recognizes that he "did something wrong, once," and for this he must die, he is speaking not of violence and theft—although he committed both and there is a noir justice to be paid for it—but much more of the pain of self-betrayal, of having allowed himself to fall in love with Kitty Collins in the commission of such acts. It is self-laceration carried out to the nth degree. Steve inevitably dies for having deluded himself into believing that the materialistic Anna loved him. And Cleve Marshall in *The File on Thelma Jordon* suffers a dubious future, blessed nonetheless to have escaped without legal penalty and with his life, after his involvement with Thelma.

The File on Thelma Jordon, like *Christmas Holiday*, has a fluid mise-en-scène that places obsession in context. Cleve Marshall falls in love with Thelma Jordon after a disintegrating but not wholly loveless marriage. His wife's devotion to her father's ambitions leaves Cleve constricted and dispirited by the illusion of happiness nurtured on middle-class convention and material security. He is thrown off course when his childhood friend, Thelma, returns to town. Like John Forbes in André De Toth's *Pitfall*, Cleve submits to an intensifying desire to experience the passion that has been drained from his life. Thelma, in turn, is a more complex variation of the noir *femme fatale* and is portrayed by Barbara Stanwyck with the ambiguity of motive and desire that she displayed as Phyllis Dietrichson. Thelma draws suspicion in her aunt's death, just as she finds herself truly falling in love with Cleve. Upon seeing Thelma's aunt's corpse, Cleve tells Thelma to wait for him by the side door as he douses the lights. Her gaze past him at that point reinforces the unknowability of the female image, for Thelma now recognizes Cleve as an accomplice as well as a potential lover. The conflict for both of them, but especially for Cleve, lies in the destructive and very wrong impulses that lace their desire and in Thelma's undependable love.

Desire, its obsession nurtured and betrayal spawned, becomes, as has been said, the eye of the storm in Siodmak's world, since it is in its throes that the greatest pain is suffered. Terror may be felt in the impending doom of Henderson's imprisonment in *Phantom Lady* or Ole's death in *The Killers*, but the numbing pain of romantic betrayal is the most direct link between Siodmak's expressionism and the romanticism

Cry of the City (1948). Shot, Martin Rome (Richard Conte) tries to escape the law with Brenda's (Shelley Winters) aid.

out of which all expressionistic impulse grew. Cast here in Siodmak's noirs, it is the dazed numbness never quite anticipated that leads to death. "It is fitting that the theme music of *Christmas Holiday* should be 'Always,'" noted Colin McArthur, "and of *Cry of the City*, 'Never.' These are the emotional polarities of Siodmak's world."[37] The Swede dies for having fallen in love with Kitty, who used him out of greed. Robert Mannette must die in Abigail's arms before she can be free of him— before the clouds literally open up to the stars and, symbolically, to her emotional freedom from his grasp. Martin Rome runs afoul of the law, escapes, and risks recapture by Lieutenant Candella in order to convince Tina Riconti to elope with him. She refuses, and he is trapped by his childhood friend, who must shoot him. But the moment that most lyrically defines the misery of betrayal unto death occurs at the end of *Criss Cross*, a film that is "nothing less than a gangland version of *Tristan and Isolde*," wrote Carlos Clarens.[38] In a classic example of betrayal by the unredemptive *femme fatale,* Anna Thompson Dundee steals the payroll money from her present husband, the money that he and her ex-husband, Steve, stole. With the promise of renewed affection for him,

Criss Cross (1949). Steve (Burt Lancaster) and Anna (Yvonne De Carlo) in their moment of final reckoning.

Steve tracks Anna down to a cabin in the country. Surprised by his appearance and annoyed that he may have been followed by her husband, Slim, she tells him that there is no future for them under these circumstances and that the money will give her alone a fresh start. Stunned, Steve cannot fathom her callousness. Slim arrives. He sees them together and shoots them as police sirens are blaring outside. Operatic and miserable, the ending of *Criss Cross* sums up the tragic implications of Siodmak's vision. A world governed by such obsessions and desire must finally turn in on itself and destroy itself. Only in this is there release.

THE INCEPTION OF THE FILM NOIR
IN THE FRENCH CINEMA OF THE 1930S

The birth and development of the film noir can be found in the distinct reflection the French screen of the 1930s held up of a changing European culture, at once impressive in its modernity and anxiety-ridden in its presentation of a world clearly spinning out of control. The realism of this reflection—named "poetic" by various film directors, critics, and historians—was revealed in a body of work that was at heart deeply romantic and often naturalistic. From Marcel Carné and Jacques Prévert, Jean Renoir, Julien Duvivier, and Pierre Chenal came films in which technique itself was a poetic product that represented the social realities of love and betrayal, poverty and crime, and the dark mood of despondency in fog and mist that complemented the brooding nights and shadows of the German screen. It would be inaccurate, however, to consider the French cinema of the interwar years as a permutation of the expressionist forces that gave rise to the German filmmaking of the twenties. Although the influences are there, the French screen of the 1930s brought into focus a much more fatalistic edge, resonant with ineluctable tragedy as well as with the tide of social forces corrupting society. Both the French and the German cinemas made crime films in the early years, with the French offering Louis Feuillade's *Fantômas* series starting in the early silent years (1913–1914) and continuing until Feuillade stopped making crime films in 1920. By the early thirties, the first Maigret stories by Georges Simenon were brought to the screen shortly after their publication: Jean Renoir directed *La Nuit du carrefour* and Julien Duvivier, *La Tête d'un homme*, in 1932. Only the year before, Renoir had made *La Chienne*, based on the La Fouchardière novel, which would be remade fourteen years later in Hollywood as *Scarlet Street*, one of Lang's great noirs.

La Chienne* showcases Janie Marèze as the greedy temptress Lulu who breaks Maurice Legrand's heart and destroys his dignity. Denying his love, Lulu is slapped by a heartbroken Legrand (played by Michel Simon) and runs out into the street, where she is promptly struck dead by a speeding car. Maurice is left crushed at the loss of his love. Whereas Lang's is a nightmarish, more punitive and deterministic vision, one very much in conflict with the vagaries of life and desire—where Chris Cross goes mad after killing Kitty March—Renoir's, by contrast, embraces these vagaries and shows their often tragic contours. "I believe that in [*La Chienne*] I came near to the style that I call poetic realism," Renoir said. "There is not a yard of dubbed film in *La Chienne*. When shooting out of doors, we sought to damp down background noise with hangings and mattresses. I soon discovered that by suitable adjustment an outdoor scene shot on a gray day could give splendid night effects. This was the method I used later in *La Nuit du carrefour*."[39] Simenon himself was originally to shoot *Carrefour*, but the project was given to Renoir instead, with his brother Claude to serve as cameraman and Jacques Becker as production manager. As one of the earliest noir films, *Carrefour* was plagued by production woes, including lack of money and missing footage that, according to Jean-Luc Godard, made for an "ineffably strange and mysterious thriller, more Simenon than Simenon himself."[40]

La Chienne, like Carné's trio of films from the late 1930s—*Le Jour se lève*, *Quai des brumes*, and *Hôtel du Nord*—and the later postwar Allégret noirs (*Dédée d'Anvers*, *Une si jolie petite plage*, and *Manèges*), expresses a fatalism peculiar to the French cinema and quite different from the determinism of the German screen of the twenties. As necessary as the German expressionist formal geography became to generate the despondent noir mood, the abstractness of the soul found greater philosophical expression in the French cinema of the thirties. The psychic malaise written on the physiognomy of the great screen star Jean Gabin—romantic fatalism at its signature best—expressed not fear and terror so much as existential resignation to the perceived inexplicability of man's longings, not terribly mutable through time and destiny. The landscape was urban, dismal, of rain and mist, and the characters were contemporary; but the vision was a precursor to that of the absurdity of man's very existence in a world of suffering and despondency that would preoccupy Camus at the time and prove to be the muse of the great isms of popular postwar French philosophy, from existentialism to absurdism.

The French cinema continued as well to bridge with relative seamlessness the brooding melancholy of the Carné films, Duvivier's *Pépé le Moko*, Jacques Feyder's *Le Grand Jeu*, and Pierre Chenal's *Le Dernier Tournant* with the postwar noirs of Duvivier, Henri-Georges Clouzot, and Yves Allégret. The Carné and Carné–Prévert films described as poetic realist infused more than sadness into their fatalistic world: these prewar films, often considered noirs, like their successors displayed the passions of characters ruled not so much by design as by the desperate attempt to subvert design to the inevitable emotion fueled by romantic desire. Theirs is the death knell sounding the impossibility of passion fulfilled, and in that failure arrives the noir disposition that leads to personal destruction. This is the link to the American noir shared ever so intimately by the French cinema that created a spiritual connection between the two from Renoir through François Truffaut.[41]

> The ideologues of Vichy proclaimed: "We have lost the war
> through the fault of Jean-Paul Sartre and *Quai des brumes*!"
> —Georges Sadoul

Marcel Carné never liked the term *poetic realism*; he saw himself not as a creator of film realism but as an interpreter of it and, as such, an "expressionist."[42] Allowing for his misapplication of the expressionist idea, Carné nonetheless understood the melodrama basis of realism and applied it to narratives that spoke of and to ordinary people trapped in often sordid circumstances and vanquished by the social forces that attenuated their prospects for happiness. In fact, the concept of a movement in a poetic noir realism bears little connection to the historical fact that Renoir, Carné, and Duvivier worked in this style to varying degrees yet never conspired to bring to the screen something approaching a common ideology. Each acknowledged the existence of the others, but none ever communed with the others to formulate the prevailing current.[43] Jean Paulhan, editor of *La Nouvelle Revue Française*, is credited with first using the phrase *poetic realism* in the 1930s to describe the novels of Marcel Aymé, author of *La Rue sans nom*, filmed by Pierre Chenal in early 1933.[44] Portraying the gray Paris torpor enveloping characters bound by a languid malaise in their lives, the mood became so infectious in the work of other filmmakers such as Carné, especially in his collaboration with Jacques Prévert, that a variation of it was often injected with a proletarian view of romantic despair. Surely factory worker Jean Gabin and flower seller Jacqueline Laurent suffer regret over the impossibility of their union in *Le Jour se lève*. The theme of fatal desire in the lives of lower-class heroes "was organized around the perceptions of a single consciousness" and "drew tremendous power from the literary traditions which fostered the climate and techniques of poetic realism."[45] Pierre MacOrlan, author of the contemporary novel *Le Quai des brumes*, influenced this cinematic style, just as Auguste Le Breton would begin to influence the *roman policier*, which in turn would influence the *film policier*.

Quai des brumes (1938). The romantic evocation of grime, violence, and the night.

However, it bears remembering, as Borde and Chaumeton noted, that the world of the working-class hero was not that of organized crime. The characters of Renoir's *La Bête humaine*, the Carné–Prévert films, and Pierre Chenal's 1939 adaptation of James M. Cain's *The Postman Always Rings Twice—Le Dernier Tournant*—are very much the representation of the Popular Front's notion of a cross between the forgotten man and everyman. They suffer as products of a landscape rife with social commentary about the interwar class distinctions that exacerbate the human drama of these characters and personalize it into a passionate portrayal of violence, betrayal, and unrequited longing. MacOrlan's term for his characters' mental activity here was *fantastique social*, "fantastic in the sense of Nerval, where visions and longing shimmer to life in the experience of the most sensitive of characters, and social in the sense that these visions are set not in some extraterrestrial or allegorical milieu but in the heart of contemporary life."[46] The Carné–Prévert films capture this, and Carné's *Hôtel du Nord* epitomizes it.

Le Quai des brumes was made into a movie in the first weeks of

1938 and came out in May. Prévert wrote the scenario and dialogue from MacOrlan's novel and transferred the setting from Montmartre to the harbor of contemporary Le Havre.[47] The film is a darkly lighted work, evoking the grime of a naturalism accentuated by a deprivation of sun and daylight and shrouded in fog. The runaway military man, Jean, played by Jean Gabin, has a sketchy past and seeks encounters with those who will not trouble it. He finds the possibility of an escape by assuming the identity of the painter Michel, who philosophically sees "crime in everything" he paints and wants to end his despondency by ending his life. Michèle Morgan's Nelly is Jean's only hope for happiness; he spends his last night with her and tells her he will send for her when he reaches Venezuela. Carné's fatalism prevents Jean from escaping by positioning him as the jealous other to Nelly's "protector," Zabel (Michel Simon) and the defender of her honor at the hands of the petty gangster, Lucien. Lucien guns him down for his interference, and he dies an example of the raw deal life has dealt him as an outsider who became involved. Jean cannot escape, as Carné shows, from the responsibility of his moral destiny. He killed someone in the past, precipitating his flight; but we understand that his action was motivated by a humane passion quite at odds with Zabel's violent possessiveness toward Nelly. Zabel, who killed Nelly's former lover Maurice and is about to kill Jean, tells her, "I also disgust myself sometimes, yet I go on living."

The hopelessness of this view of life unto death was eclipsed in *Le Jour se lève*. Few films illustrate the plight of ill-fated lovers more beautifully; and again, no one expressed its regret and implosive pain more sympathetically than Gabin. As a companion piece to *Quai des brumes*, *Le Jour se lève* eclipses it as a pinnacle moment of Carné's vision and as one of the true precursors to the techniques used in the film noir. Gabin portrays François, a factory painter and welder, who is destroyed by the pain of his love for the delicate Françoise and her humiliation at the hands of Valentin (Jules Berry), her former lover. François, provoked to kill Valentin, is sought by the authorities and remains holed up in his room on the upper floor of a residential hotel. As he fends off the apprehending police, Jean smokes his cigarettes and relives in three distinct flashback sequences the episodes leading up to the present. The film, lighted in low-key chiaroscuro, is set in a hotel whose stairway is shot to reveal an incredible spatial use, as the camera spirals up to and down from the landing of François's room, just outside of which lies Valentin's dying body, stumbled upon by a confused blind resident. The corridor

Le Jour se lève (1939). Honor and passion: Jean Gabin's François.

and stairway, the hotel's exterior from the street, the factory, and the greenhouse where François and Françoise profess their love were designed by Alexandre Trauner to evoke the discovery of tenderness shared by these two in a world of working-class drabness.

The flashback technique in *Le Jour se lève* makes it a key work in film history in its almost total preoccupation with the point of view of its protagonist as the narrative of the story. The claustrophobia of the setting achieves a remarkable liberation through François's musing, up to the desperate moment when he kills himself. Each flashback episode that he recalls ends with a slow dissolve to the present and another barrage of police fire. It also gives the film the structure of a well-wrought stage drama that comes miraculously to life, by means of the intensity of Gabin's performance, the vividness of Trauner's set design, the abstract camera angles Carné uses to capture it, and Maurice Jaubert's music, which punctuates the key moments as a melody of regret for the impossibility of happiness for François and Françoise.

Raymond Borde spoke of his generation's experience encountering such screen work: "It was the reflection, the crystallization of an anxiety that marked an age. *Quai des brumes* arrived at a time when we discovered Kafka, Sartre, Rimbaud, when one reread Dostoevski, when pallid mornings and damp streets were still shocking images."[48] This particular kind of fatalism, tinged with melancholy and the rather anemic revolt against it, was different from Renoir's passionate and abrupt intrusions of human defiance, which only added to the arbitrary violence of near-tragic endings. One need only compare *La Chienne* or *La Bête humaine* with Carné and Prévert's work to recognize the lack of sadness and regret in the Renoir films. The distinction is even more pronounced with Carné's *Hôtel du Nord*, where Prévert's talents were replaced by those of Henri Jeanson (who wrote the dialogue for *Pépé le Moko*) and Jean Aurenche, who with Jeanson rewrote the scenario based on the populist novel by Eugène Dabit.

Made between the two, *Hôtel du Nord* exemplifies Carné's work of the period to a degree rarely extolled alongside *Quai des brumes* and, especially, *Le Jour se lève*. In a crucial way, however, it marks the end of the vision of romantic possibilities tragically held by the characters in this trilogy. Its action is confined within the Hôtel du Nord (actually in existence as of 1991) and its neighborhood on the Canal St.-Martin in the tenth arrondissement. Carné and Trauner recreated the district as a microcosm of outsiders who function in a world removed from the threats to the social order affecting France at the time. The political right brought about an end to the Popular Front and placated the rabid forces within French society in what would turn out to be a tenacious appeasement of its German neighbors. But *Hôtel du Nord* sought to show that the work-

Hôtel du Nord (1938). Lower-class Eden: moments of happiness, but more of regret.

ing class and social outcasts—the pariahs of Carné's world: Louis Jouvet's gangster, Edmond, and Arletty's marvelous prostitute, Raymonde; François Périer's homosexual Adrien; the despondent lovers Renée and Pierre (played by Annabella and Jean-Pierre Aumont); and Madame Lecouvreur (Jane Marken), who houses them all—could navigate a stunning neighborhood of what must be described as lower-class beauty. Trauner's sets of canal footbridges, railroad tracks crisscrossing below, and the hotel's now-legendary exterior do not deny the hard lives of these characters but allow them to transcend their marginal status in a milieu that becomes their own Eden in Paris.

Renée and Pierre enter into a clumsy suicide pact out of despair at unemployment and a dull future, but their lives are spared through the intervention of Edmond, who falls in love with Renée. However, it is Raymonde, his mistress, who gives *Hôtel du Nord* its touching sense of loss. She cannot have Edmond, she is losing her youth but not her heart, and she will never relinquish her will: she is the prototype for every contemporary prostitute with a heart of gold. Renée and Pierre are reunited, and Edmond sees no future in a life already spent in too much misadventure and with no promise of contentment. On the lam from old accomplices out to get him, he is finally found on Bastille Day. When he enters his hotel room at the end of the film, he clearly has the gun on one of his pursuers. The camera lingers on Edmond as he contemplates the moment, after which he tosses the gun over to the man, expecting to be killed. We hear the shots fired outside the hotel amid the celebration in the street below. Jouvet, like Gabin, is Carné's vehicle of regret for a life bereft of passionate possibilities and happiness. Unlike Gabin, who palpably feels the pain of loss, Jouvet's Edmond accepts its arrival with near impassivity, his facial expression becoming the petrification of the very hopelessness he accepts.

Alexandre Trauner's sets here, indeed as much as Carné's drama, become one of the most memorable evocations of the period and cinema.[49] With *Le Jour se lève* and *Hôtel du Nord*, Trauner caught the dreamlike qualities of the working- and lower-class milieus—the *grisaille* of fog, smoke, and misty nights and perpetual dampness—and transmuted these into a pallette of sadness, which, although unaccompanied by terror (as much of noir despair is), became the Gallic precursor to a world soon to be consumed with terror. The Popular Front's cinema, ironically, was not only the liberation of a darker cinematic imagination that fused expressionism, documentary realism, and politics (if we may include in "politics" all the philosophical and social changes that visited a rapidly changing interwar French society); that cinema was prescient in its implication of doom. The honest passions and destructions so rich with noir overtones are indeed the private ones, with Gabin, Morgan, Michel Simon, Simone Simon, Jouvet, Arletty, and others suggesting in their personal dramas all that was fomenting into the impending public tragedy that would soon bring to a close this moment in film history.

Jean Gabin emerged as the hero of this French cinema and, it may be argued, a unique hero in the history of cinema that may never be reinvented. For Gabin grew, almost since the beginning of his film career, to embody a remarkable composite of qualities to which no other star can lay claim. Proletarian, urban, romantic, strong, intrepid, and sentimental, Gabin never deviated from a personality that served him well for forty years. "He incarnates the myth of the brave one driven to stealing or murder, then to despair or death, betrayed by life and love, hunted down by destiny," François Guérif wrote.[50] Or, as André Bazin so aptly put it, "[t]he public that swallows many affronts would undoubtedly feel that they were being taken for a ride if screenwriters presented them with a happy ending for Jean Gabin."[51] Gabin alone among several distinguished screen actors of the era—including Michel Simon—would translate these virtues to the detective figure in several *policiers noirs* and, throughout the 1950s, assume a stature that would be credibly labeled heroic in much the same manner as that of Bogart's after *Casablanca*.

The interwar French cinema, speculated Bazin in 1954, could well have been linked to the country's literature of that time. As he saw it, the "equivalent of the prewar *film noir* might have been a product grown for the screen out of the confluence of the post–World War I populism of Dabit and the Surrealist-inspired influence of Jacques Prévert and Jean Aurenche, as well as Existentialism."[52] Borde and Chaumeton doubted that any of this influenced the American film noir. They thought Duvivier, Renoir, and Carné were clearly speaking within the well-defined working-class social milieu of their experience, a world without excessive eroticism and violence. Except for the poetry of visual imagery (wet pavements, cityscapes, urban characters, hotels, gray mornings), there "is no evidence that a John Huston or a Howard Hawks watched a single French film of this period."[53] It is difficult to elaborate an argument for the cross-cultural influence of the French poetic realism of the 1930s and the birth of the American film noir shortly after. Unlike the German émigrés who established more than a toehold on the American cinema of the 1940s, the French artists can claim only a more diffuse and pervasive influence—namely, that worlds were colliding at a perilous time, and the spillage would permeate the humane concerns of many genre film artists henceforth. It is fair to speculate that without the melancholy and despair, without the conventional prohibitions discarded and the private rebellions enacted on screen, the scenarios that ended without sunshine would have remained trapped in a discrete period of film history. Instead, this vision became ensconced in a style that portended the irrational, the nightmarish and violent, elements that would be found in the American film noir and become those dark forces that certainly bear an affinity to the fatalism of the best French cinema of the thirties.

The Film Noir in France in the Immediate Postwar Years

From 1920 to the present, the evolution of the *roman noir* has provided the literary tableau from which the postwar French film noir was spawned, complete with the crimes and passions that one associates with the fiction of the American hard-boiled school.[54] An early variant of this is, of course, Simenon's Inspector Maigret (*Pietr-le-Letton*, 1931). From Simenon also came Julien Duvivier's 1946 *Panique*, with Viviane Romance, and Henri-Georges Clouzot's 1954 *Les Diaboliques,* with Simone Signoret and Véra Clouzot. The two significant developments during the forties that shaped the appeal of the *roman noir*, however, were Léo Malet's invention of "troubleshooter" Nestor Burma, "above all a first-rate private eye who is *French*,"[55] and the publication of the Série Noire.

Nestor Burma explored the criminal element of the day set against the Occupation and the realities of the war's aftermath. The films *120, rue de la Gare* (1943), *L'Homme au sang bleu* (1945), and *Le Cinquième Procédé* (1947) established a persona that functioned as a cross between Philip Marlowe and a provocateur out of Eric Ambler. But as popular as Malet's detective became, the enduring legacy of the *roman noir* was established with Marcel Duhamel's creation of the Série Noire for Gallimard. Duhamel published translations of the American hard-boiled masters (Burnett's *Little Caesar*, Cain's *Double Indemnity*) that rivaled in popularity anything else being published at the time. So many filmmakers were to derive their inspirations and adaptations from novels they read in the Série Noire that it is fair to say that the nouvelle vague and the careers of several of its filmmakers, notably Godard and Truffaut, would have lacked such a meteoric rise without it. Other imprimaturs proliferated throughout the 1950s in a vain attempt to cash in on Duhamel's readership. Éditions La Tarente published a series of novels that mimicked the Série's installments but diluted their cultural appeal by calling them *franco-américains*. Other imitators included collections from Lutèce and Éditions Jacquier à Lyon. Les Presses de la Cité and Flammarion also started detective series. However, the decisive influence of the Série Noire, particularly with Albert Simonin, Duhamel's successor, at the helm, shaped and gave resonance to the noir gangster in French popular literature, evoking the postwar philosophical climate. Surely Auguste Le Breton's *Touchez pas au grisbi* and *Du Rififi chez les hommes* and José Giovanni's *Le Deuxième Souffle* captured in striking relief the cinematic imaginations of Jacques Becker, Jules Dassin, and Jean-Pierre Melville. Bazin saw in Jean Delannoy's adaptation of *Dieu a besoin des hommes* (1950) the success of the Série Noire on screen.[56] Noël Simsolo wrote disapprovingly, though, that "in France, American 'film noir' has become a style, whereas in America the times have changed. The gangsters of yesterday have returned in business, the syndicate, or the political parties."[57]

Throughout the 1940s and into the 1950s, the spirit of the noir was found in the films of Henri Decoin—in *Les Inconnus dans la maison* (1941), based on Simenon, and, more notably, *Razzia sur la chnouf* (1954)—in the work of Duvivier and Clouzot (*Quai des Orfèvres*, 1947),[58] and in Yves Allégret's *Dédée d'Anvers* (1947), *Une si jolie petite plage* (1948), and *Manèges* (1950).

Violence was inevitable as an evolutionary step (or, some may say, devolutionary decline) in the postwar French noir. The hope wrought in the blind love between two lovers (say, Gabin and Morgan) was now too corroded by the wartime experience, which reminded all of the need to satisfy man's baser instincts. Harsher did not necessarily mean the poetic *grisaille* of an urban background at dawn, and when Carné and Prévert "heated up yet another brew of luxuriant melancholia in the postwar *Les Portes de la nuit* (1946), with one of Prévert's death-symbol characters stalking the streets of Paris, fatalism began to look like affectation. We had been there once too often."[59] Instead, what we now had on the French screen was Simone Signoret in *Dédée d'Anvers* and *Manèges* conveying the same hardened veneer and ambiguous affectlessness we associate with Barbara Stanwyck on the American screen. Abused by her pimp, Marco, an entranced Dédée tells her soon-to-be lover, Francesco, as both witness a vicious street fight, of the thrill she receives in watching men beat up each other—the more brutal, the more exciting. In *Panique*, Viviane Romance's Alice masochistically prostrates herself to her thief-lover upon her release from jail. "No, I liked my prison because it was for *you* I was serving time!" she insists. "I wanted to suffer more to show you how much I loved you!"[60] The landscape, although gray and misty, is less a symbol of the despondent soul than an expression of mob prejudice targeted against the pathetic Hire (played by Michel Simon). These films noirs stand parallel to the American noirs imported to France immediately after the war, which Nino Frank recognized in 1946 as a new kind of American cinema. Jean-Pierre Chartier, in the same year, spoke in *Revue du Cinéma* of the difference between what he saw as the French school of films noirs of the late thirties—*Quai des brumes* or *Hôtel du Nord*—and the recent American imports, specifically Billy Wilder's *Double Indemnity* and *The Lost Weekend* and Edward Dmytryk's *Murder, My Sweet*. The French noirs

Panique (1946). Postwar passion and betrayal: Alfred (Paul Bernard) and Alice (Viviane Romance).

Dédée d'Anvers (1947). Postwar passion and submission: Francesco (Marcel Pagliero) and Dédée (Simone Signoret).

before the war "struck fewer chords of revolt, love was passing through them like a mirage of a better world, an implicit social demand was opening the door to hope and, if figures in these films were desperate, they sustained our pity or our sympathy." About the American noir figures, he said, "There's nothing like that here: these are monsters, criminals, or sick people that nothing excuses and who act as they do only by fate of the illness which is in them."[61]

The French postwar noir in retrospect seems to be a blend of the romantic infusion of poetic realism tempered by a residual wartime grit; existentialism, as it must surely have emanated from the literary cafés of Left Bank Paris; and the recent influences of the American film noir with its roots in the hard-boiled fiction that preceded it.[62] Like many American noirs, *Une si jolie petite plage* emphasizes through the irony of its title—"such a pretty bit of shoreline"—the miserable lives of its main characters, Pierre and Marthe. These two share an emotional conspiracy of pain and regret and do so through the constant rainfall and howling wind that closes off a shabby resort and confines its guests in a gloomy atmosphere that invites depression more than menace. Gérard Philipe has fled here to his boyhood home after a sordid episode involving murder and, much like Gabin in *Quai des brumes*, is presented as among the righteous tormented of the world that live with unspoken guilt over a grim past. The laconic pursuit of him by the authorities is synchronous with the reluctance to condemn him. Indeed, the dreary atmosphere is the most evocative condemnation in Allégret's film. The low-key lighted interiors (although Philipe receives gentle, front lighting) and seemingly malevolent guests provide a punitive environment that encourages Pierre to flee again from the approaching police. His departure comes almost as a permission to exit the story, with the viewers' knowledge that he will never find solace. The resort, which held unpleasant childhood memories for him, is no less a hell for Pierre than staying on the run, and indeed it reiterates the Sartrean premise that there is no exit from oneself or the judgment of others. The part was written specifically for Philipe by screenwriter Jacques Sigurd, and his performance embodies the *tendresse* of the soul from which anguish ceases to surface and now becomes its very essence.

Manèges, released in 1950, has Simone Signoret adding greater definition to her screen image as *femme fatale*. Shot in flashbacks, it refers most perfectly to the American studio noir of the time: Signoret's

Une si jolie petite plage (1948). Image of anguish: Gérard Philipe's Pierre haunted by the past.

Dora is clearly intent on using her respectable husband, a riding academy owner (Bernard Blier), to acquire the necessary financial security and social standing to fuel further social climbing—all this with the total encouragement of her mother, played by the formidable Jane Marken.[63] Dora maintains a lover, who dumps her just as she dumps her husband. Her plans foiled, she has a near-fatal automobile accident, and the extent of her scheming is revealed to all in flashback scrutiny.

Allégret's films noirs counterpoint the appearance in the late 1940s of filmmaker André Hunebelle's series of films that, for Borde and Chaumeton, recalled the wry stylishness of Hammett's Nick and Nora Charles.[64] In *Mission à Tanger*, Hunebelle inaugurated the dashing adventurer-hero personified in several guises by the film star Raymond Rouleau, whose coolness would later suggest the more poignant characters of Jean-Pierre Melville. (Indeed, *Bob le flambeur* movingly aestheticizes this figure.) André Hunebelle was a newspaper publisher (*La Flèche*), then a master glassmaker who found himself in Nice during the war without a specific occupation. Marcel Achard steered him toward the cinema, where he became a production manager, then a producer of movies. Responsible for several big comedy successes during the Occupation (*L'Inévitable M. Dubois*, *Florence est folle*), he finally decided to take full control of his filmmaking by making a series of comedies with titles beginning with the letter *M*, after filmmaker Pierre Benoît, whose romantic heroines had first names that began with the letter *A*. Hunebelle went on to make *Mission à Tanger*, *Méfiez-vous des blondes*, and *Massacre en dentelles*.[65] Raymond Rouleau would play the role of "the perfectly amoral man of action with vaguely anarchistic tendencies, of elementary and violent pleasures yet tender memories of a social class in a state of crisis." And he would be flanked by his resourceful photographer-sidekick, Bernard Lajarrige, "a fitting eccentric in this role."[66] Michel Audiard wrote the Rouleau films and was himself a detective novelist for the Fleuve Noir label and was inspired by the rich mythology of the American private eye popularized by the Série Noire translations. His hero was defined by the formula "Thoughts and words do not necessarily kill the action."[67]

Rouleau created the prototype further extended by the second actor whose presence on the French screen in the 1950s cannot be overestimated: Eddie Constantine. As private eye–adventurer Lemmy Caution, Constantine created a popular protagonist of action and violence in such films as Bernard Borderie's *Les Femmes s'en balancent* (1953), *Cet homme est dangereux* (1953), *Je suis en sentimental* (1955, directed by the exiled McCarthy casualty, John Berry), *Ces dames préfèrent le mambo* (1957), and *Le Grand Bluff* (1957). As a kind of continental Mike Hammer, the Constantine mystique sustained a body of films that culminated in Godard's reflective 1965 paean to the cultural status of his "heroism," *Alphaville*.

Rouleau and Constantine were joined by a rejuvenated Jean Gabin, who reinvented himself in such films as *Touchez pas au grisbi* (Jacques Becker, 1953) and *Razzia sur la chnouf* as a figure of iconic significance, playing characters who navigate the corridors of the underworld as effortlessly as the venues of respectable society. Indeed, Decoin's *Razzia sur la chnouf* (roughly translated "drug sweep") takes the audience through a tour of the Paris underworld of drugs, straight and gay after-hours bars, and murder, the likes of which would not be seen on the American screen for another dozen years. Here, a woman is raped by a young Lino Ventura in reprisal for lost drug money while her husband is forced to watch, and a drug-crazed Lila Kedrova dances to an erotically charged African beat in an after-hours club as she is surrounded by a group of muscled male patrons intent on having an orgy with her on

Touchez pas au grisbi (1953). The final shootout: shades of Hollywood.

Razzia sur la chnouf (1954). Gabin twenty years later.

the dance floor. Gabin bears witness to all this, yet stands apart from it. The gravity of the Gabin figure finally becomes the subject matter here, and our fascination is with the resilience of his humane appeal almost twenty years after his explosion as the quintessential proletarian hero of the prewar French cinema. "For ten years Humphrey Bogart interpreted the same figure in the American *noirs*," wrote Borde and Chaumeton in 1955, "and no one has it in mind to hold it against him."[68] In the same manner, Gabin sustained and deepened the élan vital of his screen myth.

THE NOIR
IN AMERICA

It is perhaps most useful to consider the development of the film noir as the confluence of cinematic changes that, in themselves, are found in other kinds of films without the specific resonances and appeals that in play with one another establish the coherent mythology that we recognize as noir cinema. The nexus of these changes occurred at a crucial time in the nation's history and in the history of film. Around 1940, with war looming in Europe, the artists of film, theater, and literature who emigrated to America found the apparatus of Hollywood at their disposal; too often, however, Hollywood withheld its consent for artistic freedom. They adapted, for better or worse, to a world that was ruled by commerce but which sought to utilize the artistry it imported. The distance was essential, for these artists combined experiences distinctly at odds with the optimism promulgated by most studio fare at the time. "In fact these émigrés were all too well prepared to lend themselves to the construction of a 'world' filled with fear and distrust where survival necessitates a sardonic detachment," Robert Porfirio noted.[1] Lang, Wilder, Preminger, Siodmak, Dieterle, and later Ophüls were at the same place at the same time; and they, along with their native counterparts from Huston and Welles to Polonsky and Fuller, created the look of noir cinema in their filmmaking and practically held it accountable for the passions and unsavory destruction of their characters. Noir cinema was, in fact, born in the entertainment marketed of the big "no" to the depression-era cheeriness that movies sold as an escape valve to audiences coping with the ruder realities of American life. There were gangster films in the 1930s, but none that implicated the darker side and the universal weaknesses of modern moviegoing audiences quite the way noir characters did.

Abraham Polonsky directs John Garfield and Beatrice Pearson in *Force of Evil.*

What the American hard-boiled school did on paper, what Cornell Woolrich wrote to a sizable readership, matched perfectly the subject matter of the early films noirs. The terror of the noir landscape was explained through the increased interest in Freudian psychology—again, popularized as never before through the influence of émigré intellectuals—and the impact of desolation and dislocation stemming from the ravages of war and the philosophical investigations nourished by them. The changes ensconced in a modern world of social and cultural upheaval reflected everything from the class structure underpinning American society to the altered role of women, to the threat of organized crime; and they often contoured the human psyche in ways that showed an America quite ambivalent in the pursuit of its dream. Often little was stated of these changes—certainly not in any marketing ploy by the Hollywood publicity machine—but all these developments converged in a cinema that *suggested their essential value* in a dramatic world that appealed to the changing consciousness of the American moviegoer.

THE NOIR CITY

The city landscape envisioned as a requisite setting for the film noir symbolizes the conflict of all cities in their collection of different groups of people with competing influences and interests. But much more than this, the noir city individuates human motivations and passions, the very display of which serve as a morality tale of the course modern man has

Cry of the City (1948), opening title credit.

taken in his developed society with its institutions, values, and enticements. Within this urban world, the individual is alternately lost and at
home, a refugee from others; as a lone human spirit, the person exercises his or her will to be heard among all the other cries, making that
paradoxical claim of all noir characters for whom the city has been a
modifying existential experience: to be one among none. The quest of
June Goth in *Deadline at Dawn*, Joe Morse in *Force of Evil*, Skip McCoy
in *Pickup on South Street*, Johnny Kelly in *City That Never Sleeps*, and
Richard Widmark's Harry Fabian in *Night and the City* becomes, in the
end, a quest to locate the self lost in a world of clutter, distraction, and
noise—what Sartre recognized as the *de trop* of existence—and in the
process claim a measure of personal identity. It is the loss of self among
the masses that stimulates so many noir protagonists to confront themselves in a milieu that produces such anxiety and dispossession; and
those who do—lost souls or criminals and their pursuers—find in the
myth of a pitiless urban world an odd validation of their individualism.

The mythical noir city most often exists somewhere in the
postdepression 1940s spanning into the 1950s and bears, really, little
connection to the social verisimilitude of urban life at the time, although
it certainly draws upon those social realities to shape its voluptuousness
and resonate its philosophy. The fluctuations of the progressive period
of American economic growth in the 1920s, followed by the crash of
1929, the Great Depression, and the nation's recovery from it during the
first years of the Roosevelt administration, spawned an American public
chastened, made wise from collective suffering. "Optimism in its native
form disappeared and was replaced for a time by an equally naïve pessimism," wrote historian Leo Gurko in the early fifties. "Existence, we
now realized, was no longer the simple thing it had appeared to be at the
turn of the century but a difficult, tortuous, often painful process. A
dawning awareness of the tragedy of life and of the necessity for struggle
in the perpetual effort to master it now began to filter into the uncon-
sciousness of the American people."[2] It is this tremulousness of American urban life, rooted in historical consequence, that reverberates in the
look and the vitality of the noir city and its residents. The criminality
and passions driving many noir characters stem from the premise that
the insecurity of existence here promises little in rectitude, and so pursuing one's obsessions becomes acceptable, even desirable, in the face
of an unclear future.

Kasper Gutman devotes his life to going from city to city and country to country in search of the elusive falcon statue. We do not see him or his cohorts against a literal urban background, but we clearly accept the cosmopolitanism of their lives as very much the product of the noir city of the imagination, fraught with promiscuous excitement and danger— an ideal panorama of human weakness and vice. Just as clearly, the semi-documentary realism of Jules Dassin's *Naked City* actually shows us not an untouched real New York City but the noir city "naked" with the tension of potential violence and crime; and we see the death of an attractive young woman whose murder, lurid and mysterious, transforms her life into a quest for answers. It is in the noir city of neon signs and after-hours clubs where killer Tommy Udo can swagger like a "big man" in *Kiss of Death* (Henry Hathaway, 1947). It is in the noir city of Abraham Polonsky's *Force of Evil* (1948), with all its Wall Street architectural splendor, that Joe Morse and his brother Leo attempt to define the parameters for an ethical life in—what else?—the numbers racket. It is in the noir city evoked in *The Big Sleep* that the musty allure of pornography, nymphomania, extortion, and murder can flourish from bungalow to nightclub, and with plenty of cars and taxis available to make the connecting trips as interesting as possible—yet we see not one significant stretch of urban architecture around. It is in Robert Siodmak's jazz club and burlesque house, in the dark and menacing subway platforms during the sweltering nighttime heat, that the noir city of *Phantom Lady* takes shape in our imagination and before our eyes. And it is in Harry Fabian's running, always running, toward his death in Dassin's *Night and the City* (1950) that we see his isolation against the neon and asphalt of the noir city. In Siodmak's *Cry of the City* (1948), Lieutenant Candella shoots Martin Rome dead in the night as Rome attempts to flee on the sidewalks of their old neighborhood. It is one of the defining moments in establishing the thrall of the noir city, as violence and death mingle with the lure of the city's excitement to the musical theme of Alfred Newman's "Street Scene," a background composition used repeatedly—at least four times—in the Fox cycle of films noirs during the forties and early fifties. It matters little that Candella was ostensibly pursuing justice by shooting Rome, any more than Harry Callahan's wanton violence has feeble rationale in Siegel's *Dirty Harry* (1971) a generation later. Or that Travis Bickle exercises a distorted moral psychosis in defense of his city of New York in Martin Scorsese's *Taxi Driver* (1976). Each of them defends or fights the city against the nihilism of a noir world that in the end can promise only death. For the gangsters and criminals pursued here and in other noirs, "there is only the city," as Robert Warshow wrote, "not the real city, but that dangerous and sad city of the imagination which is so much more important, which is the modern world."[3]

ARCHETYPES—PROTAGONISTS

The two archetypes of the film noir are the pursued and the pursuer. By far the man pursued is the greater illustration of noir torment, followed by the one that pursues him, to be found in such roles as private detectives, policemen, law enforcement agents, insurance investigators, spurned lovers, and double-crossed accomplices. The pursuers are mentioned throughout this book, but some discussion that limns the role of the pursued as an example of postwar urban man is useful here.

The archetypal noir protagonist who flees externally imposed torments, by society or the law, or the paranoia that has consumed his imagination and provokes the act of running is the moral picture of a character who runs, for whatever reason, out of guilt. In noir cinema, the moral landscape becomes a murky proposition: characters, mostly men, run away to escape their complicity in some actual or perceived incident of negation. The negation may be criminal and may not be totally reprehensible. A desperate and scared Bowie flees the law with Keechie in *They Live by Night*; Jeff Bailey is caught in Kathie Moffet's pernicious web of deceit and murder and runs from a "dark past" in *Out of the Past* (Jacques Tourneur, 1947); war vet Bill Saunders, in a fit of derangement, kills someone and must assume a new identity in *Kiss the Blood Off My Hands* (Norman Foster, 1948); and Larry Ballentine, philanderer and egotist, explains his web of lies—lie after lie (really, a form of escape)—to a jury that ironically acquits him in *They Won't Believe Me* (Irving Pichel, 1947). The idea here implies not that criminality, derangement, and anarchy are to be justified—not always—but that the noir archetype is best understood as the character whose human weaknesses and passions receive no kind reception in a social order structured to deny their existence. It is not that crimes—socially destabilizing acts warranting just punishment—must be defended; indeed, too many noir protagonists lack redemptive virtues. Rather, the noir archetype is one of anxiety in a modern world that functions as a sensorium of disillusionment, of disabling human identity. But more must be said here: the noir protagonist is not a pathogen. The most extreme sociopathic tendencies found in any citizen are unhealthy for a truly free society. However, the noir protagonist skirts the contours of an accepted social terrain; he may be seen as the citizen who sees the sociopathology nascent in a world that refuses to recognize its insinuation in the creation of it.

To know the noir protagonist most accurately, we must see the broken image of modern urban man, who at his most destructive quashes a ubiquitous American optimism. John Garfield in *He Ran All the Way* (John Berry, 1951), Robert Ryan in *On Dangerous Ground* and *Odds against Tomorrow* (Robert Wise, 1959), Richard Widmark in *Kiss of Death* and *Road House* (Jean Negulesco, 1948), Cliff Robertson in *Underworld U.S.A.* (Samuel Fuller, 1961), and William Bendix in *The Blue Dahlia* (George Marshall, 1946) play nihilistic characters, destructive precisely because their enterprises are violent and criminal and because they tell us that in the face of optimism and normality there are fissures, eruptions, that speak to the intransigent dark nature of man. We recoil from such characters in real life, but the film noir asks us to look at them more closely. If they exist among us—as they surely do—then what do they have to say to us? The psychology and reformative measures of social health are exposed for their inadequacies in the presence of these characters who betray, steal, and kill because in their world they have to. The film noir does not always ask us to pity them; often it is enough that we consider them as they move about their landscape, for their reverberations are much more spiritual and moral than psychological. Why in this world can such characters not be changed? Is there a myth of destruction that they carry? If we assume a contemplative attitude toward the unregenerate and their demons, then we may certainly take pity on those blinded by their weaknesses and victimized by circumstance. These are by far the greater number of noir protagonists on screen and the ones that challenge us to redefine the contours of American life—contours now extended to include the desperate that run away from their fears in a world that gave those fears shape.

Flight assumes many forms—certainly not all of them criminal—and the noir protagonist often attempts to escape a painful past too uncomfortable to face. That the film noir gained popularity during the wartime years is no accident: many war veterans returned to a disorienting civilian life in a changed society. The war effort mechanized and modernized the landscape, and women had undertaken work and performed jobs during the war that would permanently change their status

High Sierra (1941). Humphrey Bogart as Roy Earle: a precursor to the troubled noir protagonist. With Ida Lupino as Marie.

The Killers (1946). Swede Anderson (Burt Lancaster) fondles Kitty's green handkerchief, contemplating her betrayal of his love.

Night and the City (1950). Harry Fabian (Richard Widmark): the face of noir despair.

Act of Violence (1949). Frank Enley (Van Heflin): the fear of the hunted.

in the equation of gender power. In the film noir too, their position becomes uncertain and their motives questionable in an obscure battle of lust and power. If the film noir in all its misogyny chiseled anything at all, it was the image, alternately flattering and crippling, of the strong woman driven by destructive impulses.

In this context, the anonymous urban male was further driven to anonymity as the displaced man returning from war to a new city not quite sure how to accommodate him. Here, in the noir tableau, we find Sam Masterson in *The Strange Love of Martha Ivers* (Lewis Milestone, 1946), George Taylor in *Somewhere in the Night* (Joseph L. Mankiewicz, 1946), Rip Murdock in *Dead Reckoning* (John Cromwell, 1947), Joe Parkson in *Act of Violence* (Fred Zinnemann, 1949), and Nick Garcos in *Thieves' Highway* (Jules Dassin, 1949). And then there is investigator Bradford Galt in *The Dark Corner* (Henry Hathaway, 1946), whose disorientation comes as a total mystery, who is a pursuer pursued for no apparent reason, and whose phantom pursuers only reinforce the irrational world enveloping him. Each leaves a world of certain knowledge,

The Dark Corner (1946). Bradford Galt (Mark Stevens) and his secretary, Kathleen (Lucille Ball): "I feel all dead inside. I'm backed up in a dark corner and I don't know who's hitting me!"

where he maintains a footing, a rank, an order, to enter a destabilizing world of betrayal and greed or of reckless passion. Like the noir private detective hero, the mystery comes not from the crime committed or action taken but from the corrupt or unknown motives behind it, which, because they are fragments in an unclear equation, come to symbolize the suspicious and fearful side of man. Although Cornell Woolrich's Martin Blair is not a veteran, we still need only think of him here; in *Black Angel* he fulfills the ultimate prescription for noir terror as the Oedipal pursuer for his own crime. For if the world is not populated only by the visible hunters and hunted, then certainly it is populated by a more complicated species of common man—that person who fears the malevolent forces around him, and thus within himself. He is the noir archetype, and he often runs away from both.

ABRAHAM POLONSKY (1910–1999)

Body and Soul (screenplay, 1947)
Force of Evil (1948)

Abraham Polonsky remains one of the great creative forces in noir cinema simply on the basis of two works—the definitive boxing film, *Body and Soul*, for which he wrote the screenplay, and the brilliant *Force of Evil*, perhaps the most passionate and philosophically resonant of all films noirs. No other noir filmmaker has infused his work with the specificity of moral weight in time and place as Polonsky has in *Force of Evil*, his reworking of Ira Wolfert's 1943 socialist novel, *Tucker's People*. And it must surely be recognized as one of the most fortuitous complements in screen history that Polonsky had John Garfield portray the anguished protagonists in both of these films. Garfield, the most biblically angry of all the young men of the screen for whom he must be acknowledged as prototype—James Dean, Marlon Brando, Robert De Niro—has only grown in complexity and stature as the affectations of his successors dim in light of his striking authenticity of manner.

Polonsky wrote the screenplay of *Body and Soul* for Robert Rossen, but the entire film is so infused with Polonsky's vision of the spiritually vanquished noir hero that Charley Davis provides the inevitable link and philosophical metamorphosis to Joe Morse in *Force of Evil*. When Charley betrays his mob backers and fails to throw a fight, he asks them,

"What're you gonna do, kill me? . . . Everybody dies." The resigned fatalism of this punched-out remark lays out the bleakest thesis of the film noir in its recognition of death, in whatever style, as an inevitability. It is an awareness that can only liberate and empower the living.

Polonsky also wrote the screenplay for Don Siegel's *Madigan* (1968), and, as was only recently acknowledged, he wrote (uncredited) the screenplay for Robert Wise's 1959 *Odds against Tomorrow*, when he was blacklisted from the industry.[4] But it is his screenplay for *Body and Soul* that so clearly dominates the noir tone of troubled passion in the story—almost as to redefine the power of brilliant screenwriting. For *Body and Soul* is Polonsky's voice incarnated through boxer Charley Davis's ascent in the ring as he discovers the corruption supporting it and, finally, rebels against it. James Wong Howe's cinematography, the perfect corollary for this internal struggle, shows Charley fighting in the ring, his battered face captured in low-angle shots against a low-key lighted background. His rounds are interspersed with gritty shots of excited spectators in sharp front lighting. The final ring sequences serve

Body and Soul (1947). A mother's love: Charley Davis (John Garfield), out of the ring, dismisses her (Anne Revere) advice.

not as the pinnacle of boxing glory but as the metaphor of entrapment, of suffocation, for an increasingly enlightened man. Charley's bouts for titles and money become, here, the "body" blows that condition his "soul." And in this sense, Polonsky's social consciousness, namely that bad money corrupts, achieves the grandeur of a greater theme particularly important to the film noir—namely, that corruption insidiously consumes all who participate in it, deforming their human character as it leaves them lost to reclaim what it once was. The boxing racket emerges as one more existential test in such a corrupt and seductive world. It is the condition of this world that costs Charley the lives of his best friend, Shorty, and his sparring partner, Ben. It is, in a larger framework, the world that saw Charley's father murdered by a bomb blast in reprisal for his opposition to a neighborhood speakeasy.

John Garfield, the apotheosis of the agonized noir man, displays— portends—the torment that a corrupted government would soon exercise against him. The HUAC hearings and subsequent harassment that were to kill him find no more compelling analogy than in Charley's attempt to defy his owners in that perpetual struggle of the noir protagonist: the need to stand alone in a world that rejects the quarrelsome rebel voice. In Polonsky's films, Garfield emerges as the most complete modern urban representation of this protagonist, whose moral dilemmas arise from the specific milieu of New York City and whose American Jewish identity informs us of the immigrant heritage that shaped the inner man: a more perfect meld of star and hero could not exist. Charley Davis came from a working-class family whose cohesiveness stemmed from the shared struggles of a mother and father bound together as much out of love as out of the necessity to make a life in the Lower East Side without relinquishing their humane values to the excitements and intimidations of a teeming metropolis. "Fight for something," Anna Davis tells her son, "but not for money"—just as Leo Morse in *Force of Evil* reminds his younger brother, Joe, that all his sacrifices were for him, to provide him with the law school education that has now only served to make Joe a tool of a criminal "corporation" and of Leo's own demise. "All that Cain did to Abel was murder him!" Leo rages at this brother after Joe has him arrested.

George Barnes, the canny photographer of publicity photos for some of Hollywood's more famous aging stars, shot New York City's Wall Street in *Force of Evil* with an eloquence rarely seen at the time— of on-location low-angle shots from a distance that awaken the viewer

Force of Evil (1948). Benevolent corruption: Joe Morse (John Garfield) observes his brother Leo's bookie operation.

to all the possibilities and defeats of life in this city, of its promises and betrayals. In this context Joe Morse discovers himself through a project of self-analysis that underscores every step of his actions and illustrates the moral necessity of his introspection. This introspection occurs in voice-over, and with such prominence that its strangeness is haunting. Polonsky uses it as a discrete dramatic function to state, among other things, Joe's intentions and emotions and then to restate these through his actions. But its power is intensified far beyond this aesthetic role to animate the *spirit* of a man, one Joe Morse, who loves with some difficulty his brother Leo in this city he calls his home. It is the most impressive use of the voice-over in noir filmmaking. And it is this anthropomorphizing of the city in vital tandem with the words and actions of our noir protagonist, in such a manner that Polonsky's screenplay becomes part of a near-perfect fugue of visual and aural poetry, that intoxicates us and leaves us in awe of all that such an experience in the movies can mean. No other film noir has captured the power of this particular vision of New York or so perfectly insinuated its wonder, melancholy, and tragedy.

> This is Wall Street, and today was important. Because tomorrow, July 4th, I intended to make my first million dollars—an exciting day in any man's life . . . Temporarily, the enterprise was slightly illegal.
>
> —Joe Morse, *Force of Evil*

Force of Evil came at the beginning of a period when the public was recognizing that crime had become organized like a business enterprise, and the question of its degrees of corruption is central to the film's theme. Joe speaks of Tucker's "corporation," of the consolidation of numbers banks as "the combination" in which Leo's bank can make more money as the leading depository for bets made. Leo's skepticism is old-fashioned; after all, he has maintained an intimate business, with a paternal interest in his employees and taking only modest risks for his own modest gain. "We're normal financiers," Joe tries to persuade Leo—and, indeed, he has tried to have the numbers legalized, albeit unsuccessfully, with the aim of having the business run as a more lucrative enterprise. These euphemisms and the taint of Leo's involvement in an illegal enterprise illustrate the seductive power of corruption in Polonsky's film, for they beg the question of when such involvement becomes truly unsupportable and irreversible. When, on a primal level, does it justify betrayal and violence? The seduction for Joe Morse is in the influence and the money and the power behind it, and he has contempt for Leo's lack of ambition. "It's perversion," he tells Doris Lowry. "Don't you see what it is? It's not natural. To go to great expense for something you want, that's natural. To reach out to take it, that's human. That's natural. But to get your pleasure from not taking, from cheating yourself deliberately like my brother did today, from not getting, from not taking—don't you see what a black thing that is for a man to do? How it is to hate yourself?"

In his attempt to sponsor Leo's bank in Tucker's corporation, Joe traverses the city in a quest of self-justification for the plan he has made for his life, and Polonsky shows us, again, the city that renders the brothers' lives a noir experience. Tucker's well-appointed apartment is shot in low-key lighting, with the apartment hotel sign blinking on and off through the window at night; Joe goes to Leo's apartment building, climbing the stairway shot darkly in high angle, to confront his brother about complying with the corporation; he takes Doris for a taxi ride home, during which he betrays a tenderness and a restrained guilt and anger about how his life is perceived; Leo meets his bookkeeper, Bauer, who has informed against everyone out of fear, in the neighborhood coffee shop where he will eventually be shot—an iconically appointed establishment, only as such establishments are prone to be in noir movies; and, finally, Joe and Doris go down to the East River to find Leo's body after the collapse of Tucker's scheme has cost him his life.

This scene, shot against the panorama of Manhattan's Wall Street district, becomes a glorious visual dirge for Leo's death accompanied by Joe's internal confession, revelatory and penitent. "I found my brother's body at the bottom there," he speaks in voice-over, "where they had thrown it away on the rocks, by the river. Like an old, dirty rag nobody wants. He was dead. And I felt I had killed him. I turned back to give myself up . . . because if a man's life can be lived so long and come out this way, like rubbish, then something was horrible, and had to be ended one way or another. And I decided to help." The ending of *Force of Evil* is a reclamation of one's self and one's responsibility in the world, as it illustrates the greatest awareness any noir protagonist can have the moment he stops running: to face oneself in the clarity of failure, of misbegotten ambitions, of submission to those passions that excite and then destroy—in other words, to define who one finally is in a world where one has never felt at home is to have made a lucid yet painful existential truce. "[H]aving reached the absolute moral bottom of commitment, there's nothing left to do but commit yourself," Polonsky said. "There's no longer a problem of identity when you have no identity left at all. So, in your next step, you must become something."[5]

JULES DASSIN (1911–   )

Brute Force (1947)
The Naked City (1948)
Thieves' Highway (1949)
Night and the City (1950)
Rififi (*Du Rififi chez les hommes* [1955])

Jules Dassin directed four films noirs between 1947 and 1950 that bridge the studio noir of the midforties with the semidocumentary and on-location shooting that marked the year 1947. His on-location camera work is particularly impressive in *Night and the City*, a film that displays the definitive fusion of all the noir visual stylistics. It is, quite simply, one of the great films noirs resonating despair and pity. Dassin's protagonists are rebels, and the destruction of their spirit is his theme. Their particular agendas are less important than their defiance of a seemingly presumptuous determinism. In Dassin's world the contest, struggle, or game becomes the pretext for the self-defining noir man to stand alone, anxiously fighting against his powerlessness.

The Naked City is less remarkable for displaying this theme than for showcasing New York City as the ultimate existential challenge to civilized man. We are told that the story in the movie is only one of 8 million—a rather daunting consideration given the chaos underlying it—and that the parable of the wayward son or lost girl is implicit in the city. William Daniels photographed the movie almost entirely in Manhattan; 107 locations were used, including the spectacular overhead opening shot of New York. *The Naked City* is dated in its depiction of New Yorker types, but it is nonetheless a prime example of the semidocumentary style used to shape a police procedural, here involving the murder of an ambitious young woman entangled in a theft ring. The city's lure of temptation, vice, and unforeseen peril is dissected with facile sociology to explain the crime; the film is much more a *film policier* than a true noir. ("Wanting too much—that's why she went wrong," the dead girl's mother cries. "Bright lights, theatres, furs, and nightclubs. That's why she's dead now! Dear God, why wasn't she born ugly!") Lineups, fingerprinting, and a forensics examination accentuate the realism of the police environment, and producer Mark Hellinger's voice-over narration, intoned with appropriate seriousness, is interjected throughout the story to assume the posture of other "voice-of-God" narrations in semidocumentary noirs.

His collaboration with Dassin in *Brute Force* was a much more successful fusion of expressionism and documentary realism, capturing the structure of prison life as a routine of drills, work, and solitary confinement. Dassin shows the limited possibility of individuating frustration and rage in the commitment of the five cellmates to escape through the underground drainpipe they work on—a fitting metaphor for the deeper reaches of hell. Their rebellion as a group defines their lives during the last days of their incarceration and is justified because of their sadistic treatment at the hands of Captain Munsey.

Brute Force has highly dramatic lighting that achieves a form of vital seepage in the narrative and acquires an architectural shape, with chiaroscuro spaces defined by blinking prison searchlights and created in an airless, confined drainpipe below, which, given its spatial confines and the play of light, appears to have other, discrete spaces within it. As in *Night and the City*, Dassin alternates high- and low-angle camera work throughout to distort the geography of the prison environment, from the dining hall to the grounds. After the violent shootout escape, which leaves all the principals dead, Dassin tracks past the now-quiet cell block. An expected resolution, it nonetheless remains an uneasy image, eerie and leaving the viewer to wonder how long it will be before the next explosive moment.

An upheaval ran its course here, and it was attended by some of the more vicious examples of an increasingly brutal postwar violence. Wilson, who squealed to Munsey under duress, is crushed by a steam press in retaliation—vengeance that has biblical force in such an insular society and is met with Dassin's tacit approval of its justification. Honor is marked no less. When Louie, the prison reporter, refuses to squeal on the planned escape, Munsey stages a sadistic beating with a rubber hose. Administered to the strains of an increasingly amplified classical recording, it leaves Louie hospitalized and near death. The episode quenched Munsey's propensity for "brute force," as Doctor Walters accuses. There is an undeniable homoerotic undercurrent in this scene as Munsey, newly shaved and in his undershirt, performs a domination ritual that has been exploited for pornographic effect in various contemporary knockoffs of the prison film. An equally painful moment, however, comes when Munsey, unable to solicit Tom Lister as an informant, lies to him that his wife Cora, to whom he is devoted and for whom he stole, is divorcing him. His reason for enduring prison suddenly taken away from him, Tom is unable to bear it and hangs himself.

Brute Force uses a flashback of each principal escapee and the significant woman in his past—Tom Lister and Cora, Spencer and Flossie, Soldier and Gina, and Joe Collins and Ruth. None of these men are sociopathic, and, owing to the liberal-reformist inclination of most prison films, each appears victimized behind bars nearly to the point of absolution for any civil wrong committed. The escape planned in *Brute Force* compares to the burglary planned by Tony, Mario, César, and Jo in *Rififi*. Both groups are focused on a common goal, and both function according to an internal, commonly held honor. When one of the prisoners who was originally part of the group betrays its plans to Munsey, he is the first sacrificed to the awaiting bullets of Munsey's guards. And when César—played by Dassin himself—betrays the other thieves to crime boss Grutter in *Rififi*, both he and Tony Stephanois know that Tony has no choice but to kill him.

Rififi literally defines the phrase "honor among thieves" as only a Gallic noir could render understandable, since few American caper films show the disintegration of the group consequent upon honor betrayed, but only upon self-interest to be salvaged. *Rififi* stands apart as a less desperate and nihilistic work than either *The Asphalt Jungle* or *Odds against Tomorrow*. Failure in *Rififi* lends it its noir turn, since none of the thieves, except possibly Tony, just out of jail, see the future as dim and exhausted. It is their unraveling as a cohesive unit when César unthinkingly gives one of Grutter's girls a ring from the stolen cache that makes the criminal enterprise pointless. The result brings on a domino effect of death, as each accomplice is found out and killed in gunplay with Grutter and his men. Tony, the last to die, upon returning his kidnapped godson to his mother, meets his death as an almost merciful end to a tired existence.

Rififi is a notable cinematic achievement for Dassin; it can be said of him that he is perhaps the only director to shoot a noir film on location in each of the Western world's major cities—New York, London, and Paris—and to do it with a particular awareness of the myths and flavor of each.[6] Paris has rarely appeared more fascinating on screen than in *Rififi*. More beautiful, yes, and more dismal too. But the postwar moment of Paris during its 1950s vogue offered a Paris of enormous cinematic texture, evoking the tragic remnants of its recent past just beneath a renewed vitality and displaying the sterile middle-class consumerism that would begin to engulf Parisians by the end of the decade (and in which the young nouvelle vague filmmakers would exult with both romance and cool criticism). During this time *Rififi*, Melville's *Bob le flambeur*, Becker's *Touchez pas au grisbi*, and Decoin's *Razzia sur la chnouf*—all made between 1954 and 1956—were intriguing underworld tone poems to a city that instinctively absorbed the noir sensibility, perhaps as no other outside America.[7] Dassin and his cameraman, Philippe Agostini, captured the landmarks, the storefronts, the metro stops, and the rhythm of the city's streets and *bar-tabac* life with an allure that intensifies the story's tragic irony. Street scenes shot at night and in the rain do not serve as mere set pieces in *Rififi*; they accentuate the whole of Paris as a noir universe.

Thieves' Highway (1949). Figlia (Lee J. Cobb) bargains with Midgren (Hope Emerson) as Nick Garcos (Richard Conte) observes the corruption in his trucking business.

Thieves' Highway, written for the screen by A.I. Bezzerides (*On Dangerous Ground, Kiss Me Deadly*) from his novel *Thieves' Market*, fits into Dassin's noir work by showing the rebellious indignation of returning vet Nick Garcos, quite the opposite of the fatalistic hero. Nick returns from wartime service decent and trusting, yet not too disingenuous to be an effective avenger of his father's crippling by racketeer Figlia. To reach Figlia, Nick courses past the corruption of the wholesale produce market and reenters the world of the long-hauler. Trucking and blue-collar heroes rarely reside comfortably in the noir world; their concerns are simpler, more trusting in equitable solutions, and more prone to be worked out in wide-open spaces than in the noir city. One thinks of Raoul Walsh's *They Drive by Night* and *Thieves' Highway* as the exceptions. In Dassin's film, driving is dangerous and deadly, and the criminal impulse to steal or make crooked money on a haul is far more important than the value of a life. Dassin shows this in the context of the marketplace, with its loading docks and warehouses and neighborhood honky-tonks, which generates an energy as volatile as any found in a more familiar noir neighborhood. We feel uncomfort-

Night and the City (1950). Harry Fabian's (Richard Widmark) moment of scared self-awareness—"Oh, Anna, the things I did! The things I did! . . . "

able when Nick and Rica walk along the neon-lighted side streets and alleys; we expect an incident to erupt, Figlia's retaliation. However, *Thieves' Highway* misses making that descent into a noir world where the scathed come back to us but never quite the same. Nick Garcos is restored, and to some extent Rica is, too, by the promise of happiness together. Unlike Harry Fabian, Nick sought to correct the wrongs done him, whereas Harry spent a lifetime running to forget them.

Among the great noir films, there are a handful that achieve a power of definition that projects them into their own orbit, quite apart from the accomplished body of work that defines the genre. They exist as luminous expressions in the profoundest sense of what they claim to be. *Night and the City* is one of these. In a perfect fusion of mood and character, Dassin created a work of emotional power and existential drama that stands as a paradigm of noir pathos and despair. Harry Fabian, the unregenerate schemer, comes to us as an unctuous and energetic self-promoter, and he leaves us as a man who is tired of running from those he has wronged and has accepted that his life is of little value to anyone and that the charity of his death must be his own.

"Harry's an artist without an art . . . groping for the right lever, for the means with which to express himself," Adam Dunn perceptively tells Mary Driscoll, who loves Fabian. "And that's a dangerous thing to be." Harry Fabian's existence is bound to the nighttime, to its excitements and illicit promises, and to the racetracks and training gyms, suffocating enclaves shot in murky low-key lighting. In this London setting, Dassin delineated a noir protagonist who seeks to define himself in a world of perpetual betrayal. Harry is manipulated by Phil Nosseros to fail in his attempt to control exhibition wrestling in London; he betrays Helen Nosseros in her secret plan to take over a clip joint by providing her with fake licensing; and she in turn uses Phil in a loveless but financially profitable marriage. Finally, Harry betrays his client, the great Gregorius, an aging wrestler of athletic integrity, and his death in the training ring must now be avenged by his crime-lord son, also, strangely, a man of honor. Richard Widmark has his greatest screen role in Harry Fabian, and the desperate, nervous edge he brings to his portrayal encourages our sympathy for Fabian at the end. But it is the noir landscape of London's East End and its denizens, the rawness of good and bad luck made there, the shrewdness of its takers, and the hard payments to life in the street that shape the film. And Harry, for all his cleverness, is just a man of bluff who wants "to be somebody."

In *Night and the City*, Dassin and cinematographer Max Greene fused the classic expressionism of film noir lighting with on-location shooting—from steep high-angle shots that magnify Harry at his moments of exhilarating invincibility, to a low-angle camera that captures traffic scenes and the Thames waterfront, and on to an extreme high-angle shot of the city at the end of the film that becomes a visual dirge for the lost man inside Harry Fabian.[8] The themes of running, isolation, and fear have rarely been expressed so effectively. When Kristo offers a thousand pounds for Harry's head, Harry learns just how alone he is. He runs and runs, down the lamp-lighted streets, through the alleyways, up seedy hotel stairways, and past the nightclubs that have been a part of his life. Dassin shoots his face in front lighting and alternates between delirious high- and low-angle shots of the frightened man. His flight up the lighthouse steps is a chiaroscuro fantasia. When he seeks refuge in the Fiddler's shack, we see him breathless and sweaty in close-up profile as the Fiddler camouflages a phone call from Kristo and encourages Harry to stay a while. But Harry realizes how expendable his life is—

and, indeed, has always been. "How much are you selling me for?" he asks and continues his flight.

When he finally arrives at Anna O'Leary's barge, Dassin creates a moment few filmmakers ever have created: a scene of the poignancy of absurdity and despair. There is irony here. Harry is sought because Gregorius died accidentally under his management, and not through any dubious maneuver by him (". . . An accident. Just an accident. Then everything fell apart"). However, his fate is sealed. Anna can receive him only with words of hard but soft-spoken compassion: "It's no good comin' to me, Harry. I can't help you. Nobody can help you." He remarks: "I don't want help. I just want to . . . I just want to sit down and rest. I can't . . . run . . . any more. All my life I've been running, from welfare officers, thugs, my father. See, there they are [Kristo's men]. There on the bridge. I'm a dead man. Nosseros told me that. He told me. He said, 'You got it all, but you're a dead man, Harry Fabian.'" Yet the admission of despair does not end there; it continues with Harry's wail of terror in the face of mortality. "Oh, Anna," he cries, "the things I did! The things I did . . . Oh, the things I did!" It is an audacious and pathetic gesture, and Harry Fabian emerges ennobled by its heartbreaking honesty, a stark representation of man's tragic aloneness.

NICHOLAS RAY (1911–1979)

They Live by Night (1949)
In a Lonely Place (1950)
On Dangerous Ground (1952)
Party Girl (1958)

The world of Nicholas Ray's noir films so clearly coincides with his vision of the dislocated, violent individual trapped in postwar America that it is fair to say the noir perspective displayed in these films is simply a variant of a vision apparent throughout most of his work. His characters anguish on a personal battleground where social forces structuring human discourse are internally disavowed and raged at and the most formidable opponent finally becomes one's own conflicted self trying to function in the world. The three films considered noir here—*They Live by Night*, *In a Lonely Place*, and *On Dangerous Ground*—with

On Dangerous Ground (1952). Mary Malden (Ida Lupino): the serenity of the blind lights a dark world.

notice given to the marginally noir *Party Girl*—are displays of anxiety and mood. They represent Ray's work as a whole by including elements of the city and the country, of the professional temperament (Jim Wilson in *On Dangerous Ground*) and the artistic one (Dixon Steele in *In a Lonely Place*), of corruption and innocence, and of tender love and paranoid violence. The claustrophobia so formalized in the lighting and sets of Lang's noirs is, by contrast, internalized in the lives of Ray's characters.

In his first film, *They Live by Night*, his main characters, Bowie and Keechie, live on the run from the law in fear, half expecting doom. They escape to the meager domesticity of a cabin in the country but submit to their conjugal life with a sense of trepidation. The country provides a respite, but it has not freed them from anxiety. This suffering by the naive caught in a criminal past, for which they must eventually pay, narrows the possibility of emotional ease. With Chickamaw's intrusion into their escape and Mattie's betrayal of them, Bowie and Keechie are hounded to destruction by the moral weakness of their associates and officialdom. Not that they are without guilt—Ray never posits this—but the measure of Bowie's guilt in crime and Keechie's complicity in it are exploited in outsized proportion to the innocence of their souls. This is why *They Live by Night* serves as a compelling precursor to the other "rebel without a cause" pictures that have enjoyed popularity in postwar America. Here, the escape of two people unjustly implicated in a man's murder and involved in a bank robbery accretes to form a public perception and the public's official vengeance totally at odds with the image of a scared young couple pursued. Throughout, Ray suggests a bleak prospect for them; for whatever they do, wherever they go, Bowie and Keechie become increasingly distorted figures and, consequently, victims of an unrelenting and skewed justice.

Completed in 1947 and shown in Britain the following year, *They Live by Night* was released in America in 1949. The delay was due to title disputes and Howard Hughes's takeover of RKO in 1948.[9] The chronology is important here because the social consciousness of Nicholas Ray was first expressed in 1947, that pivotal year of socially conscious filmmaking in Hollywood. But the correctives of reform, moral appeal, and fair justice, implied in other films of that year—*Boomerang! Crossfire*, and *Brute Force*, for instance—all fall short in this story. What must be dealt with relies little on the opposing forces of good and evil. Used by his accomplices, betrayed by his abettor, Bowie cannot even escape to Mexico. As Justice of the Peace Hawkins—who married Bowie and Keechie and sells much else besides twenty-dollar weddings—tells him, "In a way, I'm a thief just the same as you are. But I won't sell you hope when there ain't any." The noir perspective of *They Live by Night* approaches the tragic precisely because Bowie and Keechie are rejected by the very society they believe they can become a part of. Bowie naively retains his faith in at least the barest justice of its laws, and both have structured their dreams of a future around its illusions.

Bowie and Keechie are socially circumscribed by a world that has no place for them. It is an example of Ray's versatility that this world also cannot sustain a man who functions professionally within one of its institutions and becomes increasingly closed off to his humanity because of it. In *On Dangerous Ground*, New York City detective Jim Wilson is so enraged by the pain, crime, and injustice of his urban vocation that he shuts down the very emotional dimension necessary to mitigate the callousness of working in a corrupt world. He becomes the avatar of the violence he is paid to subdue. Wilson's anguish is consistent with that of other Ray protagonists—from the paranoia of Bogart's Dixon Steele, to the rebelliousness and despair of James Dean in *Rebel without a Cause*, to James Mason's delusions of grandeur in *Bigger than Life*. Wilson became a "gangster with a badge" precisely because his world denied humanity its redemption; it was his way of coping out of loneliness and isolation. This loneliness must pass through a moral reckoning that will eventually allow him to feel the compassion and love he has denied himself.

When forced to accept a murder case in the country, Wilson encounters a quandary in meeting Mary Malden, the sister of the young killer he is pursuing. Their first meetings are tense counterpoints between his suspicion and hostility and her gentle strength; but Mary feels the need Wilson has been unable to confront, and finally her humanity and sensitivity free him of his emotional defenses. The country, a reprieve from reality in *They Live by Night*, becomes a source of salvation for Wilson in *On Dangerous Ground*. George Diskant photographed both films and in a similar flat, darkly monochromatic style. In both, the car chases in the nighttime city display a sharper chiaroscuro cinematography, less soft-focused and more traditionally noir than we see later on when Bowie and his accomplices escape to the country and Jim Wilson maniacally speeds to his murder case outside the city. By contrast, the country sequences are shot in a dull natural light—if not real light, then one devoid of expressionistic effect. The visual dichotomy between city and country further signifies the instability of Ray's male protagonists in two critical ways. First, the sensitive nature essential in them blossoms only in the natural harmony of a country setting that Ray distinguishes as curative to the chaos of the city. And second, the characters we see here compel us to recognize the contradictory and ambivalent nature of the misunderstood human heart. As Mike Wilmington pointed out: "Mary, a perceptive artist, should not be blind; the gentle Danny should not be a killer; Brent, 'a real good man,' according to the sheriff, should not be a vigilante. And Wilson does not belong in his job; not because he is insensitive and brutal, but because he is *too* sensitive, too touchy, too promiscuously involved with the emotional states . . . of the criminals he controls."[10]

One of the key functions of Ray's women is to stabilize the potentially violent behavior of his men. This is particularly true of his noir films. Mary Malden appeals to Wilson's sense of decency in bringing her brother in unharmed. Her guilelessness and love for Danny mitigate Wilson's own vigilante impulses, and when Danny slips and falls off a cliff to his death, Mary understands the act not as one of callous entrapment but as one of divine intervention for a tortured youth. She prays, in one of the tenderest supplications ever offered on screen: "Father, hear my prayer. Forgive him. As you have forgiven all your children who have sinned. Don't turn your face from him. He didn't know what he was doing. Bring him at last to rest in your peace . . . which he could never have found . . . here." This pivotal moment for Wilson, who overhears, finally salvages his belief in the human heart. He can now, however tentatively, offer his own to another. Such stability in Ray's women as a counterpoint to the violence and paranoia of his men rarely promises much of a romantic future; it provides only privileged moments of union in which the destructive inner and social forces are kept at bay. Bowie and Keechie realize how much they can love each other at night when they talk alone, or later when they are driving away together. Jim Wilson and Mary Malden must be alone in her cabin in the country, without official police intrusion. In *Party Girl*, Tommy Farrell and Vicki Gaye, who eventually do marry, court, even though Tommy is not divorced and becomes increasingly enmeshed in mob activity. And screenwriter Dixon Steele and Laurel Gray perform their courtship rites through a mutual effort to restore his creative career in *In a Lonely Place*.

In Ray's world of the angry and spiritually discomfited, Dixon Steele is more tormented by paranoia than any of the others. Certainly the project of screenwriting as an agency of moviemaking challenges one to achieve creative expression only to see the end product so often distorted, mutilated, or made banal by commercial forces. Steele faces this but is, moreover, self-lacerated, as many of Ray's characters are, by the psychic urge to find meaning in a life personally and routinely bereft of it. This vision, cast in the noir mode and personified by Humphrey Bogart in one of his most intriguing roles, is perhaps better explained by reference to another Ray film, *Rebel without a Cause*. Victor Perkins described the planetarium sequence, as James Dean and his friends gaze upward at the universe while the narrator comments about gas, fire, and the insignificance of the planet's impending destruction. "It is against this concept of man's life as an episode of little consequence," he wrote, "rather than against society, or his family, that Dean rebels."[11] Dixon Steele emerges as a glamorous cultural variant of such rebellion. Violent but not knowing why, provocative but to what end, needful yet closed

In a Lonely Place (1950). Screenwriter Dixon Steele (Humphrey Bogart) descends into paranoia and violence, with Laurel Gray (Gloria Grahame) unable to help him.

off, cynical and ruefully philosophical, Steele is, finally, Hollywood's figure of a troubled man. And who better to personify such a postwar figure than Bogart?

In a Lonely Place shows Bogart functioning with a propensity for violence that is never explained by anything more than some sketchy references to a few violent episodes in his past. Psychology develops, as with other Ray characters, in the course of the narrative, and its aberrations in Dixon Steele are most acutely exercised when he falls in love with Laurel Gray. His paranoid rage, provoking him to severely beat another motorist and humiliate his long-suffering agent, Mel, is aroused at that point where he begins to recognize the possibility for shared happiness. Ray shows Bogart erupting in concise scenes without much suspense or warning, and he alternates them with the image of a dazed Bogart, either apologetic or feigning humor at his outbursts. Such an unpredictable personality finally undermines the love and trust Steele sought and found in Laurel. Dixon Steele did not kill Mildred Atkinson, but he has shown a murderous violence. This paradox of love walking hand-in-hand with violence sums up the mystery of Steele and other Ray characters; it is the unsatisfactory state of affairs between the turbulent soul and an unaccommodating world that forestalls contentment.

Ray's protagonists suffer their angst in an America specifically grounded in the postwar forties and fifties. It is fair to say that no one reading the headlines of today's metropolitan tabloids should be allowed to feel enormous sympathy for Ray's rather privileged sufferers; their spiritual dislocations bear little resemblance to an America perpetually battered by the social, racial, and economic ills that fuel the nightly news in the new millennium. His currency in the Truman and Eisenhower years, however, revealed the inner turmoil of a seemingly well-adjusted society where, after the American Dream delivered some measure of its promise, unfulfilled gaps in the American psyche remained untended. The characters in Ray's noir films are unhappy in a material world, and their disconsolateness remains essentially unappeased by it. Perhaps his vision aligns itself most cogently with the world of the film noir in his awareness of this existential dilemma.

ORSON WELLES (1915–1985)

The Lady from Shanghai (1948)
Mr. Arkadin (1955)
Touch of Evil (1958)

Orson Welles defines the film noir most completely through his expression of an unstable and often chaotic world of mythic morality and the dilemma of human character it exposes. There is an unholy concession made upon entry here: Welles leads us into an awareness of such character governed by the implacable needs of his protagonists, and we come to understand that each of them consumes us in a moral cosmos whose gravitational pull is theirs. Welles and the film noir do not fully intersect until late 1946, when he started shooting *The Lady from Shanghai*; in 1955 he merged the noir with international intrigue in *Mr. Arkadin*; and in 1958 he reached the apex of his noir career with *Touch of Evil*, one of the great films noirs.

Welles's films in general defy easy generic classification. Why is

Citizen Kane, for instance, not to be considered noir after its apparent infusion of noir technical style? Or *Journey into Fear* (1943) on technical, and perhaps thematic, grounds? Or *The Stranger* (1946), which is certainly dark enough? In the first case, *Citizen Kane* may logically be considered the breeding ground for several screen movements, cycles, and genre developments that, laying claim to it as a source, would scarcely satisfy claims specific to the genesis of the noir. As for *Journey into Fear* and *The Stranger*, the incompleteness of the former permits it to be considered as a Welles exercise rather than a finished product, and the latter was done rather tamely to prove to the studios that Welles could turn in a completed picture on time.

In many ways *The Lady from Shanghai* develops into the paradigmatic Welles noir in its seduction of the viewer. The story is really a weak excuse for Welles's presentation of a cast of characters whose fascination stems from their very unconnnectedness to us. Arthur Bannister, his wife, Elsa, and his partner, Grisby, are a universe of malignant tensions unto themselves and, like spiders, dare us to become ensnared in their intrigue. Bannister and Grisby are properly sinister, but Elsa, seemingly the most victimized, is deadliest. That Michael O'Hara is invited to step into this world only reinforces Welles's adventurousness in situating his naïfs in vital orbit with those who seek to destroy them. It is, of course, the same invitation extended to Robert Arden in *Mr. Arkadin* and Charlton Heston in *Touch of Evil*. Welles's own Michael O'Hara is enthralled by the spell of Elsa Bannister, just as surely as Welles was intrigued by the screen image of the star that plays her, his wife at the time, Rita Hayworth. And it is in the essential enigma of Elsa/Rita that this film displays the power of the *femme fatale* in noir cinema, a subject poeticized here in all her opaque beauty as a symbol of misogynist desire. Arthur Bannister, a brilliant and jaded lawyer, club-footed and bitter, and his partner Grisby, a psychological accomplice and leech, envenom this triangle. But Elsa, ostensibly held hostage in marriage to Bannister because of her dubious past, vapidly submits to his malicious humor as a creature of unreachable spirit. This mysterious essence becomes Michael's lure, one that he cannot help pursuing and one that he will never possess.

The voice-over/flashback technique in *The Lady from Shanghai* establishes not only a reference to this memory of which Michael speaks but also one of detached consciousness at odds with another, elusive, half-known consciousness of who is preying upon whom. For when the

The Lady from Shanghai (1948). The fun house 1: where illusion masks illusion in betrayal. Michael O'Hara (Orson Welles) and Elsa Bannister (Rita Hayworth).

murder plot is finally stated, there still exists the unknown factor needed to explain the characters' loyalties and motives. Michael tells the parable of the sharks that, in a blood-lust frenzy of feeding, finally feed on each other until nothing is left but blood and death. Now "this loss of certainty about his world underscores an even larger problem facing Michael," J.P. Telotte pointed out, "a loss of certainty about the self that reflects on both his shark parable and, more significantly, his whole narration."[12] Welles locates the noir dimension here in the film and shows it with ever-increasing violence by entrapping Michael in the lethal dynamics between Elsa and her husband.

Having determined to rid herself of all these men, Elsa proceeds to kill Michael, who learns that he cannot accept or abet her murders and tries to escape her. However, the hall of mirrors in the Crazy House sequence illuminates too many images of her, too many guns, and too many mysteries of a woman whose gaze can never be penetrated. Welles

The Lady from Shanghai (1948). The fun house 2: where illusion masks illusion in a maze of surprises.

the magician plays with us here, as his own Michael O'Hara finds himself surrounded by a multiplicity of images—of Elsa, Bannister, and himself—none of which is completely reliable and all of which threaten to kill. When Bannister shoots at each mirror reflecting Elsa poised with her gun, he fails to easily destroy the very object symbolizing Welles's thesis in the film: specifically, that the illusionary index that names our desires, that gives them shape and voluptuousness, seeks an objective correlative. Elsa has been empowered to destroy, and significantly so, by men. If her soul cannot be known, then her opaqueness is fascinating precisely because Welles has taken the image of Rita Hayworth, iconic in power, and rendered it alluring, mysterious, and dangerous. "As a lady from Shanghai," the film and art critic Lawrence Alloway observed, "she speaks a Chinese dialect that helps her in the final chase after the hero in San Francisco's Chinatown. The worldliness and malaise of the fatal woman appear here in terms of a restless itinerary and exceptional linguistic powers."[13] The mirror sequence in the Crazy House illustrates Welles's difficulty in deconstructing the Elsa/Rita image. It is the film noir's ultimate moment of violence against the image of the *femme fatale,* since no one refraction of it can obliterate the unknowable whole.

The enigma of character that so fascinates Welles and gives mythic scope to his films invokes the moral questions explored by the ancient Greeks. Myth here is transferred to the screen through his grandiose protagonists in a baroque style expressing their fears, desires, and appetite for power. From *Kane* and *The Magnificent Ambersons* to the Shakespeare films and *Mr. Arkadin* and *Touch of Evil*, Welles's protagonists are shown in low-angle, often tilted, shots with grotesque distortions of the human proportion—especially the faces in close shots—to propel a moral drama largely fueled by an exercise of hubris. If Elsa Bannister is the image of feminine mystery, then Gregory Arkadin and Hank Quinlan are the products of the malevolent male ego. The misogyny in this distinction supports the power wielded by the actions of his men—men who destroy—against the lethal attraction of a female like Elsa, a Circe-like creature created to lure men to their destruction.

Gregory Arkadin, in contrast, not only lures Guy Van Stratten into his intrigue; he also sets out to destroy him and all who come in contact with him. Arkadin is both the subject and the architect of his enigmatic legend, and the fatal moment for Van Stratten comes when he decides to unravel its mystery. This is grand, undiluted irony, and Welles expresses it to the hilt, with costumes and makeup unabashedly overdone and with a variety of grotesque characters (and wonderful character actors such as Akim Tamiroff, Mischa Auer, and Katina Paxinou) to lend exoticism to the proceedings. The noir sensibility in *Mr. Arkadin* arrives later, when Guy finally realizes that he is a marked man, that he knows too much about Arkadin to be allowed to live. This moment is much like the one in Carol Reed's *Third Man* (1949) when Holly Martins finally learns the grim truth about his old friend Harry Lime (played by Welles). The adventures begin to sour now, with an understanding that the puppeteer's humor has always been of a deadly kind.

Gregory Arkadin and Hank Quinlan distort reality in their attempts, really, to recreate it, and Welles's camera displays this through the use of an 18.5 mm wide-angle lens, favorable both to depth of field and to rendering a spatial distortion of the human body. "An actor walking toward the camera appears to be wearing seven-league boots," André Bazin noted.[14] In *Mr. Arkadin* the treatment is relished largely as self-parody, as Arkadin looms over Van Stratten in early scenes and in the delirious costume ball he gives where Welles-as-Arkadin tells his party guests the now-famous scorpion fable—a fable that may be as much the key to Welles's cinema, especially his noir films, as Rosebud is to Kane. "Now, I'm going to tell you about a scorpion," Arkadin begins:

> This scorpion wanted to cross a river, so he asked a frog to carry him. "No," said the frog, "no thank you. If I let you on my back you may sting me, and the sting of the scorpion is death."
>
> "Now where," asked the scorpion, "is the logic of that?"—for scorpions would try to be logical. "If I sting you, you will die, I will drown." So the frog was convinced to allow the scorpion on his back. But, just in the middle of the river, he felt a terrible pain and realized that, after all, the scorpion had stung him. "Logic!" cried the dying frog as he started under, taking the scorpion down with him. "There is no logic in this!"
>
> "I know," said the scorpion, "but I can't help it. It's my character."

No protagonist defines the grandeur and intransigence of such a character as Sheriff Hank Quinlan does in *Touch of Evil*. The leitmotiv of largeness—in life, cinema, and invention—practically necessitated that Orson Welles play this role, for Welles created himself as a screen presence no less in his performances than through his direction. Quinlan's flamboyant dismissal of due process, his bigotry, and his lament for the fear and respect he can no longer so effortlessly command fall in step with other outlaw figures whose very blindness denies recognition of a

Touch of Evil (1958). Orson Welles as Hank Quinlan: the grotesqueness of the grandiose.

changed world with no room for them. The same hubris that signals the downfall of Johnny Rocco in Huston's *Key Largo* (1948) or Cagney's Cody Jarrett in Walsh's *White Heat* (1949) infects Quinlan as he soon becomes a pariah in his own kingdom. "The creation of myth is not only a means by which the Welles hero conceals his moral weakness from himself and others," wrote Joseph McBride; "it is also the creation of a more easily manageable rationale for his actions."[15]

Quinlan, the remnant of a past world that has changed into a noir border town, encounters lewdness and half-breeds, suggesting illicit pleasures and their attendant violence. Everyone he knows has grown older here: Tanya, the madam of the local brothel; Quinlan's sidekicks; and "Uncle" Joe Grandi with his absurd toupée and his delinquent nephews. The old accommodations of graft and corruption no longer thrive so easily. Welles creates the garish world of Los Robles with some of his flashiest camera work: crane and dutch-angle shots fusing expressionism and action, with flickering neon signs of bars, strip joints, motorcycle gangs, and cheap hotels in the sweltering summer night. All this was edited in the beginning of the film, without Welles's permission, to the beat of a neurotic Latin jazz score by Henry Mancini.[16] It is, according to Henri Agel's description, "that romantic night of a certain American cinema at once magic and sticky, in any case, menacing."[17] Characters are constantly overlapping their dialogue, a Welles trademark but rare in the film noir, and the wide-angle tracking shots of Grandi's boys tailing Vargas around town make Welles's direction look peculiarly modern.

This is Welles's noir perspective, something that Maurice Bessy saw as much more than social critique. "This particular drama has to do with overwhelming disorder and nausea," he wrote, "a sense of the absurd, which washes over men like Welles when confronted by a certain kind of contemporary confusion."[18] As Hank Quinlan is slowly disoriented by Vargas's encroaching authority, as he missteps by leaving his cane in the hotel room where he murdered Uncle Joe, and, indeed, as he kills his old friend and betrayer, Pete Menzies, we see his stature reduced to that of one of the frailest victims of noir fate. Quinlan is shot, and the grotesqueness of his corpse appears a funny, bloated testament to egotism. When Marlene Dietrich, equally grotesque in her fortune-teller's getup as Tanya, remarks, "He was some kind of man. What does it matter what you say about people?" it might well have been the perfect epitaph for the myth of Orson Welles.

THE HARD-BOILED FICTION INFLUENCE

From the early 1920s and continuing throughout the war years, the hard-boiled fiction of the pulp magazines and booklets, published cheaply and selling briskly, attracted a readership all too familiar with the emotions, crimes, and violence that would find expression in the film noir. This literature as a body of work spoke in a language that alternately described a cold, cynical, and grimly ironic world and the obsessive, overripe passions consuming its characters. Often sordid, fatalistic, and quite punitive, it was just as often expressive of a failed romanticism, contemptuously accepted by those caught short in life. Hard-boiled fiction largely includes and overlaps detective fiction. The appellation is broad enough to permit several literary genres and subgenres space under its umbrella: detective fiction, crime thrillers, some proletarian fiction (Ira Wolfert's *Tucker's People*, Budd Schulberg's corruption stories), and a few political thrillers and spy novels (Graham Greene's *Third Man*). Dashiell Hammett (*The Maltese Falcon*, *The Glass Key*), Raymond Chandler (*The Big Sleep*; *Farewell, My Lovely*; *The High Window*; *The Lady in the Lake*; *The Little Sister*), James M. Cain (*Double Indemnity*, *The Postman Always Rings Twice*, *Mildred Pierce*), and Cornell Woolrich (*Phantom Lady*, *Black Angel*, *The Black Path of Fear*, *I Married a Dead Man*, and many others) are among the seminal influences of the hard-boiled school that gave shape to noir cinema, with others such as Horace McCoy (*Kiss Tomorrow Goodbye*), Dorothy B. Hughes (*Ride the Pink Horse*, *In a Lonely Place*), David Goodis (*Dark Passage*, *Nightfall*, *Down There*), and later Jim Thompson (*The Grifters*) and Ross Macdonald (*The Moving Target*, *The Drowning Pool*) contributing.

The style of its terse, mainly first-person, action prose has roots in

The Postman Always Rings Twice (1946). Cora (Lana Turner) and Frank (John Garfield): MGM's glamour of the tawdry.

the fiction of both Hammett and Ernest Hemingway, but the existential context is decidedly modern urban American—usually New York City, Los Angeles, San Francisco, and their environs—and its characters are doomed by temperament and circumstance to face irrevocable consequences for bad actions taken against themselves and others. James M. Cain, whom Raymond Chandler regarded contemptuously as "a Proust in greasy overalls" (even as he adapted Cain's own "Double Indemnity" for the screen), brought a literary challenge to recognize unbridled lust and greed in the pages of his sensational novels.[1] In *The Postman Always Rings Twice*, Cora and Frank lack the glamour of Lana Turner and John Garfield in Tay Garnett's 1946 version of the novel: sex here is instinctively satisfied and its gratification often disgusting, yet it is even more desired because of that. Loosely based on the sensational 1927 murder of Long Islander Albert Snyder by his wife, Ruth, and her lover, Judd Gray, *Postman* weaves sex, love, and money into a fabric of betrayal and death.[2] The same elements shape the lethal dynamic between Walter Huff and Phyllis Nirdlinger in Cain's story, "Double Indemnity," serialized in *Liberty* magazine in February and March of 1936. The films noirs made from these and other hard-boiled stories and novels are discussed throughout, but it is important here to recognize that the characteristics of this literature—in the patter of these writers' vernacularisms and the roughness of their characters' actions, actions driven by passion and in quest of elusive happiness—inspired and helped define a portrait of the noir world on screen.

"Thriller literature is situational literature, crisis literature," wrote Ralph Harper in his study of the subject. "In the language of Karl Jaspers' existentialist philosophy it is the literature of boundary situations. Man is always in situation, but only occasionally for most men is life reduced to total questionability by any particular situation." Pasted on the modern urban tableau, "the anxieties of death and fate, guilt and condemnation, meaninglessness and emptiness (each pair containing an absolute and a relative threat)" find easy accommodation in the plots of thriller fiction compared to those of other genres.[3] Among the first identified hard-boiled literature is the pulp fiction that appeared in the 1890s; the Nick Carter stories were collected in the *Nick Carter Weekly*, which first appeared in 1891. The detective hero, a departure from the inspector of gothic mysteries and a distant precursor of Hammett's Sam Spade, found a convenient home in the world of the hard-boiled.[4] *Detective Story Magazine* began publishing in 1915 (its editor was named Nicholas Carter), and *Black Mask*, surely the best of all pulp magazines, was started in 1920 by H.L. Mencken and George Jean Nathan as a profitable hedge against the losses incurred in publishing Mencken's much more exclusive and sophisticated magazine, *Smart Set*. It was only after Joseph T. Shaw became *Black Mask*'s editor in 1926 (continuing until 1936) that the magazine developed its reputation. Dashiell Hammett published his first short story, "The Road Home" in its December 1922 issue under the pen name Peter Collinson and went on to publish installments of most of his more famous fiction there (*Red Harvest, The Maltese Falcon, The Glass Key*) and many of the Continental Op stories, whose detective-operative hero was a predecessor to Sam Spade. Raymond Chandler published "Smart-Aleck Kill" (July 1934), "Nevada Gas" (June 1935), and the wonderful "Goldfish" (June 1936) in *Black Mask* before having extracts of *The Big Sleep* appear there. Horace McCoy, Erle Stanley Gardner, and Cornell Woolrich also saw their short fiction on its pages.

During Shaw's stewardship, the magazine defined the best of American detective and hard-boiled fiction in a departure from the older conventional detective story, "to reflect the violence of American society and the vivid colloquialisms of American speech."[5] Naturally, other detective and mystery pulps arose to proliferate the market of the time—*Dime Detective, Dime Mystery, Detective Fiction Weekly, Action Detective*, and *Strange Detective Mysteries*—but none came to enjoy the reputation of *Black Mask*. The pulp magazines, named so because of the cheap wood pulp used to produce them, pretty much died along with the B movie in the early 1950s when the growing popularity of anthology television took away their readers. But during their time, they fed a rebellious and often subversive literary vision to the mass consciousness while helping to shape its cinematic taste, and they usually did so at no more than twenty cents a copy.

CORNELL WOOLRICH

The hard-boiled fiction of the 1930s and 1940s was by no means overtaken by the primacy of detective literature. Apart from Cain's novels of greed and sordid sexual entanglements, Horace McCoy wrote of chiselers, corrupt politicians, and assorted down-and-outers (*Kiss Tomorrow Goodbye, No Pockets in a Shroud*, and *They Shoot Horses, Don't They?*), and Cornell Woolrich wrote of people caught in circumstances, arbitrary and destabilizing, that provoked fear, often unto terror, and the feeling of utter helplessness in the face of it. No writer describes this interior world more vividly than he, and the psychology of Woolrich's characters, often facile in itself, is complicated by the subtle modulations of impending dread, of that sinking feeling that always anticipates doom.

Cornell Woolrich's life (1903–1968) was itself an odyssey of bleakness and despair: the possibility of happiness was forestalled early on by divorced parents, a self-hating homosexuality and a failed marriage, and later the parasitic love-hate relationship endured with his mother—living with her for more than twenty years in a near-reclusive state at a residential hotel on Manhattan's Upper West Side. He rarely left his apartment and died there of a stroke. He had already lost a leg to gangrene that developed from diabetes.[6]

His short stories in the thriller genre began to appear in the 1930s in *Detective Fiction Weekly* ("Walls That Hear You," August 18, 1934), *Dime Mystery* ("Dark Melody of Madness," July 1935), and *Dime De-*

tective ("Kiss of the Cobra," May 1, and "Red Liberty," July 1, 1935). He sold his first crime story to the movies in late 1937 when Columbia Pictures decided to film "Face Work," which appeared in that October's issue of *Black Mask*, as *Convicted*, a fifty-four-minute B film released in 1938. Woolrich wrote *The Bride Wore Black*, his first full-length thriller, in 1940, and with it he initiated a series of novels with "black" in their titles—the "Black Series." The series was extolled by Marcel Duhamel as the inspiration for his Série Noire, published in Paris after the war, which included translations of Woolrich's novels (e.g., *The Bride Wore Black*).[7] Woolrich wrote in much the same hard-boiled idiom as Chandler and Cain. Detectives were "dicks," women hard, money and love betrayals violent. In his 1935 short story "Hot Water," one unregenerate con woman is "a tough-looking little customer, with jet-black hair and layers of paint all over her map that you could scrape off with a spoon."[8] In "Kiss of the Cobra," a particularly lethal exotic vamp provokes the detective protagonist to speculate in fear: "She is what she is, either of her own free will—maybe a member of some ghastly snake-worshiping cult—or without being able to control herself. Maybe her mother had some unspeakable experience with a snake before she was born. In either case she's more than a menace to society, she's a menace to the race itself."[9]

It would be a mistake, however to write off Woolrich as a hardboiled misogynist. In his early fiction, often written in the first person and in the present tense, thereby establishing a powerful authorial suspense, his characters, male and female, are delineated best in terms of the anxiety and terror aroused by nightmares, hallucinations, strange twists of fate, mistaken identities, and misunderstood moral transgressions. The murderer Paine fears the deformity of his character in "Momentum"; he finds that "one's conscience, after all, is the most dreaded policeman of the lot."[10] In the novels, characters are excavated with much sensitivity to the despair they live out. In *I Married a Dead Man* (1948), this is felt entirely by a young woman, one Patrice Hazzard, formerly Helen Georgesson, who finds the familial bliss she never knew possible in the Hazzard family—a family co-opted from a couple recently killed in the train wreck she herself survived—by pretending to be their previously unseen, newly married and then widowed, daughter-in-law. Patrice savors every moment of family warmth and security and dreads that her deception will be exposed and all this taken away from her. At the beginning of the story, Woolrich writes in Patrice's voice, lyrically yet

Phantom Lady (1944). Jack Marlow (Franchot Tone) about to strangle Cliff March (Elisha Cook Jr.): shades of expressionist psychosis.

with the subtlest melancholy, of the love and contentment she has found with the only family she has ever known and as the wife now of their other son, and of how happiness should indeed be the providence for such a family. Then with equal power, he follows each of these opening musings with a single-sentence paragraph: she concludes, "But not for us."[11]

The essence of Woolrich's sensibility is found, finally, in the suspense of impending doom, in the fear of the helpless human being caught—often in nothing more than his own paranoia. Woolrich makes his readers feel the interior world of these quasi-damned characters who must yet complete their journey to a final hell. And the hell may never exist in much greater design than in its anticipation. In his brilliant story "Three O'Clock," Woolrich has a man suspect his wife of infidelity and, festering in muted rage, plan to bomb her when she is home alone. Surprised by burglars while he is in the basement assembling the explosives, he is gagged, tied up, and left there alone, soon to die. His wife comes home and goes about her daily chores and reveals to us that her rendezvous have not been with a lover but with her escaped convict brother. Stapp is trapped, his misbegotten suspicion apparent now, now that it is too late. As the hour of the explosion approaches, Woolrich writes:

> Another vagary was that this ordeal had been brought on him as punishment for what he had intended doing to Fran, that he was being held fast there not by the inanimate ropes but by some active, punitive agency, and that if he exhibited remorse, pledged contrition to a proper degree, he could automatically effect his release at its hands. Thus over and over he whined in the silence of his throttled throat, "I'm sorry. I won't do it again. Just let me go this one time, I've learned my lesson, I'll never do it again."[12]

Within minutes of the blast,

> He couldn't *feel* any more, terror or hope or anything else. A sort of numbness had set in, with a core of gleaming awareness remaining that was his mind. *That* would be all that the detonation would be able to blot out by the time it came. It was like having a tooth extracted with the aid of novocaine. There remained of him now only this single pulsing nerve of premonition; all the tissue around it was frozen. So protracted foreknowledge of death was in itself its own anaesthetic. (107)

Finally, the clock is about to strike three:

> Something deep within him, what it was he had no leisure nor skill to recognize, seemed to retreat down long dim corridors away from the doom that impeded. He hadn't known he had those convenient corridors of evasion in him, with their protective turns and angles by which to put distance between himself and menace. Oh clever architect of the Mind, oh merciful blueprints that made such emergency exits available. Toward them this something, that was he and yet not he, rushed; toward sanctuary, security, toward waiting brightness, sunshine, laughter. (108)

The power of Woolrich's style here, as Francis Lacassin saw, is in "the art of transporting the anguish of the imaginary universe to the consciousness of the reader."[13] It is precisely this experience that was compellingly transcribed on the noir screen in several movies based on Woolrich's stories. The films based on his writing that can claim contribution to the noir cinema are *Street of Chance* (Jack Hively, 1942; based on the novel *The Black Curtain*), *Phantom Lady* (Robert Siodmak, 1944; based on the novel), *Deadline at Dawn* (Harold Clurman, 1946; based on the novel), *Black Angel* (Roy William Neill, 1946; based on the novel), *The Chase* (Arthur Ripley, 1946; loosely based on the novel *The Black Path of Fear*), *Fall Guy* (Reginald Le Borg, 1947; based on the October 1940 *Black Mask* story "C-Jag" [retitled "Cocaine"]), *The Guilty* (John Reinhardt, 1947; based on the story "He Looked Like Murder"), *Fear in the Night* (Maxwell Shane, 1947; based on the story "And So to Death"), *Night Has a Thousand Eyes* (John Farrow, 1948; loosely based on the novel), *The Window* (Ted Tetzlaff, 1949; based on the story "The Boy Cried Murder"), *No Man of Her Own* (Mitchell Leisen, 1950; based on *I Married a Dead Man*), *Obsession* (Jean Delannoy, 1954; based on the February 1943 *Black Mask* story "If the Dead Could Talk"), *Rear Window* (Alfred Hitchcock, 1954; based on the story "It Had to Be Murder" [later retitled "Rear Window"], published in *Dime Detective*, February 1942), *Nightmare* (Maxwell Shane, 1956; a remake of Shane's 1947 *Fear in the Night*), *The Bride Wore Black* ([*La Mariée était en noir*] François Truffaut, 1968; based on the novel), and *Mississippi Mermaid* ([*La Sirène du Mississippi*] François Truffaut, 1969; based on the novel *Waltz into Darkness*).

THE PRIVATE DETECTIVE

Gilles Deleuze makes an important distinction between the detective film and the crime film, which may often also involve detective work. "What distinguishes the two types," he observes, "is that in the crime formula, one moves from the situation, or the milieu, towards actions which are duels, while in the detective formula one moves from blind actions, as indices, to obscure situations which vary entirely or which fluctuate completely, depending on a minuscule variation in the index."[14] The difference must be appreciated not only for its application to noir cinema in general but also to set apart the detective film, which almost always means the *private* detective film, as a narrative structure establishing an archetype that has become the indispensable embodiment of the values and mystique challenged in the noir world. The private detective protagonist of literature claims the certitude of a morality or a moral value distant or highly mutable in those he encounters, and he establishes in a world of corrupt motives and desires an impenetrable cell of individualism. Many have called it honor, decency, a kind of dark knighthood for right,[15] but in the film noir, the private eye has much more often displayed what his appellation describes—a "private eye" of calibrated moral distance that attempts to decipher the world it sees. The moral distinction here requires emphasis, for the private detective on screen, from Sam Spade (*Falcon*) to Jake Gittes (*Chinatown*), is less a hero of sanctity than one of shrewd innocence that acquires sight, who renders clarity—or comes to see the impossibility of rendering it—in his pursuit of truth in a world of obscurity, duplicity, and half-hidden motive. The classical role of such a man (for they have been, until fairly recently, only men) stems from his heritage of displaying the Aristotelian dramatic function of *hamartìa*, where the tragic flaw arises not from moral failure or egregious error in judgment but from the simple mistaken direction one follows in pursuit of the truth. "The mistaken person may or may not be rescued," wrote drama historian Richmond Lattimore, "but the mistaken truth must be."[16] It is this pursuit, structured as it is on an inquiry in a dark, uncertain world—dark of visual design, uncertain in the malevolence of characters too vivid to forget—that distinguishes the Sam Spades, Philip Marlowes, Lew Archers, Mike Hammers, Easy Rawlinses, and others of noir cinema from their counterparts on the printed page.

In relation to the noir world of the private eye, Raymond Chandler wrote as well as anyone has about crime as an activity compelling characters to clearly face previously obscured passions. For Chandler, "good and evil seem part of the same dark ocean, one in which we are always trying to keep our heads above, one in which we'll do anything to stay afloat," observes Raymond Obstfeld in his analysis of motive in detective fiction. "Suddenly motives were not just for money for the sake of money. If someone killed for money it was because it represented more than just minks and Cadillacs. *It often represented a means by which to buy back the past, or to keep it hidden.*"[17] This is the key to Chandler's world; in all of his novels the criminal antagonists strive to make a tabula rasa of their existence in order to refuel that nullity with fresh animus. Marlowe traffics among these obscurantists and seeks to uncover the meaning of the passions that drive them and destroy others. Like Hammett's Sam Spade, who orbits a more visibly corrupt and venal milieu, Marlowe, in *Farewell, My Lovely* and *The Little Sister* particularly, finds a world of people active in masking their own guilt and regrets as they—perhaps unconsciously—ask him to uncover disturbing truths implicating their own guilty past. Velma Valento in *Farewell, My Lovely* must eradicate her past as a prostitute and a betrayer of Moose Malloy in order to secure her present and future respectability as Helen Grayle, wife of Judge Lewin Lockridge Grayle. She hires Marlowe on the pretext of wanting to find a late friend's murderers but really in order to locate Moose, who, by the end of the novel, is the only character who can identify her as Velma, the woman he did time for. In *The Little Sister*, Orfamay Quest hires Marlowe to find her missing brother, only to have Marlowe expose her as the extortionist of her brother in his blackmail scheme. In *The Big Sleep*, Colonel Sternwood wants Marlowe to stop the blackmail of his nymphomaniac daughter, Carmen; his other daughter, Vivian Sternwood Regan, intervenes to handle the matter and ends up revealing herself to be a blackmail victim as well, in her attempt to protect her sister from being exposed as the murderer of her husband, Rusty. Rusty Regan, it turns out, rebuffed Carmen's advances, and Carmen is to be seen as someone sick and in need of treatment.

These machinations of deceit and chary disclosure of guilt are part of the noir world as much as they are of Chandler's, as Marlowe becomes increasingly disenchanted with the capacity for genuine human connectedness unsoiled by corruption. At its finest, Chandler's writing ruminates on this existential awareness. In *The Little Sister*, a tired Marlowe laments to himself on his drive back from Mavis Weld's: "Who am I cutting my throat for this time? A blonde with sexy eyes and too many door keys? A girl from Manhattan, Kansas [Orfamay Quest]? I don't know. All I know is that something isn't what it seems and the old tired but always reliable hunch tells me that if the hand is played the way it is dealt the wrong person is going to lose the pot. Is that any of my business? Well, what is my business? Do I know? Did I ever know? Let's not go into that. You're not human tonight, Marlowe. Maybe I never was or ever will be. Maybe I'm an ectoplasm with a private license. Maybe we all get like this in the cold half-lit world where always the wrong thing happens and never the right."[18] Here, Marlowe assesses a strange life that compels him to go on without any apparent reward, as a kind of heroic fool who sees virtue only in its own value and consequently finds himself spiritually dispossessed in a world that offers little human redemption.

To be sure, these private eyes maintain a code of personal honor, but it has been less proscriptive and judgmental than is usually held to be the case, not like the medieval Christian heroes. The heroic stature of Sam Spade (a principled but not always likable man), Philip Marlowe (sometimes blinded by his romantic self-image), or J.J. Gittes (who, alas, is not prepared for the hard, unredeemed evil of Noah Cross) comes from the need to know the truth with conclusiveness, finality, to the extent possible in their noir journey. This is the hard deal they strike with those in their orbit. Bogart's Marlowe in *The Big Sleep* persists because, although in Howard Hawks's film, who did what to whom remains a confusing tangle, it cannot remain so for Marlowe: he simply wants to find out where Sean Regan is. After all, he has been beaten and has dodged bullets in his efforts to learn this, a job he was paid to do. It is interesting that even a jaded iconoclast like Robert Altman cannot free himself from expressing this need in his 1973 adaptation of Chandler's *Long Goodbye*. Every deviation in contemporary Los Angeles encountered by Elliott Gould's Marlowe is "fine" by him; people are, after all, free to do as they choose (the perfect 1970s anodyne). What propels his inquiry is the quest to figure out why *he* must be victimized by the actions and motives of these gratuitous others (in this case, Terry Lennox and Eileen Wade). And the punishment is often his to take for disrupting the malevolent elements that wish to prevail. After doing prison time on a frame-up by his ex-partner, Bradford Galt in *The Dark Corner* is released only to be implicated in the man's murder. "I feel all dead inside," he exclaims to his secretary. "I'm backed up in a dark corner and I don't know who's hitting me!" His frustration, like Marlowe's, defines the objective of the "seeker-hero" protagonist, who, only upon discovering the origin of the corruption from which he can no longer stand apart, earns his status as a man from those who want to destroy his strength as a lone inquisitor.[19]

Spade, Marlowe, Brad Galt, Lew Archer in *Harper* (Jack Smight, 1966) and *The Drowning Pool* (Stuart Rosenberg, 1976), John Klute in *Klute* (Alan Pakula, 1971), Jake Gittes, and Harry Moseby in Arthur Penn's 1975 *Night Moves*—all of them—move through a maze of deliberate obfuscations that modify their frustration and concerns with each effort to solve their cases. And in the process of such quests, they be-

Murder, My Sweet (1944). Dick Powell's Marlowe—"Philip. Philip Marlowe.
A nice name for a duke. You're just a nice mug."

come defined by narrative demand as peculiarly modern, urban variet-
ies of hero.

In the classic American film noir, Raymond Chandler's Philip
Marlowe was portrayed on more occasions by more actors than any other
private eye, and in timely fashion too. Four of Chandler's novels were
adapted for the screen within a few years of their writing, in the early
period—the pre-1947 period—of noir cinema.[20] Edward Dmytryk's 1944
Murder, My Sweet (based on *Farewell, My Lovely*), with Dick Powell,
showed us the most abused Marlowe, beaten, tied down, drugged, and
left hurt and hallucinating; he details in voice-over and to sardonic effect the sensation felt with each body blow he takes. "Philip. Philip
Marlowe," Mrs. Grayle ridicules him. "A nice name for a duke. You're
just a nice mug." Hawks's *Big Sleep*, released in 1946, stars Bogart, to
whom the role of Marlowe is bound by myth—a myth about which more
shall be said. The year 1946 also had Robert Montgomery directing himself as Marlowe in *The Lady in the Lake* and using a subjective camera

Chinatown (1974). J.J. Gittes (Jack Nicholson) and company: echoes of Chandler.

at that, an experiment of limited satisfaction, with Montgomery portraying Marlowe in a leaden manner. However, it was George Montgomery's portrayal in *The Brasher Doubloon* (John Brahm, 1947) that was perhaps the least effective of the period: the detective was translated as a cross between a smug womanizer and a matinee idol. It was not until 1969 that Marlowe would reemerge on the big screen, in Paul Bogart's *Marlowe*, based on *The Little Sister* and the first Chandler novel filmed in color. James Garner quite convincingly evoked the cynical weariness the private eye as a screen entity would convey in the late sixties.

By now the model of private detective—and, it may be argued, the only noir tableau depicted in post-1968 Hollywood until a resurgent interest in making films noirs followed in the early seventies—came with the filming of *Marlowe* and Ross Macdonald's Lew Archer novels (*The Moving Target* [as *Harper*] and *The Drowning Pool*). The Archer films, especially, attempted to contemporize the noir detective by replacing a Chandlerian disgust with a rueful sadness for those troubled amid corruption.[21] But the weariness of these men would turn into the garrulous boredom of Altman's Marlowe, played by Gould as if he lived in a state of chronic hangover. This film, as well as *Klute*, *Chinatown*, *Night Moves*, and *Angel Heart* (Alan Parker, 1987), displays a shift in Hollywood filmmaking style and attitude, and the protagonist-detectives in all of these films are reinvented as part of the desire in the 1970s and 1980s to reinvent genre myths or play with the romance of the noir filtered through a contemporary, often hip, context.

Humphrey Bogart, Spade, Marlowe, and the Film Noir

> In all manner, Bogart has always been a passenger of the night.
> —Henri Agel, *Romance Américaine*

Few examples of the total identification of a star with his roles exist to equal that of Humphrey Bogart with Sam Spade in *The Maltese Falcon* and Philip Marlowe in *The Big Sleep*. We bear witness here to the convergence of a screen image, a performance style, a fictional character, and the ineffable chemistry that binds them, in the creation of a role so complete that the perpetual transference of these qualities from star to role and back is activated with each rescreening of these movies and lives in the popular imagination long after the stories have become pleasant, but diluted, memories. The Bogart persona in these films defined the capacity of romantic involvement that we could have with the allure of the noir detective and his world. As Stanley Cavell pointed out, "if those films did not exist, Bogart would not exist, the name 'Bogart' would not mean what it does."[22]

The Maltese Falcon was John Huston's first directorial effort. The book had been filmed twice before, as *Dangerous Female* by Roy Del Ruth in 1931 and as *Satan Met a Lady* by William Dieterle (a curio of nondescript style from him) in 1936, starring Bette Davis. George Raft, then Warner Brothers's major star of crime dramas, was asked to take the lead of Spade in Huston's version. "[H]e turned down the picture because he didn't want to do it with an unknown, inexperienced director, which I can't blame him for at all," Huston recalled. "So I thanked God when I got Bogart."[23] Huston's script was so faithful to Hammett's novel that the dialogue was practically lifted from the page and little was done to the plot until the ending, when Effie Perine, Spade's secretary, has her moment of disappointment and muted contempt for him eliminated. The significant difference in this version was that Sam Spade was rendered as a morally troubled man who does right in the name of his murdered partner but is left rent by the emotional betrayal of Brigid O'Shaughnessy. He tells her: "When a man's partner's killed, he's supposed to do something about it. It doesn't make any difference what you thought about him, he was your partner and you're supposed to do something about it. As it happens, we're in the detective business; well, when one of your organization gets killed . . . it's, it's bad business to let the killer get away with it. Bad all around. Bad for every detective everywhere." The emotional ambivalence mitigating Spade's decision becomes the most touching complication in Huston's film: he is torn, not by what is right and wrong, but by the sadness of moral obligation. He has been made to feel affection for Brigid, and the difficulty of retreating from such feelings aroused for a killer is the source of his regret. "Yes, angel," he tells Brigid, "I'm gonna send you over. But chances are you'll get off with life. That means if you're a good girl you'll get out in twenty years. I'll be waiting for you. If they hang you . . . I'll always remember you."

Bogart first revealed the possibility of delineating the more interesting human complexities of such characters in his role of gangster Roy Earle in Walsh's *High Sierra*, released earlier in 1941; he developed it in such films as Michael Curtiz's *Casablanca* (1942) and Howard Hawks's *To Have and Have Not* (1944); and when he returned to the private eye noir in *The Big Sleep*, he enriched it with wisdom, humor, and generosity. Shot in 1944–1945 and reedited and released in 1946,[24] *The Big Sleep* was the second teaming of Bogart and Lauren Bacall, who were so sensational together in *To Have and Have Not* that Warner Brothers decided reteaming them could only produce more box-office fire. The alteration of the novel occurred precisely to accommodate this; with Bogart playing Marlowe, the result was a dynamic between two stars rarely achieved in film and one never exceeded in equanimity and romance. It has been argued that the deviation detracted from a fidelity to the Marlowe figure. Nothing could be further from the truth, since Marlowe, in pursuit of Sean Regan for Colonel Sternwood and in the thick of blackmailers, pornographers, a nymphomaniac, and killers, never relinquishes his strength of independence and objectivity. He perceives the world around him as a humane survivor and with a sarcasm that never betrays bitterness. This broadened dimension of the Marlowe character on screen could only have been brought out by a female counterpart of comparable intelligence and attractiveness. It is Bacall as Vivian

The Big Sleep (1946). Bogart and Bacall in signature form.

who is able to face Marlowe with uncallous self-confidence in protection of her sister Carmen, to be seductive through her independence and charm as she is seduced by his, and to provoke in the process the capability of the Bogart private eye to instigate a mating dance between them as two equally matched opponents and lovers. That Howard Hawks had an expert hand in this is undeniable; that Bogart and Bacall created a unique chemistry in noir cinema of prevailing love is equally undeniable. It is one of the rare examples where it triumphs in a climate of corruption, greed, and sexual exploit, and because these two smart characters gravitate among such elements, there is little illusion at the end of the film that they leave the bloodstained Laurel Canyon house to enter a world much changed because of their romance. It is simply that their relationship for us, the spectators, has been so immensely satisfying in an otherwise unregenerate world that we feel momentarily renewed.

The French critics in the 1950s were among the first to notice the distinctiveness of Bogart's very modern style. When Bogart died in 1957, André Bazin compared him to the Jean Gabin of *Le Jour se lève* and *Pépé le Moko*, noting that "both men are heroes of modern cinematographic tragedy" but that "the fate of Gabin is precisely to be duped by life," whereas "Bogart is man *defined* by fate . . . absurdly victorious from the macabre combat with the angel, his face marked by what he has seen and his bearing heavy with all he knows."[25] Few, however, have described the Bogart ethos more perceptively than Henri Agel, when he observed:

> He knew how to reinvent, little by little, the internal elegance of the dandy. He elevated to a sort of plastic dignity the most modest manifestations of existence: taking off his jacket, lighting a cigarette, opening a door. With greater reason, the ritual gestures whereby he celebrates the office of the *film noir*—picking up the telephone receiver, handling a revolver, kissing a dangerous woman—attain with Bogart a concentration and a bald nobility. . . . The physiognomy of Bogart evokes that of Albert Camus—of a Camus who always would have remained in the first part of *The Myth of Sisyphus*, who would not have found consolation in a somewhat nebulous humanism. These two men are really contemporaries by their controlled reverie and the acuteness of their gaze.[26]

THE GANGSTER FIGURE AND THE NOIR

When we speak of gangsters and their official pursuers—police detectives and federal agents—and the noir environment, it becomes easy to dismiss police crime as a distinct portrayal of American society, one that lacks the moral anxiety and strange animus that give the noir protagonist the special associations that we attach to troubled individuals. Crime pursued by civil authorities is, after all, a mixed bag: sometimes portrayed as a commendable rebellion by some desperate enough to commit it, it is nonetheless an act of individuation that condemns them for the very anarchy they display in defiance of civilized institutions. And if criminals have a dubious status here, the police have their own dubious distinction: simultaneously corruptible and incorruptible, men of civil authority yet protectors of vice, lords of peace in a landscape that rewards their power with violence and death. The film noir traffics in many of the dilemmas faced by the good and the evil here, and although no gangster film or police drama is necessarily noir cinema, several have gone beyond presenting the professional concerns of crime fighting found in the *film policier* to probe the obsessions and nihilism afflicting the gangster as he attempts to survive his pursuers in an increasingly desperate chase. Martin Rome in *Cry of the City*, Shubunka in *The Gangster* (Gordon Wiles, 1947), Johnny Rocco in *Key Largo*, Cody Jarrett in *White Heat*, and Nick Scanlon in *The Racket* (John Cromwell, 1951) stand among the finer examples of such a noir character.

The first gangster film per se was Edwin S. Porter's 1903 *Great Train Robbery*. In this landmark of early narrative filmmaking, crime joins a frontier railroad setting in what was undoubtedly received as a contemporary crime story at the time, and a departure from an old west narrative was presented on that most modern of inventions, a movie screen, to become a "crime" film for its urban audiences. Throughout the early silent years, gothic crime serials, simple melodramas of maidens in distress pursued by villains, proliferated. During the 1920s crime on screen depicted a decidedly urban vice of street thuggery, poverty, and extortion. The Volstead Act, sponsored by Minnesota congressman Andrew Volstead, inaugurated Prohibition in 1919, which made the transportation and consumption of alcohol illegal except for medicinal and religious purposes. Prohibition was the rather desperate last draw of frontier rural American civilization to assert its dominance over American urbanism with the accompanying increasingly ethnic diversity and cosmopolitanism. Before congressional repeal on December 5, 1933, Prohibition spawned the great myths of urban and organized crime with all their social ramifications, depicted in American movies as different as Josef Von Sternberg's *Underworld* (1927), Mervyn LeRoy's *Little Caesar* (1930), William Wellman's *Public Enemy* (1931), and Howard Hawks's *Scarface: The Shame of a Nation* (1932). The myths retained their vitality all the way up through Francis Ford Coppola's *Godfather* films and Martin Scorsese's *Mean Streets* (1973). Coupled with the poverty and economic inequities spurred by the depression, the effects of Prohibition and its temptations of vice and gangsterism outlasted Repeal and were reflected in a cycle of late-thirties Warner Brothers gangster and juvenile crime dramas—*Bullets or Ballots* (William Keighley, 1936), *Dead End* (William Wyler, 1937), *Marked Woman* (Lloyd Bacon, 1937), *Angels with Dirty Faces* (Michael Curtiz, 1938)—that pretty much culminated in 1939 with Walsh's *Roaring Twenties*. Organized crime on screen from the beginning of the forties to the present day has assumed the legacy of these screen images, modified repeatedly to accommodate a changing modern landscape, where the lucre of crime after Repeal shifted from booze to extortion, narcotics, prostitution, the numbers racket, and politics, and where the veneer of criminal activity began to look more and more comfortably ensconced in respectability.

There was an irony—one wholly characteristic of American commercial enterprise—in the case of such entertainment being produced by Hollywood in the early thirties and held in contempt by the selected arbiters of social and consumer morals, who were often appeased by the very industry they condemned. In 1934 Will Hays, president of the Motion Picture Producers and Distributers of America (and Warren Harding's postmaster general and chairman of the Republican National Committee), and Hollywood censor Joseph L. Breen established their famous code for assessing the moral value of films released in answer to the outcry of civic and religious groups against the growing incursion of violence on screen. In April of that year, a committee of Catholic bishops formed the Legion of Decency "to alert Catholics as to which movies to avoid," and it received ecumenical support.[27] From 1934 to 1937, the Legion was so successful in its drive that few crime films were produced. It mattered little that no violent criminal in Hollywood cinema ever escaped the appropriate punitive ending. The idea that "actors concentrated on learning how to talk out of the side of the mouth and around a cigar" and that "the most popular prop in the studio was the machine gun" temporarily silenced the industry mythmakers.[28]

The gangster in his clash with law enforcement approached the noir world as a rebel, a violator of the social order; he was a rebel of the self against the world. "[W]hat matters is that the experience of the gangster *as an experience of art* is universal to Americans," wrote Robert Warshow in his famous essay on the gangster as tragic hero. "In ways that we do not easily or willingly define, the gangster speaks for us, expressing that part of the American psyche which rejects the qualities and the demands of modern life, which rejects 'Americanism' itself."[29] What Johnny Rocco and Cody Jarrett envision is a lawful civilization ripe to be plundered for their own exciting and violent gratification, a civilization whose conventions never accommodated their volatility and megalomania. At the close of the classical gangster film cycle—in 1949 with *White Heat*—Raoul Walsh can still have Jimmy Cagney climb to the top of a gas tank just before its explosion and, as deranged Cody Jarrett, exclaim to his dead mother and the world: "Made it, Ma! Top of the world!" And Edward G. Robinson as Rocco in *Key Largo* knows one certain thing until his dying breath: that there is only one Johnny Rocco;

there will never be another. The grandiose presumption is sad and broken here, and touching in its cowardice. It echoes another famous gangster's bullet-riddled demise, at the end of *Little Caesar* eighteen years earlier, when Robinson asked the world with near-classical astonishment: "Mother of Mercy! Is this the end of Rico?" These valedictory moments signal the obsolescence of the Warners gangster, filtered through a postwar world, at a moment when the rage of desperado individualism to be heard has just passed. From now on gangsterism adopts a more sophisticated capitalist approach that "ambiguously mirrors a world in which the individualistic ethos no longer satisfactorily explains and orders society for most members of the public. . . . The drama of the criminal gang has become a kind of allegory of the corporation and the corporate society."[30]

The changing depiction of criminality from unvarnished gangsterism to organized crime appeared throughout the 1950s in noir cinema, from *The Enforcer* (Bretaigne Windust, 1951) and *The Racket* to *The Godfather II* (1974) and is discussed throughout this volume, with attention given to the films of certain noir directors reflecting it (Samuel Fuller, Phil Karlson, Don Siegel) and the Kefauver crime hearings. But if it did nothing else, the gangster film nourished noir cinema by presenting a character type who acted out his fantasies of a destructive "no" against a modern world that was daunting in its increasing mandate for conformity and success. Warshow recognized it well when he observed: "The gangster movie with its numerous variations . . . sets forth the attractions of violence in the face of all our higher social attitudes. It is a more 'modern' genre than the Western, perhaps even more profound, because it confronts industrial society on its own ground—the city— and because, like much of our advanced art, it gains its effects by a gross insistence on its own narrow logic."[31]

JOHN HUSTON (1906–1987)

The Maltese Falcon (1941)
Key Largo (1948)
The Asphalt Jungle (1950)

The characters in John Huston's noir films function in such striking accord with the fatalism of the noir world that Huston emerges as the appropriate progenitor of the film noir in Hollywood cinema. Less than the doomed fatalism of Lang or Siodmak, Huston's involves characters blinded by their weaknesses as they exercise the impulse toward some folly of optimism. The fat man in *The Maltese Falcon* is driven by "the stuff that dreams are made of," while Sam Spade observes with doubt Gutman and company's prospects. Spade himself becomes a hapless victim of illusion, having fallen for Brigid O'Shaughnessy, but he maintains his moral bearing and honors his murdered partner by turning her in, because, after all, when one private eye suffers, all do. This honor, naive perhaps in the noir world, is necessary in Huston's world; for if there is truly honor among thieves, as Dix Handley, Doc Riedenschneider, and Louis Ciavelli collectively affirm in *The Asphalt Jungle*, then the failure to scheme the future of one's dreams must be a matter of the stars. It is this kind of fatalism that finally delineates the noir perspective of Huston's vision.

The Maltese Falcon initiated the possibilities on screen for a new behavior in a new kind of environment, where people appear, often not too convincingly, to be something other than what they are, with vague motives not easily defined but suspicious and suggestively corrupt. When Brigid O'Shaughnessy apologizes for her initial deception of Spade and Archer, Spade remarks that they never really believed her, but only believed in her money. The amplitude of shrewdness is important here: if Spade—and Humphrey Bogart in his legend-making performance of him—helped inaugurate the noir cinema on the American screen, it was precisely because of this rude assurance that established his individualist stance in the face of the unknown. "[W]hat makes someone a type," Stanley Cavell noted, "is not his similarity with other members of that type but his striking separateness from other people."[32]

Huston used Bogart here as a force contending with mysterious characters never really revealed in motive and subversion. When Spade encounters Joel Cairo, he is amused by him; when he meets Kasper Gutman, he is intrigued; but the fascination developing around Brigid finally culminates in disappointment and hurt that send him back into his orbit of the wizened, suspicious loner. Huston reveals these characters with remarkable fidelity to Hammett's narrative style—detached, in a slightly bemused manner. That style finds its cinematic equivalent in the static medium and close shots that almost always have Bogart/Spade in two-shot with the subject/object of his inquiry. The tension, heightened by such inquiry, rarely reaches a crescendo; instead, it plays out in scenes of comparatively subdued linearity—this probably a hold-over from the Warner Brothers gangster films of a few years earlier. (Here, however, character actor Barton MacLane, a perennial favorite in those movies, does not shout his incomparably better-written lines.) What Huston added to this studio influence that makes *The Maltese Falcon* such a distinctive work of its era and, really, of our popular consciousness, is the modulated pacing of action, which advances the detective narrative and calibrates the growing dynamics between characters and at the same time uncovers that which is not known and cannot be known. As Huston's camera pans from character to character in quest of answers and coherence to the mystery of the lost black bird, the infectious siren call of Adolph Deutsch's score and the patina of Arthur Edeson's shaded, but really not too dark, cinematography give a heady aromatic quality to the unfolding narrative. It is as if some of Joel Cairo's sickeningly pungent perfume spilled over onto the proceedings. And once this particular Maltese falcon has been discovered to be a fake, the drama is not satisfyingly completed: Spade is left bitter, spent of the cynical humor he has maintained throughout the story. This is the accord between Hammett and Huston that makes their union perfect. Gilles Jacob saw the irony, so appropriate to the styles of both, when he asked in 1950: "What is so much the point of murderers, of rough combats, of tests, if the hero takes possession of this Holy Grail so quickly? It comes doubtlessly in the notion of the Grail not being ever even conquered, especially at the moment when it is so close."[33]

After the war Huston cowrote in the noir or intrigue vein *The Killers* with Anthony Veiller for Siodmak and *Three Strangers* (1946) with Howard Koch for Jean Negulesco. He worked uncredited with Veiller and Orson Welles on the screenplay for Welles's *Stranger* (1946). Then in 1948 he made *Key Largo*, a postwar variant of the prewar gangster film. It was, however, sufficiently infused with a noir mood that had developed in the intervening years, and it presented the now-legendary image of Bogart and an elegiac role to Edward G. Robinson's career of playing gangsters.

Key Largo reverses Huston's technique of enveloping characters in a web of circumstances that constrict the possibility of rebellion and force the inevitable conclusion of the story. Unlike *The Maltese Falcon*, where the black bird and Brigid are exposed, or *The Asphalt Jungle*, where illusions and fate entrap or vanquish the thieves, *Key Largo* presents characters in the dilemma of hostages quite early in the story.

Key Largo (1948). Noir hubris: Johnny Rocco (Edward G. Robinson) challenges Frank McCloud (Humphrey Bogart).

Huston's camera encloses beautiful two- and three-character compositions throughout, showing equally the captives' responses to the gangsters and the tensions erupting among the hostages themselves. The necessity here, especially for Bogart's Frank McCloud, becomes one of maintaining dignity and rebellion under suffocating circumstances and the threat of violence by asserting a delicate equipoise of individual strength and submission. Robinson's Johnny Rocco emerges, finally, as the pathetic, blind thug, touching as much as he is vicious in a display of hubris that brings about his downfall. Like other Huston characters, Rocco's blindness further ensures his doom by a lingering sentimentality for the unshakable image of the Rocco that was and the stability of the times that were—a tragic implication that neither was ever much more than the megalomaniacal illusion of a broken-down gangster. The old-fashioned Rocco, fleshed out through Edward G. Robinson's performance, is no match for Bogart's McCloud, a war veteran whose social code puzzles Rocco. Having shared common reference points in the old gangster cinema, Robinson must now step aside for Bogart, who has come to symbolize the "modern" somber hero of a decidedly postwar existential shade.

The Maltese Falcon initiated the detective noir, but "the stuff that dreams are made of" found its fullest expression in Huston's *Asphalt Jungle*. As in *The Treasure of Sierra Madre*, the price paid through folly and fate delineates the weakness of those joined in unholy alliance. *The Asphalt Jungle*, however, is set in an increasingly desperate noir world of costlier suffering and death. The network of flawed characters, each trapped by his own lure, finally fragments, and their best-laid plans of escape after a jewel heist disintegrate. Doc Riedenschneider, the gang's sage mastermind, observes: "Put in hours and hours of planning, figure everything down to the last detail . . . then what? Burglar alarms start

The Maltese Falcon (1941). Sam Spade (Humphrey Bogart) and the usual suspects: Kasper Gutman (Sydney Greenstreet), Joel Cairo (Peter Lorre), and Brigid O'Shaughnessy (Mary Astor).

going off for no sensible reason. A gun fires of its own accord and a man is shot. And a broken-down old house no good for anything but chasing kids has to trip over us! Blind accidents. What can you do against blind accidents?"

The blind accidents that foil their getaway are eclipsed by their sad, pathetic, and often poignant dreams. Doc only wants to retire in Mexico surrounded by the young girls willing to satisfy his lecherous fantasies. It is his lechery that finally allows him to be caught. Louis Ciavelli only wants to remove his family and expectant wife from the cramped, noisy tenement that stifles them. "If you want fresh air, don't look for it in this town," he says bitterly. For his effort, he takes a bullet and dies. As the police sirens blare louder in pursuit of the others, his widow Maria, depleted with fear and grief, remarks, "It sounds like a soul in hell." But Dix Handley's dream is saddest of all: he dreams of returning to the innocence of his boyhood home and horses. Doc gives such vain hope the critical noir perspective when he tells him, "You can always go home, and when you do, it's nothing. Believe me, I've done it. Nothing." Dix flees shot with Doll to Oklahoma, only to die when they get there. Such moments define the noir vision of Huston's films, exacerbate the hopelessness produced in misbegotten endeavor to realize a dream. ("After all, crime is only a left-handed form of human endeavor," observes Alonzo Emmerich early on.) The pathos in *The Asphalt Jungle* inevitably arises from its characters' efforts to come to the paltriest and most transient of contentment in an antagonistic world distorted by the hopes and illusions they have created. "One way or another," Doc Reidenschneider says, "we all work for our vice."

There is a link between the mythology of the ancients and the noir world that John Huston created. Unlike the films of directors like Siodmak, Preminger, or Joseph H. Lewis—to take three different examples—Huston's characters run the inexorable course of disappointment, failure, or destruction in pursuit of some sort of cosmic definition and of a privileged place envisioned within it. Cobby, Emmerich's private eye in *The Asphalt Jungle*, in contrast, wants in on the heist take only for the money. Huston quickly dispenses with such a character. Emmerich kills Cobby out of fear, for he was a poacher, "a parvenu among aristocrats."[34] Sam Spade probes in his milieu, searching for answers; Brigid, Gutman, and Joel Cairo chase the black bird in lust and duplicitous misalliance; Johnny Rocco pursues his immortality ("You're not big enough to do this to Rocco! . . . You'll never bring me in! Never!");

The Asphalt Jungle (1950). Dix Handley (Sterling Hayden) and Doc Riedenschneider (Sam Jaffe) lie low after their job.

and Doc, Dix, Emmerich, and Ciavelli are driven by the need to create the world of their dreams. Their gestures all form the noir world of a director for whom *pursuit* becomes the thematic device culminating in defeat. Unlike Fritz Lang, who entraps his characters in paranoid torment, Huston entices his with a light at the end of the tunnel, only to show us that it was but a chimera of their own desires.

VIOLENCE IN THE NOIR

> I told the art director I wanted those stairs, because I liked the
> idea of Widmark pulling Kiley down by the ankles, and the
> heavy's chin hits every step. Dat-dat-dat-dat-dat: it's musical.
> —Samuel Fuller on the making of *Pickup on South Street*

Violence is the most consistent motif in the film noir; virtually no noir is without it. Its importance is complicated and often explained in sociological terms to justify its aesthetic power. As a statement in itself, violence in noir cinema claims a distinctive use. Whereas its purpose in the pure gangster film has often been to explain the sociopathic breeding and greed of thuggish personalities who reach power and control, violence in the noir is less explicable and more arbitrary, less a matter of historical cause and effect than an unexpected and intense exercise of rage. It became increasingly brutal after 1946 when graphic realism on screen was accompanied by a matching violence, often stylized, to offer an equally novel and sensational experience. The brutality of a Tommy Udo in *Kiss of Death*, who pushes wheelchair-bound Ma Rizzo down a flight of stairs, or of a Rick Coyle in *Raw Deal* (Anthony Mann, 1948), who throws a flaming chafing dish in a woman's face, has an appalling, hideous immediacy rarely seen in the prewar gangster film. *Brute Force*, *White Heat*, *The Big Heat*—each has moments of violence that jar us by their cold-bloodedness, occasionally terrify us in their perverseness. Sadistic prison matron Evelyn Harper (in a superb performance by Hope Emerson) strangles a kitten in *Caged* (John Cromwell, 1950) because it is the only symbol of vulnerability and tenderness that sustains Marie Allen's will. She then advances her wicked domination of the prisoners by brutally beating Kitty Stark into disfigurement. We see neither action take place, but we gasp at the images that remain. Such images of violent acts as those performed by Udo, Coyle, Captain Munsey in *Brute Force*, and the disfigurements of Vince Stone in *The Big Heat* are all in the context of criminal or outlaw enterprise but depart from the active pursuit of it long enough to suggest a darker, crueler impulse.

In the films noirs of private detectives and conspiratorial domestic tragedy, violence has a less palatable expression than it had in the boudoir or, before it, gothic melodrama. There is a big difference in sensibility between Gregory Anton poisoning his wife Paula in *Gaslight* (George Cukor, 1944) and Canino in *The Big Sleep* forcing a poisoned drink upon a frightened Harry Jones as we watch him drink it, knowing he will die. Or in Hitchcock's quasi-noir *Shadow of a Doubt* (1942), where small-town life takes on a decidedly pernicious patina as we watch Charley Oakley attempt to throw his favorite niece off a train. Mildred Pierce is willing to go to prison for her daughter Veda, but more unsettling is the fact that Veda would let her. Such violence still disturbs the viewer fifty years later. The most immediate impact in a historical context was in the quality of violence displayed in so many postwar dramas that came to be recognized as films noirs. The sadism that satisfied a number of sociopaths, or the amorality of an Ellen Berent's vacant re-

Brute Force (1947). Reprisal for squealing: new, more brutal postwar violence.

sponses to the pain of dying and manslaughter in *Leave Her to Heaven* (John Stahl, 1945), implied something new at the time: namely, that violence can be disturbingly recognizable, a perversion arising from the rupture of psychological balance that both subdues and unleashes it.

Violence after the studio-period noir of 1944–1947 changed from the casual amorality of Chandlerian violence to the punched-gut variety refined—if that is the word—throughout the fifties. Jon Tuska suggested that audiences nurtured on the violence of newsreel footage during World War II (violence that "had *never* been filmed before") developed a curiosity if not an appetite for its depiction.[35] We know a similar argument was made about the coverage of the Vietnam War. The difference between the two is that World War II was the inaugural war; before it the world was a far wider place, and the moviegoer's consciousness was less challenged by the increasingly tightening circle of world horrors seen before a double bill. Violence a generation later not only was depicted more vividly but also had lost its remoteness for audiences too willing to accept its undercurrent coursing through recognizable civilized culture. Postwar noir cinema, particularly, depicted a visceral and often highly exciting violence culminating in more imaginative exercises in killing and death. More and more, audiences accepted it. Alfred Appel remembered that the prison stoolie's sadistic death under a steam press in *Brute Force* delighted *Life* as well as the audience in his neighborhood theater. They delighted "in the scene's novelty, its *inventiveness*."[36]

The graphic screen violence escalating throughout the fifties and sixties aroused the indignation of other audiences, who, like the voices of public morality during the depression, protested its corrupting influence. However, "bigotry, envy, treachery, aggressiveness, repression, and hate are consonant with virtue," Jack Shadoian wrote in his 1972 essay on Phil Karlson's 1953 *99 River Street*. "If one wishes to understand America now, one could learn a good deal from films like *The Line-Up*, *Kiss Me Deadly*, *Scandal Sheet*, *Murder by Contract*, *The Big Heat*, *The Brothers Rico*, and others like them. They were telling us something. What it was is perhaps clearer now."[37] The same caveat applies today to a much different style of film culture. In retrospect, the stylized violence of films like *Bonnie and Clyde* and *The Godfather* makes less of a personal impact and instead creates a distance from the reality of violence. The best films noirs have always had the opposite effect; they have allowed the incursion of violence unannounced, arbitrary—often unsettling precisely because of this—to affect the audience's perception of the violence around them. (Quentin Tarantino's *Jackie Brown* [1997] weaves such violence with dark humor in a particularly contemporary expression of this.) From the endings of *Chinatown* and *The Long Goodbye* in the seventies (these, too, stylized, but with a sensitivity to the startling quality violence can assume) to the menacing river of violence throughout James Foley's 1986 *At Close Range*, noir violence happens as a force without agenda. And it continues so through the nineties, as we see, for example, with Lilly Dillon, who accidentally slashes the throat of her son, Roy, at the end of *The Grifters* (Stephen Frears, 1990) and quickly regains her composure to collect his bloodied dollar bills and effect her getaway. We are compelled to absorb the image of her face, an exquisite enigma of maternity and violence.

SAMUEL FULLER (1911–1997)

Pickup on South Street (1953)
The Crimson Kimono (1959)
Underworld U.S.A. (1961)
Shock Corridor (1963)
The Naked Kiss (1964)

Have you ever killed anyone?
Have you?

The dilemma of man in society in Samuel Fuller's noir films—consistent with the immediate, high-impact style of his best filmmaking—brings a vulgar innocence into conflict with brutal corruption. His use of heavy-handed close shots, often abruptly edited into sequences of contrasting long takes, emphasizes the sensationalism of his melodramas and stylizes his vision of a noir world full of thrusts and jabs, of violence that reveals social injustice as often as it betrays the sensitive nature of his main characters. Fuller's is a tabloid vision, nurtured by his youthful experience as a big-city crime reporter, and it finds expression in five films that place him in the noir cinema—*Pickup on South Street*, *The Crimson Kimono*, *Underworld U.S.A.*, *Shock Corridor*, and *The Naked Kiss*.

Fuller's world is a place where the institutions and conventions of America as defined by its middle class become ambivalent social constructs, perverted by the hypocrisy and corruption that keep them powerful forces, yet often redeemed by those who are among society's least desirable representatives. "Paradoxically, bourgeois America is often defended in Fuller's films by the pariahs of American society," observed Colin McArthur.[38] And, it would seem, with little irony intended. For Fuller, a staunch anticommunist, gives us in *Pickup on South Street* two pickpockets to help authorities break up a Communist spy ring and then allows these two—two badly used and cynical marginals—a compassionate intimacy implying a future best spent together. Skip McCoy and Candy, denizens of a rather gritty underworld, ennoble the core decency of grifters and cons, who, even they, would not sell out to the Commies. It is a stunning proposition here, played out against the perpetual violence of their background. Skip and Candy, much like Kelly in *The Na-*

ked Kiss, and even more like Tolly Devlin in *Underworld U.S.A.*, have shrewdly assessed the system that hounds them and in the end concluded that complicity with its authority is as much a reluctant moral necessity as it is an expedient choice. That Tolly Devlin pursues with the law's tacit approval the men who killed his father, or that Kelly faces trial with town sentiment suspicious of her alleged motive for killing their scion, Grant, only heightens the moral authenticity of these outcasts who are asked to aid the very institutions that persecute them. More, however, is meant in McArthur's observation, which goes to the heart of Fuller's intentions and ambivalence as a noir filmmaker: the characters in *Pickup on South Street, Underworld U.S.A.*, and *The Naked Kiss* dream against hope of having the kind of life that is denied them. Beyond the realization that "respectable" society repudiates people like them, Cuddles and Tolly, Kelly, and Moe, too, attempt to create what society refuses them—the right to ordinary happiness—in every attempt to simulate the movements of conventional life. Cuddles repeatedly tells Tolly that she wants to marry him, to make a home with him and have his child. Tolly, in stereotypical fashion, plays the resisting male. Kelly, who cannot have children, renounces her past as a prostitute and becomes a nurse's aide working with children. Joe Kojaku, the Nisei detective in *The Crimson Kimono*, desires romantic happiness with the Caucasian Chris but must overcome his neurotic conditioning in a racist society to obtain it.

It is a domesticity quite consistent with Fuller's larger vision for a fraternity of the diverse coming together to live and work in harmony in the truest definition of what the fabric of a strong and just America must be. And it is the most difficult goal to achieve in a nation ostensibly dedicated to its mission. In a striking example of the formal paranoia in Fuller's work, Joe Kojaku and his partner, Charlie Bancroft, compete in a ceremonial kendo competition, as they have for several years since they fought together in Korea. But Joe's suspicion that Charlie's professed affection for Chris is more acceptable than his own dooms a friendship nurtured in wartime trust. As the pacing of the match, precise and ceremonial, accelerates, so does Fuller's editing in close-up, until the face of one of the Japanese judges registers disapproval at Kojaku's increasingly violent breach of competition decorum, which destroys his fraternal bond with Charlie.

It is from the subversion of this vision, in fact, that journalist Johnny Barrett comes to learn of madness in this society during his stay in a mental hospital in *Shock Corridor*, surely one of the most lurid "exposés"

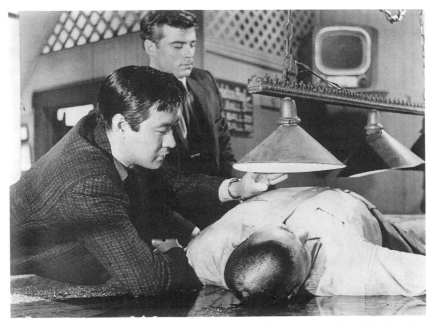

The Crimson Kimono (1959). Charlie Bancroft (Glenn Corbett) and Joe Kojaku (James Shigeta) investigate not only murder but also the basis of their own relationship.

of institutional confinement in the annals of American cinema. What confronts Johnny, who seeks answers to a suspected murder, hushed up in the hospital, is nothing short of the shock of encountering the extreme gestures of paranoia and psychosis that are nurtured in the torments of racism, abuse, and the dislocated creative impulse. During his stay, he is subjected to nymphomaniacal assault, violent attacks from the other patients, and restraint with subsequent electric shock treatments by the hospital authorities, until he is no longer able to function independently and objectively as a sane man. Shot in manic, violent scenes in an oppressive set designed by Eugène Lourié, Jean Renoir's set designer,[39] *Shock Corridor* is lighted in a cascade of gray and darker gray chiaroscuro by Stanley Cortez, often evoking his intoxicating lighting of Welles's *Magnificent Ambersons*. Cortez's cinematography is so baroque in its use of shadows that it suggests the psyche trapped in a noirlike institution, a sort of mental facility analog to the iconographic noir hotel room where so often the protagonist is holed up in fear. In this setting, Johnny meets Trent, a black student persecuted into madness by the integration struggles of the South, and Stuart, a racist bigot taught against his youthful will to hate. Phil Hardy correctly noted that "they, not Johnny, talk about America. In their speeches, Fuller once more addresses the audience, but the mood this time is of desperation: these are failed men."[40]

After *Underworld U.S.A.*, fewer close-ups appear in Fuller's work; this is the case in *Shock Corridor* and *The Naked Kiss*. The hallucinatory quality of the set and lighting in *Shock Corridor* stylizes the narrative into a delirium of time and place (beautifully displayed in a dream striptease sequence in which a miniaturized Cathy flirts with a now-deranged Johnny), as Johnny becomes catatonic in an institutional setting that, in a grimly humorous manner, serves as a microcosm of the very real conflicted world he must certainly cover as a newspaperman. But the price paid to excavate the "truth" here has pushed his own capacity for self-knowledge to a terrible cancellation, since now Johnny cannot bear the loss of personal control as he drifts into his own psychic prison.

To speak, in fact, of Sam Fuller's tabloid sensibility is not to forget for a moment that he was a cigar-chomping newspaper reporter à la Hecht and MacArthur who covered the crime beat as a seventeen-year-old. His pictures reflect a taste for the sensationalized and often clumsily exaggerated truth about crime and violence. Shots of newspaper headlines announce criminal mayhem, syndicate crackdowns (*Underworld U.S.A.*), manhunts for murdered strippers (*The Crimson Kimono*), and ex-prostitutes on trial for murdering pedophiles (*The Naked Kiss*). The opening sequence of *The Crimson Kimono* is a flagrant display of violence, staged to the blaring accompaniment of a frenzied jazz soundtrack (by Harry Sukman) as the stripper Sugar Torch, scantily clad and running in terror down a neon-lighted street, is finally struck dead. And to top the shock value of this sequence, one need only watch the comparably flagrant opening of *The Naked Kiss*, where a bald-headed prostitute (Kelly) beats up her drunken pimp, takes money from him, and leaves. Indeed, Johnny's extreme act of having himself committed to solve a murder arouses in him the exciting possibility of winning a Pulitzer Prize for it. Hardy again saw it best in some of the earliest and best writing on Fuller's cinema: "Fuller, knowing that America's secrets lie in the gutter, that the surface *is* reality if correctly viewed, disrupts the surface and builds his case, not by a judicial weighing-up of the facts, but through a reporter's intuitive grasp of the salient features of the problem—however contradictory those features may seem to be."[41]

Pickup on South Street (1953). Moe (Thelma Ritter) sells neckties but not information. With Candy (Jean Peters).

The connection between "reporting" this reality as a filmmaker and the violence that gives it dramatic force brings Fuller into the realm of the film noir, as an abettor of violence as well as its condemner. In *Pickup on South Street*, Moe has been selling information to the authorities to make money for the only goal in her dismal life: to buy a decent burial. Informing—the prostitution of knowledge—is really a relative transgression; to the police it is good, to the Communists bad, and in the end it buys Moe nothing but a bullet in the head. "Look, mister, I'm so tired you'd be doin' me a big favor if you'd blow my head off," she tells her killer. And while the strains of an old song on the record player bring her a wisp of nostalgia for the unfulfilled long-past promise of happiness, she is shot dead.

In *Underworld U.S.A.*, bookkeeper Mencken's young daughter is viciously run down on her bicycle in an act of intimidation, and a crime lieutenant suspected of informing is trapped inside his torched car. ("Give me a light," says syndicate boss Gela, as he smokes a cigarette, watching from another car a short distance away.) But it is the violence in Tolly that is most compelling, as he sees his father murdered in horror and the hate spawned from this childhood trauma, symbolized in a close shot of his clenched fist, becomes the memory that fuels his revenge and brings about his own brutal death. It is a death stylized in characteristic Fuller fashion, by a ludicrous, operatic slow-death-in-stages collapse at the end of the film. KEEP THE CITY CLEAN, says the sign on the garbage can Tolly knocks over as he dies with Cuddles and Sandy by his side, but in Fuller's world such "good" fights are endless. The underlying despair of his dark view suggests the questionable value of individual action if the summit of all human actions leads to impotence or horrible death. The crippled passions of his noir victims betray the cruel agenda of a society at odds with its own values.

ROBERT ALDRICH (1918–1983)

World for Ransom (1954)
Kiss Me Deadly (1955)
The Big Knife (1955)

Robert Aldrich places his characters in a world disoriented by the vigor of amorality and violence, where the exercise of personal responsibility ends up being a cruel joke of character in those whose conception of the human condition is modified by a faith in personal will. In the sphere of noir cinema, Aldrich presents three protagonists who exercise confidence and control or power only to see them vanquished by the obsessions and actions of others who are determined to upset the moral assumptions of the social order. It is interesting that two of these men— Mike Hammer in *Kiss Me Deadly* and Mike Callahan in *World for Ransom*—function in a fifties atmosphere threatened by nuclear destruction. The nihilism underlying both films generates the ultimate noir perspective in all of American cinema: the impulse toward heroic self-definition becomes a presumptuous exercise in a world reeling further away from a recognizable moral center toward destruction. In a more grandiose and melodramatic vein, Charlie Castle in *The Big Knife* displays a similar but more volatile egotism in Aldrich's depiction of Hollywood as a state of moral malaise, tellingly wrought to just that state of tension that never degenerates into a pure hell but always remains a hell-like trap that lures its participants into a mutually flagellating relationship from which, it seems, no exit is truly desired.

"Half-idealism is the peritonitis of the soul," movie star Charlie Castle's rival cautions him in an accurate description of Charlie's dilemma after submitting to the blackmail of contract renewal with tyrannical producer Stanley Hoff. *The Big Knife*, claustrophobic and overbaked, is one of Aldrich's first films to capitalize on the grotesquerie of temperament, temperament displayed as violently as the dangerous incidents encountered by Callahan and Hammer in their quests.[42] But Charlie's violence—internalized, self-lacerating, and a product of the shame and self-loathing only a sellout can muster—expresses the anguish of an artist who came to do honorable work in a film industry regulated by corruption and its brokers.

The Big Knife is based on Clifford Odets's 1949 Broadway play that starred John Garfield in the role of Charlie Castle, a role modeled in part after Garfield himself. Set mostly in the living room of Charlie's Bel Air ranch house, the film, interestingly, fails to capture the best expression of Odets's anxiety. Aldrich presents instead a half-successful dilution of Odets's moralism and a parody of neurotic method acting, especially with Rod Steiger's performance as Hoff. Of the socially conscious urban morality tales infused with noir nihilism, Abraham Polonsky still captures the most accurate sensibility of an Odets-like passion with existential anguish in his noir classics *Force of Evil* and *Body and Soul*.[43] Garfield, of course, starred in both of these, and Aldrich was the assistant director on them.

World for Ransom, an often neglected early work, is loosely based on Dan Duryea's *China Smith* television series of the early fifties, on which he played a private eye adventurer and for which Aldrich directed several episodes. But there are expressive noir elements here that place it among Aldrich's darkest and most melancholy films. Shot in very low light, the Singapore setting of *World for Ransom* is an exotic transplant of the noir urban milieu, full of cheap bars, B-girls, and the bustle of a

World for Ransom (1954). Noir Singapore.

Casbah-like atmosphere with its secluded alleyways and illicit danger. Duryea is the loner Callahan in the middle of it, whose only aim is to win back his former girlfriend, Frennessey, by answering her request to extricate her husband and his friend Julian from sinister Alexis Pedaras's scheme to kidnap a nuclear physicist for ransom to the highest bidder in the West or behind the Iron Curtain. The very plot of the film augurs Aldrich's apocalyptic *Kiss Me Deadly*, made the following year, yet *World for Ransom* retains in Callahan the capacity for disillusionment that Mike Hammer can no longer have; for by the end of Hammer's search for the mystery behind "the great whatsit," he has arrived at total denial of any illusion for world salvation.

Callahan's romantic disillusionment comes with the increasing knowledge of *his* world, reckoned with and accepted with a measure of complacency until Julian is killed and Frennessey blames him, claiming that she could never love Callahan because of his idealized image of her.[44] Julian accepted her and her past as a prostitute. However, there is little indication that this would have mattered much to Mike, and he leaves rejected, hurt, and humiliated and with his cynicism confirmed. Frennessey was indeed the pivotal influence in Callahan's life, as he quested to recover the possibility of happiness lost with her years before. "[A] white knight in a very grubby business," Richard Combs described him, with the action, gunplay, and tawdry exotica making *World for Ransom* a kind of low-budget postwar intrigue tale with Callahan its seeker-hero.[45] There is a cartoonish quality in the proceedings that attempts to undermine the noir threat of a world hanging precariously in the balance by a madman, but it is, finally, just this image of Callahan that lingers in the hokeyness of these mysterious "Singapore" shadows. Unlike him, Mike Hammer affects a cool detachment with regard to murder and displays a curiosity relatively free of the moral concerns that other private detectives have. He seeks knowledge much less for justice than to exercise control, and it is in this sense that the myth of the private eye undergoes a significant detour.

Kiss Me Deadly is one of the definitive films of the 1950s because of the peculiar, yet uninterrupted, line it follows from the classical figure of the private eye as seeker of truth to the complications that follow when the language of truth is no longer recognizable. The film has found a cineast's allure ever since its release. The French almost immediately recognized in it—indeed, bestowed upon it—the reverence of a prophetic talisman, demonic, mysterious, almost a caveat for the cavalier hipness it dares to assume. Beneath such arrogant grace, however, lies a narrative as enigmatic as the curious black box itself; for *Kiss Me Deadly* is also a caveat for the danger found in what cannot be said, for that which could not be spoken that results in the death of nine people—and if we include Mike and Velda, eleven. Cosmic apocalypse is reduced to a "whatsit" because it speaks of knowledge uncontainable and as yet incomprehensible. Mike Hammer cannot hear what he cannot recognize, and the terms of his quest are merely a hip, formal inquisition, an exercise in the narcissism of tough-guy bravado. "Bet you do pushups every morning just to keep your belly hard," Christina teases him.

Three key strategies delineate, and separate, the story from other noirs of the period and lend claim to *Kiss Me Deadly* as one of the first modernist expressions of the classic film noir. First, Mike Hammer pursues the case of Christina's death by, essentially, *making* the case. No one has approached him with a job or given him a compelling personal motive to pursue her murder. "If she hadn't gotten in my way, I wouldn't have stopped," he tells Pat Murphy about her hitchhiking. The fact that she was tortured to death merely arouses him to respond, "Must be some-

Kiss Me Deadly (1955). Mike Hammer (Ralph Meeker): victim of a violent and abstract noir mystery.

thing big." Given that he is a private investigator of the sleazier kind (he literally becomes a pimp for his secretary, Velda—"real woo bait"—to entrap cheating husbands), the motive here is simply without remuneration, but not without reason. It allows Mike Hammer, unlike Sam Spade, Philip Marlowe, or Lew Archer, to revel in the style of a private eye as it has become ritualized over the preceding two decades. He has the jargon down and displays the nonchalance of an unruffled player. He is, in the eyes of his acolyte Nick, unremittingly cool. Motive without personal motive here is accompanied by a second strategy of creating a quest without reference.[46] Initially, there is nothing in the story apart from Christina's murder that leads anywhere. Strange people want to hurt or kill Hammer, and he builds his case by deflecting their menace. Only after people whom he approaches to learn about his danger die is his curiosity challenged, and only after Nick is killed and Velda kidnapped are his sympathy and anger aroused. Private eye Mike Hammer, in Aldrich's film and as played by Ralph Meeker, is a modern variant of detachment in search of a role to play. The third strategy in the case Hammer makes for his pursuit is seen in the clues, inchoate and urgent, that elude and frustrate his recognition. Unlike his private eye predecessors, Mike Hammer must deal with the pursuit of an unknown object, never defined except with scary allusions, a "whatsit." These strategies sideline the issues of motive, detection, and moral imperative precisely because Aldrich's film deals above all else with the impossibility of communication.

J.P. Telotte, in his excellent essay on the film, speaks of the rupture of language in postwar society and of how Hammer cannot communicate with others because of the cultural dispossession of language as another example of our lack of human connectedness. This work, he writes, "depicts an inexorable movement toward destruction resulting from the failure of our talk, from a decreasing ability—individually and culturally—to speak 'so as not to die.'"[47] However, Telotte's emphasis is on the breakdown in communication that prevents us from reaching a common human ground. Aldrich really shows us something else: that the impossibility of language stems from the impossibility of human experience to connect to a world it no longer recognizes in familiar forms. Soberin warns Lily as she steals the box: "Listen to me, as if I were Sybaris barking with all his heads, at the gates of Hell, I will tell you where to take it. But don't . . . don't open the box!" She does not understand and she shoots him. For her there is only greed.

> *Pat:* Now listen, Mike. Listen carefully. I'm going to pronounce a few words. They're harmless words. Just a bunch of letters scrambled together. But their meaning is very important. Try to understand what they mean. Manhattan Project. Los Alamos. Trinity.
> *Mike:* I didn't know . . .

Hammer goes through his investigative rituals fairly blind to his own inadequacy to change the world—destiny—and this is what makes *Kiss Me Deadly* the portentous and silencing film noir it has remained to this day. Searching for what his secretary Velda called "the great whatsit" and driven by the hitchhiker Christina's haunting caveat—"Remember me"—Hammer functions in a noir environment drained of comprehensible human connectedness, a fifties moderne setting in southern California "so spiritually parched that a single match struck at the wrong moment could unleash the fires of hell."[48] The landscape functions as a presentiment to the final scene in the film when—as everyone interested in the film noir knows by now—the black box Dr. Soberin killed for and Hammer recovers is opened by Lily Carver to unleash a nuclear blast with poetic ambiguity. In a world where Los Angeles "looks terminally irradiated," one need only recognize that Aldrich stylized his film to highlight forms of social encounter devoid of much emotional weight in Hammer's world, where a booze-bottle mourning follows his friend Nick's murder and the only worry generated, in a mocking concession to private eye chivalry, comes with Velda's abduction.

Aldrich's narrative is episodic, yet it is methodically plotted and woven with no loose ends and few diversions irrelevant to its climax. The sense of coolness in the story stems very much from the need to show human action objectified at a step removed from genuine human contact, and this disturbing manner of narration only emphasizes the impossibility of ever negotiating such contact. Hammer defines a latter-day noir image of the private eye, one whose detachment is ironic in a film that begs to be "heard." For *Kiss Me Deadly* is awash in the elusive power of language: the pre-Raphaelite poetry of Christina Rossetti inspiring hitchhiker Christina's riddle "Remember me" and her admonition to Mike that "when people are in trouble they need to talk"; the second-rate tenor Carmen Trivago singing along to a Caruso recording of Flotow's *Martha*; auto mechanic Nick's words of warning to Mike, animated by his arousal of engine power and voluptuous women ("va-va-voom!—pow!); and Velda's quizzical frustration over Mike's fascination with "the great whatsit." Language here functions as a Greek chorus; it exists as a corollary to the blindness and violent gestures of our "hero" Hammer, who cannot hear its appeals or warnings. The deceptions, lies, thefts, and murders weaving together Christina, Lily Carver, Nick, the mobster Evello, Soberin, Velda, and Hammer are the stuff of film noir, but, as Alain Silver described, "the graphic threat of machine-gun bullets traced in the door of a house on Laurel Canyon (*The Big Sleep*) is superseded as a beach cottage in Malibu becomes ground zero."[49] Beyond this even Aldrich's violent purgatory can offer no redemption.

Don Siegel (1912–1991)

The Big Steal (1949)
Private Hell 36 (1954)
Riot in Cell Block 11 (1954)
The Lineup (1958)
The Killers (1964)
Madigan (1968)
Dirty Harry (1971)

Don Siegel's world is made up of law enforcers and their counterparts, criminals of often sociopathic inclination who are in perpetual contest with them. Hostile and sometimes irrational, Siegel's detectives are the mutations of an American society that asserts its legitimate power to subdue eruptions of individual terror; it seeks to do so quite disturbingly in skewed affirmation of the American mythos that encourages expressive individualism. The noir implications in his films arise precisely from the conflict between institutional authority (the law, the penal code) and the lawless and sociopathic elements it seeks to vanquish. What these camps of power betray far more than the violent challenges to each other are the weaknesses and corruption within each.

Siegel's law enforcers are defined by their frustration and rage, and they incorporate these feelings into the role of beleaguered cops fighting the law enforcement establishment in order to fight crime better. "They are your streets," we are in effect told, "and it takes someone like us to keep them safe." Dan Madigan is the archetypal Siegel law enforcer, with Harry Callahan as his more off-balance first cousin. For both men law enforcement is an ambiguous vocation and definitely a calling. Both bend the rules—Madigan perhaps less irresponsibly—just as both are constrained by them. Madigan complains of his commissioner, "With him everything's either right or wrong; there's no in-between." But Commissioner Russell has his own dilemma: whether or not to demand the resignation of his longtime friend and chief of detectives in a minor corruption probe. Since decency and corruption are relative values in this world, the moral quality of the power judging them becomes relative as well.

In *Madigan* and *Dirty Harry*, morality is a constantly shifting value within civil institutions; it finds its truest expression in the personal gestures of his heroes. Throughout *Madigan*, beautifully shot in technicolor by Russell Metty (but with a blaring, dated "mod" soundtrack by Don Costa), Madigan and his partner, Rocco Bonaro, traverse New York City in search of a psychotic low-level mobster, mindful of not violating anyone's Miranda rights in their rather unkempt pursuit. In *Dirty Harry*, a similar cinematic terrain is covered by detective Callahan as he tracks down San Francisco's Scorpio Killer with calculated vengeance. We are often distracted from the noir implications of these scenarios by the scenes of gunplay and car chases—spectacles of these "men at work," so to speak—that punctuate the protocol of routine police work. Such moments recur, however, to emphasize the precarious urban world that mirrors these protagonists' temperament, their volatility and cynicism. The precursors to these men are found in Siegel's fifties police drama *The Lineup*, where police protocol evinces a specialized world peopled by seasoned investigators who pursue drug smugglers and hit men.

The Lineup has much of the on-location shooting that became standard for Siegel's sixties police thrillers. Hal Mohr, one of the notable noir cinematographers (*Underworld U.S.A.*), shot few scenes here with low-key lighting; in the semidocumentary style of the narrative, like that of many fifties police exposés, the noir perspective is revealed through theme and character type, both colder and more ruthlessly violent, rather than the settings and iconography as in earlier films noirs. The exterior shooting of *The Lineup* is also a precursor to the landscape of speed and violence that will reflect the rage festering in Harry Callahan as much as the anarchy of lawlessness run amok. Here the movie opens with a police car chase that ends with the death of a policeman. Throughout the story, the police pit their professionals in a relentless battle against organized drug dealing. It is a classic Siegel situation, but uncomplicated by the more difficult moral questions his sixties work provokes. "We meet a lot of people in unpleasant circumstances," one of the detectives remarks simply and stonily upon questioning the first innocent heroin pigeon. When a cop is killed in this milieu, the negation of a life is questioned little, for there "is no rhyme, no reason."

The simple identification of the law enforcement mission is complemented by the project of the hired killers, Julian and Dancer, who are out to perform their job with similar dispatch. Siegel stages a marvelous set piece of gunplay and police pursuit at a rendezvous at the San Francisco Aquarium, and, as in *Madigan* and *Dirty Harry*, innocent bystanders figure prominently in fleshing out the chaos of a society terrorized

The Lineup (1958). Dancer (Eli Wallach) and Julian (Robert Keith): one's a killer, the other's a philosopher.

by its villains. The car chase finale ending in Julian and Dancer's death is the social—and cosmic—justice avenging a policeman's manslaughter in the beginning of the film. The pathology of these two killers is certainly given novel reinterpretation a few years later by—if it may be so said—a more thoughtful cold-bloodedness in Charlie Strom in *The Killers*. Dancer is a rabid sociopath without Strom's rational demeanor and intellectual inquiry. As the philosophical Julian explains to their hostages about his companion's disturbed personality, "[o]rdinary people don't understand . . . the criminal's need for violence."

What in such police thrillers bespeaks a noir vision, with its specific tensions emanating from the themes of pursuit, obsession, and violence? In *The Lineup* law enforcement is heroic; in *Madigan* it is still heroic but less so, and beleaguered; and in *Dirty Harry* the heroism has given way to personal obsession. Siegel portrays the noir man in his law enforcers by the very doomed mission of their vocation: to defend an urban civilization that has lost its mooring. These are not merely cowboys of the urban frontier; they are figures who have understood the inextricable link between pacifism and violence represented by institu-

Madigan (1968). The hazards of the job: Dan Madigan (Richard Widmark) and Rocky Bonaro (Harry Guardino) in a tight spot.

tionalized authority attempting to monitor civilized society and challenged by the disruptive behavior of its antisocial elements, each of whom, in his or her fashion, seeks to be heard. Furthermore, the very institutions of civil order they represent are often plagued by bureaucratic ineptitudes and petty corruptions that impede the noble fight. The tableau challenges the perseverance of these protagonists and inspires their pessimism.

Siegel's out-and-out disgruntled, loner criminal cop first appears in *Private Hell 36*, his most conventionally structured and intimate noir. Here Cal Bruner falls for nightclub singer Lilli Marlowe, who informs him that she needs money and security from any man she would commit to, but then she decides Cal's love is enough to sustain a future together. It is too late, however, since he and his partner have stolen confiscated loot, and now Cal plans to run off with it and Lilli. Bruner has become the compromised detective and is willing to murder his uneasy partner for all of the stolen money. *Private Hell 36* retains much of the traditional noir look, with Burnett Guffey's camera work capturing the shadowy menace of a drugstore robbery in progress during the film's opening. Cal Bruner catches the addict thief, to whom his partner compares him less favorably after they steal the money, since, after all, an addict cannot help himself, whereas they submitted to greed.

Written by Collier Young and Ida Lupino, *Private Hell 36* displays the noir elements of betrayal and greed and an interesting variation of the *femme fatale*.[50] Lupino portrays Lilli Marlowe as unashamedly materialistic but not consumed by the impulse to do anything for money. She falls for Cal just hard enough not to want him caught for the theft she knows he has committed. The ambiguous personality of this woman, not so hardened by life that she denies herself the possibility of future happiness, is a departure from the classic *femme fatale* of the immediate postwar years. And Lupino was among the first Hollywood stars to redefine her, as evidenced by her dazzling role as Lily in Jean Negulesco's *Road House* (1948). Cal Bruner, however, is enough of a cipher to leave doubt about the extent of his criminal nature. Much like William Bendix's Captain Blake in *The Big Steal*, he assumes the potential for violence before actually displaying it.

Bendix is perhaps the best reason for considering *The Big Steal* even a marginal film noir. Vincent Blake is also part of the authoritarian establishment he steals from—the army's security police—and in his greed he takes on a vicious impersonation without hesitating to be brutal in his attempts to reclaim the money he stole from a fellow officer. The tone of the film has much more in common with a comic-suspense chase film (like Hitchcock's *Saboteur*) than with the Robert Mitchum–Jane Greer noir classic it followed, the appeal of which it strains to recapture: Jacques Tourneur's 1947 *Out of the Past*.

These early works prepare the way for the disillusioned protagonist we see in Dan Madigan and Harry Callahan, tense embodiments of the official man often on the verge of exercising a violent bigotry. The determination of these men matches toe-to-toe the violent natures of the evildoers they pursue. In *Dirty Harry* Callahan tracks down a rapist and murderer with single-minded fury because of what this monster has done and represents: the defilement of goodness and virtue represented here by the little-seen violated Ann Mary Deacon. Abhorrent as the crime is, Callahan has distorted it into the symptom of a wicked world, one that can be redeemed only by his gritty determination to right this wrong in the violent terms to which it responds. It is in some measure the same desperation that provokes Dunn's prison revolt in *Riot in Cell Block 11*, a reformist prison melodrama first and foremost, but with a decidedly dark view of the corrupted human behavior behind bars and having as its animus the callous disregard of prison conditions by the state's penal officials. But as with the other early films, this aggression underlies a vaguer disturbance of personality that seeks violent expression, and what we see are the human faces of precisely those antisocial elements that Madigan and Callahan pursue.

It is interesting that Siegel's villains are opaque, without psychological development, and function as a *force* to display chaotic as well as organized evil. The Scorpio Killer in *Dirty Harry* is simply a mad sociopath; in his destructiveness, he could have been conceived as a crude science fiction alien threatening the local populace. In *The Lineup*, Julian functions as a Greek chorus to Dancer's proclivity to violence, whereas Dancer is simply deranged. And in *The Killers*, Charlie Strom and Lee become modernist versions of the coolly professional and detached hit team, totally amoral; but Strom is intellectually teased by what it is in racecar driver Johnny North that allows him to submit so willingly to his impending execution. *The Killers* is Siegel's most interesting depiction of the unfettered execution of violence, which gains in the process a strangely compelling dynamic as it is carried out by Strom and Lee in an unobtrusive, clean, and quiet (they use silencers) manner. Here killing has been both elevated and reduced to a style, and the only disruptive feature is the greed to which Strom submits. This was not part of the original game plan, Strom learns, as he is staggering to his death with a broken briefcase releasing stolen money to the wind. He did not properly calculate the devotion of Sheila Farr to Jack Browning, erstwhile echoes of the ruthless *femme fatale* and her equally ruthless criminal lover. It was his lethal mistake, part of the noir equation he never saw.

Sexuality in the Noir

Any discussion of the film noir must at least implicitly recognize the function of sexuality as a frequently active component in its narrativity. And, of course, no discussion of this topic can be limited to a brief essay: far too much in the area of sexuality—indeed, sexualities—ranges throughout the film noir to circumscribe the subject for the purpose of survey commentary. Consequently, sexuality in noir cinema, considered from a historical perspective, may be best observed as an objective device of narrative development, one that oscillates from the foreground to the background and then back again to acknowledge the animus of human desire that ignites the noir universe and its characters. In this sense, sexuality modifies not only morality (to do right or wrong in the context of sexual arousal) and mortality (to live or die in the quest of sexual satisfaction provided by the other) but also the temptation to reach the ultimate satisfaction of one's unquenchable, even unspeakable, passion. Hence, as a tool that drives the story, sexuality is central to films noirs as diverse as the 1948 *The Accused* (William Dieterle), where the repressed sexuality of Professor Wilma Tuttle arouses guilt and fear; to *Road House*, made the same year, where, as Susie observes, vocalist Lily can "do more without a voice than anyone I ever heard"; and on to *The Pushover* (Richard Quine, 1954), where Kim Novak plays the sensual lure that distracts and corrupts Fred MacMurray ten years after Barbara Stanwyck did the same in *Double Indemnity*.

And these are less typical examples than the commonly cited ones. It is clear that there would be no *Double Indemnity*, *Gilda*, *Scarlet Street*, *Lady from Shanghai*, or *Gun Crazy* without the sexual provocation mixed with violence that drives these dramas to their destructive ends. The complicated sexual energy in *Gilda* (Charles Vidor, 1946) alone—between Ballen's lust for Gilda and for Johnny, her desire for Johnny, and Johnny's torn attraction and devotion to both—is the real theme of that narrative. The homosexual relationship between Mingo and Fante in Joseph H. Lewis's *Big Combo* is no less explicitly entwined in the violence they wreak than Bart and Annie Laurie's attraction is in his *Gun Crazy*. And, as midcentury cinema tied homosexuality to violence, a similar argument holds for the depiction of Julian's fascination with Dancer in *The Lineup*. Homosexuality seen as a perversion—and this without irony—is the true destructive force that accounts for the blackmail and demise of a politician in Gordon Douglas's *Detective*, one of the most luridly fascinating depictions of homosexuality in American cinema. Disfiguring in its logic and thereby quite revealing, the 1968 film offers self-loathing and suicide for this "aberration," which is only further extended by a plea for tolerance by Frank Sinatra's detective. The hysteria of *The Detective* suggests the anxiety that bedeviled mainstream American cinema—just one year before the Stonewall riots in New York City that launched the gay liberation movement—about how to represent homosexuality on screen, and the result is tendentious, pathetic, and insulting. The homoerotic violence in the Mingo-Fante relationship, unencumbered by misguided sociological sentiments, is still

Gilda (1946). The emblematic *femme fatale*: Rita Hayworth as Gilda.

stereotyped psychosexuality—offensive enough on another score—but it is raw and consistent with the noir world.

The privilege of noir cinema, as distinguished from other genres, lies in the latitude these films were permitted in exploring sexual power and its ambiguity, and the reason is apparent: as the cautionary cinema of the great negation of a "healthy" puritanical American vision, the film noir almost mandates a depiction, however perverse, of those repressed impulses reigning hand-in-hand with the anarchy that drives its protagonists to violence and paranoia. Unrepressed sexuality alongside these characteristics is far too messy to contain, so it must be vanquished. When it is particularly threatening, one may be sure that there is a woman involved.

> [*Double Indemnity*] . . . created a tense climate dominated by a perverse eroticism where woman, to be angelic and demonic, recovers under the appearance of voluptuous ecstasy, the devastating attraction of Eros and Thanatos.
> —Jean Mitry, *Histoire du Cinéma*

> As they remain locked in their embrace, he shoots her: she looks surprised. The eroticism of death in the final scene of the flashback confirms a universe where access to desire is only a repression: the impossibility of a radical heterogeneity represented by the feminine.
> —Claire Johnston

In films noirs ranging from *Double Indemnity*, *Gilda*, and *Lady from Shanghai* in the 1940s to *Angel Face* (Otto Preminger, 1953) in the 1950s, to *The Killers* and *Point Blank* (John Boorman, 1967) in the 1960s, to *Klute* and *Chinatown* in the 1970s, to neo-noirs like *Body Heat* (Lawrence Kasdan, 1981) in the 1980s, to John Dahl's *Last Seduction* in 1994, fierce sexuality identified with the female image reinforces the misogyny behind the male construction of such a dangerous woman who clearly threatens the power of her male rivals. And these men are indeed rivals in a tango of power, since their apprehension of the *femme fatale* stems from a position of assumed dominance. This presumption is the first step in their downfall, for noir cinema treats the dangerous woman as an unknown quantity of the male projection that intrigues and entices by its capability to destroy. The "tragic" error such men make, recurrent throughout the tales of *femmes fatales*, is in their attempt to control, to tame, the female image that at once arouses and threatens them.

   The Lady from Shanghai is a classic example of this at its finest, as are *Double Indemnity* and *Angel Face*. Elsa Bannister is a multiplicity of elusive images—literally—and a woman confounding Michael O'Hara by her mystery. Always seen and described through the eyes of a man in the story, never those of a woman, her repeatedly inexplicable actions intensify her mystery. The most disconcerting component of her image is her sexuality, shown in high relief but never flaunted. Bannister finally kills his wife, who also kills him, in a mirrored funhouse by a haze of bullets intended to obliterate not one Elsa but every Elsa, all Elsas. The threat created by the male conception of her is given life (almost like a Frankenstein monster) to then be destroyed when such independent eroticism becomes malevolent.[51] At the heart of the *femme fatale*'s destructive passion is, finally, not so much the projection of a male need for her to be bad but the display of a freedom granted her to be nihilistic and to be so in a noir world already at odds with an ordered society. In Alan Pakula's *Klute*, a hip, early-seventies attempt at noir filmmaking, Bree Daniels is no longer the classic *femme fatale*; she has "won her liberation," in a manner of speaking. But her sexual freedom has nonetheless enveloped her in violence and fear, incurred not by her sexual libertinism (since prostitutes engaged in kinky sex long before) but by the manner of her comportment. What Bree sells is her independence; it matters little what her psychological weaknesses are. She says to her psychologist, "I think the only way any of us could ever be happy is to let it all hang out . . . you know, do it all, and fuck it." This is exactly the attitude for which she must be reviled, for it supplies the terms of truly risky behavior provoking any oppressor with illusions of domination.

FAMILIES IN THE NOIR

The treatment of the family in the film noir, most often inextricably tied to the depiction of the noir woman and her connection to family-rearing, highlights the tension and violence that undermine the security attached to home life and the retreat to it. It has been noted that gangsters in the gangster films almost never have fathers, so necessary is it for the enraged son to replace the powerless old-world father.[52] By the same token, noir characters enmeshed in the anxiety of their world do not have the solace of family to comfort them. Family—and the concept of the nuclear family in particular—often emerges in noir cinema as the vehicle for muted rage, long-bred resentments and jealousies, and the possessiveness that becomes a mother's (or father's) obsession with a child.

Roman Polanski's *Chinatown* is the great example of familial perversion, as Noah Cross's incest becomes the now-spoken taboo that exposes his evil lust in every sense. However, the contempt for the emotional demands of the family or the obsession to control it arises during the late 1940s as a decided exposé in itself of the fissures underlying the wholesome image of American family life promulgated in American entertainment throughout the following decade. In all of the Raymond Chandler screen adaptations, which Polanski's film evokes to an intoxicating degree, family is at the root of malcontent and evil. *The Big Sleep* presents it as a desiccated institution in which two daughters are clearly the products of the rotted old Colonel Sternwood. In *The Brasher Doubloon*, Mrs. Murdoch murders her husband for his money. In *Marlowe*, the Quests become entangled in murder.

The theme of brother against brother underlies the drama of *Force of Evil,* as it does that of Joseph Mankiewicz's *House of Strangers*, made the following year, in 1949. In that film the entire Monetti fraternity reaches the tense moment of arranging to murder their brother, Max. In *Bunny Lake Is Missing* (Otto Preminger, 1965), Keir Dullea's incestuous devotion to Ann provokes him to kidnap and plan the murder of his unseen niece, Bunny. In *The Naked Kiss*, the illusion of wholesome love for a child is tainted by the discovery of Grant's pedophilia. In Ida Lupino's quasi-noir, *The Bigamist* (1951), traveling salesman Harry Graham destroys both of his families when one learns of the other. In Delmer Daves's 1947 *Red House* and Joseph Losey's 1951 *Big Night*, fathers cripple their children with half-remembered traumas. Bette Davis's Rosa Moline cannot bear the thought of sustaining a pregnancy—so intrusive is it to her plan to escape to the thrills of Chicago life—so she induces a miscarriage in King Vidor's *Beyond the Forest* (1949). And of course Cody Jarrett's mother complex is justly notorious in *White Heat*, when atop a burning water tank he screams with pride to his presumed dead mother that he is "on top of the world."

"Everyone has a mother," Veda replies in *Mildred Pierce* (Michael Curtiz, 1945) when a fellow stripper remarks that she never thought of her as having one. As discussed elsewhere, Cain's dissection of a devoted mother was matched by his conception of an ungrateful and unloving child. Joining *Mildred Pierce* is an equally revealing depiction of motherhood in the 1949 film noir made by Max Ophüls, *The Reckless Moment*. Unlike Mildred Pierce, Lucia Harper emerges as the victim of unpleasant circumstances and desperation, cloaked as they are in a mother's fear for her frightened daughter's fate after the girl strikes a greedy lothario who, dazed, falls through a railing and dies. That the

The Reckless Moment (1949). Mother knows best: Lucia Harper (Joan Bennett) covers up her daughter's crime.

man was contemptible cannot mitigate the easy absolution Lucia gives her daughter, and the focus quickly becomes Lucia's frantic attempts to mask the crime and protect her. *The Reckless Moment*, shot by Burnett Guffey, is a domestic noir in a palette of grays. Unlike André De Toth's *Pitfall* (1948), it is devoid of brightness; the California seaside town of Balboa closely resembles the noir-infected Los Angeles nearby. Lucia's behavior, too, becomes increasingly mired in subterfuge and furtiveness as she covers her daughter's connection with the dead man and her own tracks in the disposing of his body. The dichotomy in homemaker Lucia

Harper lies precisely in such behavior: she finds herself thinking and acting like a protective tigress while attempting to fend off the extortionists who have her daughter's letters to the dead man. She aggresses against her blackmailer-turned-partner, trumps his suggestions, often tells him no, and then instructs him accordingly. "It's my way of doing something that's made everything wrong," an overwhelmed Lucia frets to Donnelly. However, it is all this that transforms her from a fierce mother to a compelling force not without sexual appeal. Critic Mary Ann Doane observed that as Lucia becomes increasingly concerned about her family, Donnelly becomes increasingly attracted to her. "The film is, in a sense, a fantasy about the power of mothers—even criminality is confounded and subdued by the maternal."[53]

But the noir environment of the story does much more: in the construction of Lucia Harper, we see a mother who becomes charged by the dark side of her capabilities precisely to the repudiation of all she strives to save—namely, family and reputation. She becomes the quick, calculating animus of the narrative, arousing Donnelly as she weakens him (he even offers her part of his blackmail money) by redefining herself as an inexorable and possessed *femme fatale*, one who in this case can wear an apron as easily as she dons the various-shaded glasses that heighten the tension of her clandestine movements. Donnelly pays for his "seduction" at the end of the story, slashed by his blackmailing accomplice, Nagel, as he tries to prevent him from extorting all of Lucia's money for the letters. He skids off the road in his attempt to get away after killing him and, dying, reassures Lucia that now she has nothing to fear. The closing shot shows Lucia receiving a call from her husband abroad; choking back tears, she talks to him about Christmas decorations. Ophüls's tracking creates a complex image here, since Lucia cries out of stress, relief—and guilt. No one can know the extent of her obsession to save her family from calamity except the one man who grew to love her in her moment of dark glory. The tragedy of Lucia's life has become her entrapment in a false normality. The noir world into which she entered, although certainly not desirable, forced her to confront herself and experience the weight of responsibility in a tenuous dance with life and death. "Everyone has a mother like me," Lucia modestly tells Donnelly when he extols her maternal protectiveness. He tells her no. The desperation of those shadowy movements transform her into a formidable creature of survival, much more than she ever imagined possible.

Pitfall (1948). John Forbes (Dick Powell), husband and father: caught short after one wrong step taken. With his wife, Sue (Jane Wyatt).

A provocative cautionary tale of all that can threaten the happy family appears in André De Toth's *Pitfall*, as John Forbes experiences the inadequacy of postwar suburban life, for him a limbo of predictability and boredom where each household matches the other and the lives within have ceased to function in expectation of anything exciting. The entrapment of war vet Forbes is real, chosen, and rather sad, and his attempt to revitalize his existence in the company of Mona Stevens is one of the more sympathetic messages in American noir cinema. Here, "one wrong step taken" exacts a jolting response from a family man who almost loses his safety net to experience the exhilaration of desire. It is a conservative moral on the surface but a subversive message narratively, for John Forbes hungers for the very energy made so palatable in the vulnerability and enigma of an attractive young woman. Mona is not wicked, simply in trouble, and her disruption of John's life—through his encounters with Mack and Mona's boyfriend in prison and as he helps her with her debts—counterpoint his orderly life. *Pitfall*, adapted for the screen by Jay Dratler (*Laura*) from his novel and lighted so brightly that one can argue effectively about its ironic necessity here, tells us that the ambiguous Garden-of-Eden lure of the unknown, of the new, of all that rebels against the conspiracy of safe, placid, domesticity to neuter our more dangerous human responses, can command a huge price. Yet what must be said of what remains? The landscape of Forbes's suburbia rarely appears in noir cinema, and to infect it with the darker appeals of human behavior allows us to view it uncomfortably. John's wife, Sue, and their little boy are likable, and Sue is witty and attractive, but for John the malaise of achieving the ordinary leaves a psychic void no doubt felt by many returning vets, who, under the GI Bill, found "paradise in Shady Glen."

JOSEPH H. LEWIS (1900–2000)

Gun Crazy (*Deadly Is the Female*), 1950
The Big Combo, 1955

We go together like guns and ammunition!
        —Bart Tare to Annie Laurie Starr, *Gun Crazy*

If Joseph H. Lewis had made only *Gun Crazy* and *The Big Combo*, he would still deserve distinction for his noir sensibility, among the strongest in its appeal to violence and sex as the raison d'être in noir filmmaking. Lewis displayed them more seriously than any of his imitators, and to the exhilaration of his audiences: speed, violence, and the erotic reservoir of gunplay enmeshed in lawlessness had rarely been seen in such wanton display. The most notable films noirs have explored violence and self-destruction from the fugitive theme (*They Live by Night*), as social protest (*You Only Live Once*), as rabidly violent quasi-gangster/noir films (*White Heat*), or as the stylized (or bracketed) work of modernist cinema (*Bonnie and Clyde*, Peckinpah's *Getaway* [1972], several of Godard's films). *Gun Crazy* remains an unadulterated expression of harsh realistic violence, and it should be reviled or lauded for its intention and the execution of it. For in no other film has the manner of violence and sex been so effortlessly presented—and, it would appear, accepted into the noir canon without undue controversial notice. The only movie that approaches *Gun Crazy*'s thrilling premise is Lewis's own *Big Combo*, where it becomes almost pornographic to see Susan

Gun Crazy ([*Deadly Is the Female*], 1950). The thrill of the kill: Bart Tare (John Dall) and Annie Laurie Starr (Peggy Cummins).

Lowell hopelessly submit to what is surely suggested to be an act of oral sex performed by her crime-lord boyfriend, Mr. Brown. But Lewis is no pornographer; he is a sensualist in the most serious way. No other works in American film until the 1960s broached the acknowledgment of these carnal hungers as a life-enhancing dimension of dangerous living—indeed, in living a short, intense life unto quick death. One must look to Godard a few years later in France to see Anna Karina die fast, violently, and be beautiful, and to be redeemed for a life lived in a world without redemption. It is apt to invoke Godard here, because Lewis created under similar low-budget circumstances something less meteoric than Godard's modernism—which helped launch a cinema movement—but in a style of comparable "raw" immediacy and honesty and of illicit pleasure found in the vitality of art that works the sensorium before it permits contemplation.

Barton Tare grows up in a small California town learning respect for firearms; they are his focus in a rite of passage to manhood that defines strength, self-reliance, and independence from others. Bart could be a poster boy for the National Rifle Association, so complete is his devotion to and need of guns. Annie Laurie is a carnival performer equally adept at their use; and when the two encounter each other in a shooting match during a carnival's stopover in town, their attraction is immediate and palpable. Written by MacKinlay Kantor and adapted for the screen by Dalton Trumbo—who, blacklisted during the period, was "fronted" by Millard Kauffman—*Gun Crazy* is told in relatively unfettered moral terms. Guns here create mayhem and are very much a part of the American mythology of individual power in defense of law and order as well as of lawlessness. Lewis and Trumbo understood the potent symbol at the heart of their story, and when Annie Laurie and Bart marry, their union preserves a vaguely appropriate frontier patina—as if Annie Oakley were joining forces with Buffalo Bill. Russell Harlan's lighting is bright throughout much of the film, a rare occurrence in the film noir, clearly showing us two kids who turn bad for no more convincing reason than the momentary joblessness that finds them with too much time and imagination to play with their guns. "Two people dead just so we can live without working!" exclaims a distressed Bart after their first deadly armed robbery. It is this cold-bloodedness that makes *Gun Crazy* a compelling noir portrait of the amorality spawning senseless acts of violence akin to those we see on the nightly news. And Lewis understood this in 1949. For Bart and Annie—especially Annie—guns answer the satisfying need to feel alive in a world that, by its very orderliness and predictability, quells this darker and highly charged impulse. Both radically deny reasonableness in display of anarchy. Bart claims he does not want to be a killer but is seduced by the power of firearms, especially in combination with Annie Laurie, who will "try to be good" for him. In a moment of angry bewilderment, Bart asks her, "Why do you murder people! Why can't you let them live!?" It is, in a terribly destructive and unappeased way, how a noir vision can be ludicrously expressed, caught here in a society of daylight and bright-eyed kids.

Both *Gun Crazy* and *The Big Combo* are sexually defined by the discursive violence of the external world—so much a corollary for the violence of passion that Lewis and screenwriter Philip Yordan can barely mask the story of *The Big Combo* as merely another sensational example of the extent to which organized crime corrupted postwar American life. Shot in the dramatic chiaroscuro of John Alton at his best,

The Big Combo (1955). Mr. Brown (Richard Conte) *(seated),* McClure (Brian Donlevy), and Diamond (Cornel Wilde): syndicate violence as a cruel fetish.

silhouetted figures in shadowy light stand before explosion fires and run out of the range of menacing car headlights. A blaring jazz soundtrack clearly identifies the story as a lurid urban tale. Richard Conte's "Mr. Brown" is not known by any other name, suggesting an enigmatic history too horrible to be spoken of yet which must be exposed. However, in his imaginative brutality, Lewis bridges violence to the audience's darker, vicarious desire to see pain inflicted on the screen: for instance, Leonard Diamond is tortured by alcohol intoxication and with McClure's hearing aid; and then later, Mingo and Fante gun down McClure after Brown turns off that very hearing aid so that, like him, we only see a silent spray of bullets fired at him.[54]

Lewis made several low-budget thrillers during the forties—*My Name Is Julia Ross* (1945), *So Dark the Night* (1946), and the police procedural *The Undercover Man* (1949). Each has noir elements, from the use of amnesia in *Julia Ross* and *Somewhere in the Night* to the *policier* semidocumentary element in *Undercover Man*. But these minor works lack the depth of noir tension that *Gun Crazy* and *The Big Combo* display. Mr. Brown remarks to a neophyte boxer unlikely to be corrupted that "number one is somebody and number two is nobody" and the driving force to be first is in the capacity to hate. At the end of *Gun Crazy*, Bart and Annie Laurie are trapped in a mountain marsh. Their capture by the authorities is inevitable, yet like struggling animals they resist entrapment. Annie Laurie raises her gun to shoot herself free, overcome by the delusion that compels her to believe escape possible. But Bart sees better, and before she can harm anyone, he shoots her as he is then shot by his childhood friend, a law enforcer. Lewis caught this moment in a beautiful series of images that display the abstractness of fear—fear among the reeds and stalks and dirt where Bart practiced target shooting as a boy. The camera work is exquisite, highlighting the despair of these two lovers caught in the exhausted frenzy of their own violence. And it is unmatched in its artistry; no scene in noir cinema lingers over impending death quite this way.

WOMEN AS SEEN
IN THE FILM NOIR

Sexual power is defined most clearly in the context of gender conflict, and noir cinema illustrates this in all its creative tension and tragic consequences as few other film genres do. Bracketing the treatment of women in noir cinema is a dubious and faintly rewarding exercise, for women are an essential part of the noir world; their depiction as harbingers of destructive passions or heartless self-interest combines all too well with the weaknesses of their male counterparts to form an explosive and often corrosive dynamic. Women in the film noir are created and seen through the eyes of men, and the perception of them stems, as has often been written, through the power they wield in disorienting the male object.[1] There is misogynic intent, to be sure, in many portrayals of such women: the *femme fatale* is cinema's destructive force sine qua non, offering her men mystery and temptation predicated upon sexual desire. But the search for female identity in the noir extends beyond simply this type or force, and it delineates the emerging female character as she struggles to hear her voice in a rupture of the role women have conventionally played in screen melodrama. Here, bad women, desperate women, determined women, or women blind to the destructive passions that motivate them are, much like their male counterparts, consciousnesses accruing the individuality and power to command recognition on their own terms. The *femme fatale* may indeed be wicked, but she is also fascinating, because she does not (or does not easily) acquiesce or suffer the traditionally imposed travails of her subordinated function in a male-dominated society.

The handiest image among many is Phyllis Dietrichson in Billy Wilder's *Double Indemnity*. An encounter with such a character in the noir world can promise nothing but a fatal demise. Yet Phyllis presumes to reveal that the mystery behind her motive to rid herself of her husband and have his money is much more than murderous and greedy, and we are left with the image of a bullet-stricken blond falling into Walter Neff's arms, not quite sure whether she loved him unto death despite all that drove them apart out of mutual suspicion. This striking image of her belies any easy answer, and it is precisely her opaqueness that defines the inadequacy of our attempt to dismiss her as merely a cold-blooded murderer. Christine Gledhill noted it with remarkable acuity:

> The generic features of the *noir* thriller which locate strong women in image-producing roles—night-club singers, hostesses, models, etc.—encourage the creation of heroines whose means of struggle is precisely the manipulation of the image which centuries of female representations have provided.
>
> Thus, though the heroines of *film noir*, by virtue of male control of the voice-over, flashback structure, are rarely accorded the full subjectivity and fully expressed point of view of psychologically realist fiction . . . their *performance* of the roles accorded them in this form of male storytelling foregrounds the fact of their image as an artifice and suggests another place behind the image where the woman might be.[2]

Performance is indeed the key here, in tandem with the role performed, since Barbara Stanwyck's signature role as Phyllis Dietrichson is not her only foray into the world of noir heroines. Martha Ivers (in *The Strange Love of Martha Ivers*) and Thelma Jordon (in *The File on Thelma Jordon*) are both women who inflict pain on their men and families precisely because of their ambiguous identities and torn self-images. Neither can freely commit to love, yet neither can live without its validation. Gledhill goes on to note that "in the *noir* thriller, where the male voice-over is not in control of the plot, and on the contrary represents a hero on a quest for truth, not only is the hero frequently not sure whether the woman is honest or a deceiver, but the heroine's characterization is itself fractured so that it is not evident to the audience whether she fills the stereotype or not" (18).

What the film noir has done, as perhaps no other genre has done, is

Double Indemnity (1944). Walter Neff (Fred MacMurray) is slowly seduced by Phyllis Dietrichson (Barbara Stanwyck).

to show the remonstrations of the female image filtered so completely through the male imagination. This has been the locus of our fascination with the noir *femme fatale*: the constant struggle between the female consciousness suppressed and that consciousness heard only through the destructive consequences to which she leads her male cohort. Hence Anna Thompson Dundee in *Criss Cross* is at the pivotal center of a battle between Steve Thompson and Slim Dundee that ends in a double killing—in her name, really; she and Steve are left shot dead in the crossfire of possessive male egos. In Tay Garnett's *The Postman Always Rings Twice* (1946), Cora cannot be allowed to have the passion she so intensely feels for Frank because it crosses the boundaries of marriage, fidelity, and, really, safe sex. That her needs are expressed with intense desire is a rebellious act that can only be punished by her death and that of her lover.

The latter example brings us to the treatment of James Cain's women in noir cinema, for in many ways they are the most challenging female roles of the classical period. Phyllis Dietrichson, Cora Smith, and Mildred Pierce form a trio of protagonists who breathe the mythic rages of trapped women and consequently respond in radical denial of their social destiny. Phyllis is the avaricious but romantic cipher; we know only what we see of her in the moment—of her plotting against Mr. Dietrichson, of her presumed desire for Walter, of her possession of a gun at the end. Cora is determined to have financial security. Calculating and smart, yet disoriented by her lust for Frank Chambers, she is the dichotomous projection of male desire and female possessiveness: she will give herself, but only if she gets what she wants in return. Mildred Pierce has emerged as one of the most emblematic modern women characters in American movies, and she has been excavated for feminist study many times.[3] As portrayed by Joan Crawford, she has become an icon of the melodramatic heroine of the last fifty years, for she has run the length of the race, experienced every facet of modern womanhood, and triumphed as a tragic example of the born gender victim who survives her victimhood. Critics who have tried to level Mildred as the self-sacrificing mother of all time who has cruelly paid for her misguided

Mildred Pierce (1945). Mildred (Joan Crawford) and Veda (Ann Blyth) Pierce: noir mother and daughter.

maternal devotion have missed the point of Cain's heroine. Surely he would have seen the deficiency in such a skewed creation.[4] Mildred Pierce emerges in noir cinema, above all, as an anxious figure alone in the world, who faces the responsibility of supporting and rearing two children. Her strength is hard won and her resourcefulness admirable. No male character in the history of American cinema has ever faced such domestic challenges; it is her very success in meeting them that blinds her to the yearning heart that needs tending. That she is the "good" woman in the story, counterpointed by her daughter Veda, the emerging *femme fatale*, is the cruelest irony found in any film noir, and its underlying implication becomes all too clear: what every mother nurtures to emerge as the best expression of herself becomes the nightmare of all that can go wrong. Mildred finds in Veda her competitor, her opposite, and the very reason to repudiate all her best efforts to do well for herself and her children.

But the idea here is greater than that of self-sacrifice: Mildred, in Cain's novel and in the screen adaptation of it, was doomed not to "have it all" because, consistent with the noir universe, the passionate need for Monty Beragon corrupted her and dulled her decent impulses. (After all, in the movie she attempts to set up Wally Fay, her one consistent supporter, for Monty's murder, something Mildred would never have considered doing in the past.) Desperation wrought the confused sense, the dazed moment, of a woman who lost her lover to the arms of her daughter in an entirely sinister turn of human desire infecting an otherwise misguided mother's love. The murder of Monty Beragon was added to the film version, and quite aptly for the proper noir environment. Cain's novel is an astute depiction of a burgeoning southern California suburban culture that would flourish after the war, but Curtiz's film has taken Mildred out of that milieu and placed her in a more urban business setting, less reminiscent of southern California than of the noir city. In this context, parental regard and fealty for loved ones are notoriously underrepresented and expressed in extreme terms when they are shown. We need only think, for example, of Lucia Harper in *The Reckless Moment* or Gino Monetti and his sons in *House of Strangers*. Throughout most of this story, Mildred's failing is her vulnerability to Veda's cruel taunts that she is nothing more than a "business woman" (with its implication here of being little more than a glorified waitress), a point some critics have used against her construction, saying it shows her shackled to the bonds of motherhood complete with the unrequited love of a brutish child. In this vulnerability, however, Mildred never *fails* her responsibilities as a mother. Willfully blind as she may be, she succeeds on her own terms as an enterprising breadwinner, a caring parent, and an increasingly attractive woman. Wally Fay sees this, and in his notable transformation (largely through the marvelous, underrecognized performance of Jack Carson) from sexual wolf to supportive friend, encourages her. In the end it is precisely this commitment to responsibility, this need to summon one's best survival instincts and show ingenuity, that defines Mildred Pierce as a courageous figure in the face of genuine heartbreak and tragedy. Joan Crawford, incapable of giving her greatest role anything less than the Metro gloss of nobility she carried over to Warner's with her, could justly indulge in its comportment. Mildred is indeed heroic.

Several descriptions apply to the females characterized in the film noir through the mid-1960s and intermittently thereafter, descriptions that lend themselves to analysis and argument but in themselves remain indisputable:

1. The leading female character, although not necessarily a *femme fatale*, creates a sexual tension by almost always being a woman in her most sexually active years—roughly between twenty and forty-five. (It makes no difference what the age of the actress portraying the role is. Indeed, Stanwyck and Crawford played leading roles until the age of almost fifty.)

2. The leading female character, whether or not she is a *femme fatale*, has an independent or rebellious will. If she does not defy her man, then she betrays his dishonesty out of the greater need to save him from himself and to love him. If the betrayal is not selfless, it is done to protect herself against his villainy. It is done after a thorough rebuke of his life and her infection by it and often, too, out of a reformative impulse appealing to a moral/legal principle of righteousness and its awakening in her. (Leonora Ohlrig in *Caught* [Max Ophüls, 1949], Lorna Hanson Forbes in *The Damned Don't Cry* [Vincent Sherman, 1950], Kathleen in *The Dark Corner*, June Mills in *Fallen Angel* [Otto Preminger, 1946], Thelma in *The File on Thelma Jordon*, Lane in *Flamingo Road* [Michael Curtiz, 1949], Peg Dobbs in *He Ran All the Way*, Mildred in *Mildred Pierce*, Kansas Richman in *Phantom Lady*, both Pat and Ann in *Raw Deal*, Lily in *Road House*, and both Cuddles and Sandy in *Underworld U.S.A.* are examples.)

3. If she is not the *femme fatale* or the devoted lover, she is the ingenious and clever conservative wife or girlfriend. (Peg Born in *Body and Soul* [1947], Lorna in *The Damned Don't Cry*, Kathleen in *The Dark Corner*, Irene Jansen in *Dark Passage* [Delmer Daves, 1947], June in *Fallen Angel*, Lane in *Flamingo Road*, Laurel Gray in *In a Lonely Place*, Mildred in *Mildred Pierce*, Kansas in *Phantom Lady*, Sue Forbes in *Pitfall*, both Pat and Ann in *Raw Deal*, Susie [as the girlfriend wannabe] in *Road House*, Rica in *Thieves' Highway*, and Lucia Harper in *The Reckless Moment* are examples. Sally Lord as the former girlfriend in *Sorry, Wrong Number* [Anatole Litvak, 1948] also functions this way. Irene Bennett in *House of Strangers* starts out as a *femme fatale* and then turns into a romantic interest.)

On a destructive note:

4. Three things motivate the *femme fatale*: a lust for exciting sex, a desire for wealth and the power it brings, and a need to control everything and everyone around her. (Diane Tremayne in *Angel Face*, Helen Brent in *Born to Kill* [Robert Wise, 1947], Vera in *Detour* [Edgar G. Ulmer, 1945], Phyllis Dietrichson in *Double Indemnity*, Stella in *Fallen Angel*, Thelma in *The File on Thelma Jordon*, Annie Laurie Starr in *Gun Crazy*, Lilah Gustafson in *Johnny Angel* [Edwin L. Marin, 1945], Kitty Collins in *The Killers* [1946], Sheila Farr in *The Killers* [1964], Sherry Peatty in *The Killing* [Stanley Kubrick, 1956], Elsa Bannister in *The Lady from Shanghai*, Brigid O'Shaughnessy in *The Maltese Falcon*, Veda Pierce in *Mildred Pierce*, Kathie Moffet in *Out of the Past*, Mona Stevens in *Pitfall*, Cora Smith in *The Postman Always Rings Twice* [1946], Kitty March in *Scarlet Street*, Martha in *The Strange Love of Martha Ivers*, Claire Quimby in *Tension* [John Berry, 1950], and Jane Palmer in *Too Late for Tears* [Byron Haskin, 1949] are examples. Lucia Harper, as the homemaker intriguing Martin Donnelly through her ruthless control of the circumstances following her daughter's crime in *The Reckless Moment*, and Leona Stephenson, as the controlling hypochondriac wife in *Sorry, Wrong Number*, also function in this manner.)

5. The opacity of the *femme fatale* is a projection of the male desire to retain her in the role of the mystery woman—an enigma that satisfies as it arouses the unknowability of her hidden destructive powers (the mythic Circe). (Evelyn Mulwray in *Chinatown*, Anna in *Criss Cross*, Phyllis in *Double Indemnity*, Kitty in *The Killers* [1946], Sheila in *The Killers* [1964], Elsa in *The Lady from Shanghai*, Laura Hunt [when assumed deceased, and then later when discovered alive] in *Laura* [Otto

Preminger, 1944], Kathie in *Out of the Past*, and Martha in *The Strange Love of Martha Ivers* are examples of this. *Secret beyond the Door . . .* creates this enigma through the description of Mark Lamphere's deceased first wife.)

6. The *femme fatale* must inevitably die—or, at the very least, be mortally injured or be arrested for her crimes. The implication in her arrest is a moral one as much as a legal one: she has committed a crime against the healthy image of society's female, and she must be punished for it. (Examples include Diane in *Angel Face*, Norah Larkin in *The Blue Gardenia*, Helen in *Born to Kill*, Evelyn in *Chinatown*, Anna in *Criss Cross*, Vera in *Detour*, Phyllis in *Double Indemnity*, Stella in *Fallen Angel*, Thelma in *The File on Thelma Jordon*, Annie Laurie in *Gun Crazy*, Lilah in *Johnny Angel*, Kitty in *The Killers* [1946], Sheila in *The Killers* [1964], Elsa in *The Lady from Shanghai*, Veda in *Mildred Pierce*, Kathie in *Out of the Past*, Cora in *The Postman Always Rings Twice* [1946], Leona in *Sorry, Wrong Number*, and Martha in *The Strange Love of Martha Ivers*. In *The Big Heat*, Debbie Marsh's death reaches a dimension of near-sanctification for having made the conversion from bad girl to good woman.)

The different perceptions of women in the noir have one common denominator: these women are radical disrupters of the status quo or, in the case of Lucia Harper in *The Reckless Moment*, an extreme defender of it. Mildred Pierce's disruption of the conventional order in pursuit of independence and security arises from an impulse born, ironically, out of conservation, in defense of family and survival. But these radical disruptions, for whatever social and psychological reasons, are consistent with the concept of the great "no" that underlies all noir stories, and the extent to which they are expressions of negation is seen in these women's extreme actions that end in destruction. Lilly Dillon in Stephen Frear's 1990 film of Jim Thompson's *Grifters* crystallizes the image of the opaque yet haunted noir *femme fatale*. When she kills her son Roy for the very money she needs to escape, her malevolence and instinct to survive merge into the problematic definition of the evil woman. It is a disturbing moment in noir cinema, one never before extended to quite this degree. After she kills Roy, Lilly stands back from the act she has just committed and wails. Then after a dazed moment, she summons her composure to quickly collect the scattered and bloodied money. Her emotions retreat, and in a horrible scene of wordless gestures, she packs the loot and other possessions of her son's and goes to drive away in her

The Grifters (1990). The power of women: Roy (John Cusack) caught between Myra (Annette Bening) and Lilly (Anjelica Huston).

car. Lilly continues to drive into the night, her eyes focused on the road and her face rigid with lost emotion, perhaps never to be recovered. No ending in a film noir has ever unsettled the viewer quite like this one, for it deprives us of any familiar consolation. In its radical pronouncement that every mother's son can now no longer retreat to the maternal womb for the protection too trusted to have ever been questioned before, Lilly Dillon redefines herself as a kind of asphalt Medea-cum-Jocasta whose fatal charm even she might not have imagined before.

OTTO PREMINGER (1906–1986)

Laura (1944)
Fallen Angel (1946)
Where the Sidewalk Ends (1950)
Angel Face (1953)
Bunny Lake Is Missing (1965)

Otto Preminger's noir films are studies in the ambiguous nature of appearance. A cool, expressionist-styled realism generates a tension between the appearance of his characters and their inner reality, which is often at odds with it. As a result, Preminger's perspective on their destructive actions often emerges in some of the more perversely forgiving gestures he makes toward his fallen angels. The exception—and a distinctive one at that—is found in *Angel Face*, where Diane Tremayne commits sudden suicide in the driver's seat of her sports car, an action taken without expectation or fanfare. His great films noirs—*Laura, Fallen Angel*, and *Where the Sidewalk Ends*—show us curious, half-known characters that arouse interest in those around them. Columnist Waldo Lydecker in *Laura* illustrates the type well. He has fashioned Laura Hunt with the touching arrogance of someone who demands to be loved by his creation. And Laura, assumed murdered throughout half the film, mesmerizes Detective Mark McPherson as only a living embodiment can. The critic Eugene Archer many years ago observed McPherson's perverse attraction to Laura Hunt as "a sadistic study in necrophilia, on the illusion-and-reality theme the director has pursued throughout the remainder of his career."[5]

Laura (1944). Fantasy meets reality: Detective Mark McPherson (Dana Andrews) meets Laura Hunt (Gene Tierney).

Dana Andrews, who plays McPherson, became the archetypal Preminger protagonist in three of the director's films noirs—*Laura*, *Fallen Angel*, and *Where the Sidewalk Ends*—in each embodying the confused state of a man compromised by his weaknesses. If Detective Mark Dixon is the detective who crosses the line of duty in rage in *Sidewalk*, then Detective Mark McPherson has crossed the boundary of desire in *Laura*. No Preminger noir displays the elusive nature of existence quite like this one: Preminger shows that existence is essentially distorted by ego and desire. It is interesting that we do not see the living Laura Hunt for almost half the film, and when we finally do, the descriptions of her by Waldo Lydecker, Ann Treadwell, and even her maid Bessie, have achieved two narrative developments. First, they have defined Laura in psychological and moral terms, as well as in terms of her physical beauty and grace. David Raksin's haunting theme evokes not Laura, but an aura of her, a captivating, ineffable entity that has already ensured its appeal. And second, Laura's appearance disturbs the sphere of reality in which the narrative seeks to clear up a mystery with, essentially, another mystery. For Laura Hunt is known to be alive only by Shelby Carpenter and, of course, Waldo Lydecker. Mark McPherson has wrestled with his growing attraction for a phantom and now faces the upsetting reality of investigating a young woman. Waldo is correct in telling him that he has fallen in love with a corpse. The appeal to hallucination in *Laura* not only disorients us but also underlies the accompanying deception. McPherson must now reconcile his feelings for Laura Hunt, and he must do so while uncovering a narrative of deceit that he hopes has not involved her in murder.

His polar opposite, Waldo Lydecker, has also loved Laura, and the distinctions between vulgar cop and effete critic so often cited with regard to them are less compelling than the nature of their mutual attraction to her. The Lydecker character has always been assumed to be homosexual, or at least asexual, with Laura's attention to him like that of an acolyte to a mentor. However, in his desire to have Laura *as a possession*, Waldo Lydecker is not that distant from McPherson. In his desire to own his creation of her image—the very image McPherson desires to possess in the flesh—Lydecker lusts. It is not a sexual arousal as such, but nonetheless an aesthetic one, erotically charged, that causes Waldo to recoil when he thinks of Laura in the arms of another man. It is the focus and obsession of the fastidious and controlled Waldo Lydecker that brings *Laura*, with its intoxicating fusion of love, desire, and destruction, into the noir realm. For if the passion in creating the image of Laura Hunt can no longer be sustained, then the subject/object of that image must be destroyed.

Joseph La Shelle's cinematography for Preminger's noirs is an exquisite display of studio chiaroscuro lighting design. In *Laura* it displays the ambiguity of Laura Hunt as an object of thrall, as in the scene where she wears an elegantly striped dress in the kitchen of her apartment, superimposed by another striped pattern created by the light rays filtering through the venetian blinds.[6] In *Where the Sidewalk Ends*, La Shelle's camera work restates the classic neon-lighted urban scenes of Mark Dixon's world that foment his growing sense of guilt. In *Fallen Angel*, La Shelle lighted Preminger's most austere film noir, a rigorous study in appearances and guilt and the transformative power of love, by designing precise rays of light and darkness emanating from venetian blinds and highlighting the blinking neon sign of the hotel where Eric and June stay on the run to an uncertain future. Its lighting pattern is more emphatic and precise than the one he used in *Laura*. Preminger

Fallen Angel (1946). Eric Stanton (Dana Andrews) is redeemed by June Mills's (Alice Faye) love.

tracks beautifully in this setting, especially when Eric must perform his con artistry on June, her sister Clara, and the townspeople by presenting Dr. Madley's phony spiritualist act; when June and Eric walk through this small town with its white-painted church; and in the café where Eric and June arrange a date. His interior tracking is equally impressive through the sisters' Victorian house and in the diner, where Stella exhibits the sullenness of a cynical waitress who has found few rewards in a life of selfish mediocrity.

June Mills (Alice Faye in her finest screen performance) falls in love with grifter Eric Stanton (Andrews), marries him, and in the process of learning about his plan to bilk her after their marriage, she persists in defending his honor when accused of murder; she does so out of the noblest desire: love. June's total commitment to Eric not only redeems him but inevitably awakens him to the capacity for love that he has been unable to share. *Fallen Angel* is probably the most Bressonian film noir ever made. True to its mission, the narrative transforms Eric from an *homme fatal* to a man redeemed by love through the impossibility of escape. Stanton is presumed guilty of Stella's murder and would be the likeliest victim of such misjudgment to be sent up for it. "Even when I was a kid," he confesses to June, "I was beaten up for things I didn't do." Here Preminger develops the relationship between Eric and June by persistently denying June a condemnatory voice. The dynamic that changes their phony marriage into the beginning of a love affair stems from her silence and patience. In this, June, assumed gullible by Eric, understands him far better than he understands himself, and her strength overcomes his weakness. She is smart and good and the anchor that redeems his self-esteem.

Preminger's noir characters challenge us with the moral question of motive and imply in the process a dubious if not sinister guilt. He frames this most strikingly in such close shots as those of Diane Tremayne in *Angel Face*; as either the ultimate *femme fatale* or the ultimate romantic, she gazes into the camera challenging the viewer to decipher whether she is remorseful about killing her father and stepmother or manipulative in disguising her muted rapacity for love, money, and control. That she is ultimately capable of taking Frank Jessup's life and her own does not answer the question; rather it only reinforces the mystery of motive and the ambiguity of character. *Angel Face* is one of Preminger's most fascinating dissections of these concerns. Shot languorously and with hardly any musical soundtrack, it is a curious study in murky morality. For if Diane Tremayne does not quite damn herself after her crime—displaying an odd remorse of sorts at the awareness of pain in death—the ease of killing accommodates her well. She is indeed better defined as a creature than as a human being.

In a similar manner, but with a less ambiguous and much more morally satisfying resolution, Detective Mark Dixon anguishes over the accidental killing of Ken Paine in *Where the Sidewalk Ends*. Living in muted rage over his policeman father's criminal past, he has tried to vindicate himself from the legacy of being "Sandy Dixon's son" by channeling his rage through law enforcement in pursuit of those hoods his father consorted with for profit. Hostility leads to the blow that kills Paine, an honored war vet with a steel plate in his head and implicated in a murder carried out by Scalisi and his mob—the same Scalisi who bought off his father. Mark Dixon now faces his dilemma and does so in close shot, in the face of the camera: Preminger shows Dixon to be a man of weak honor, a man who works to put "a lot of nickel rats" behind bars and now finds himself having committed a crime with no motive. When

Where the Sidewalk Ends (1950). Dana Andrews's Mark Dixon: guilt, commitment, and a badge.

Mark Dixon looks into the camera, how is he to be judged? Preminger posits no answer at this point. Ben Hecht's screenplay of *Where the Sidewalk Ends* is a judicious construct of *policier* and psychodrama—far more effective than Wyler's *Detective Story*, for example, precisely because the main character's personality is at issue not in itself but because of the crime involved that gives it moral consequence.

The film is visually beautiful and displays the studio elements of classic noir filmmaking, with the low-key lighting of a gorgeous neon-lighted urban setting accompanied by the refrain of Alfred Newman's "Street Scene" composition. There is no music except for this, and the credit shots to its strains are among the most emblematic in all of noir cinema. The opening credits end literally where the sidewalk ends: refuse is being washed into a street-corner gutter, and the credit titles are written as chalk graffiti. It is the final destination in reaching the truth—a place compromised by "nickel rats" and the violence of a detective whose zeal exceeds the law in pursuit of them.

On the surface, *Bunny Lake Is Missing* appears to be a version of the absent subject/object of narrative concern. The child Bunny Lake is never seen until the end of the film, yet the story is an exposé of the characters encountered in search of her, including her mother and her uncle. Bunny Lake's absence serves two narrative functions: to promote the search for answers surrounding her disappearance and thereby establish the characters in the story, and to establish the very existence of the child, whose identity, much like Laura Hunt's, is rendered by what others say about her. *Bunny Lake* becomes a noir experience in the terror it arouses of the unknown as a provocative animus of control and malevolence—by Stephen over Ann and by the strange, unsettling eccentrics she encounters in her moments of panic. The movie suggests Hitchcock in design and evokes Woolrich in fear.

The question of illusion over reality hinges on the emotional understanding of Ann and her brother Stephen. The superintendent must find proof of Bunny's existence in this environment of psychological disturbance—this environment that renders Ann and Stephen as two involved in an emotionally incestuous relationship where ambiguity stems from that which is fantasized (the role of Bunny as an imaginary childhood friend of Ann's and as the intrusive entity in Stephen's relationship with her that has to be killed and buried) and reality, the missing daughter and niece of whom no evidence can be found. The extraordinary scene in the doll hospital, with its abstractly composed shots and frenzied chiaroscuro tracking as it burns, underscores the terror: for the broken bodies and smashed faces and necks of the dolls in disrepair are a noir nightmare of the only images we can presume to identify as the emotional objectifications of the missing Bunny Lake.

The linchpin of all of Preminger's noir films is located in our need to decipher the enigmatic persona. The mystery of human motivation is rarely recognized in isolation from the mystery of the story told, but in Preminger's cinema it is just this that is the ultimate mystery, one against which no actions can ever be fully understood.

4

NOIR PRODUCTION

The films noirs produced in Hollywood were not identified as such, and even well into the fifties they did not receive generic definition by the industry. They were very much a part of the melodrama/thriller films, often of B-movie status, financed by the studios. The stylistics of these movies, discussed in this chapter and intrinsic to the styles of their directors (at least in certain periods of their work), find a pattern of generic development emerging—in theme, of course, but also in technique, through the use of voice-overs, flashbacks, expressionistic lighting and set designs, and low- and high-angle camera work. This last feature, ubiquitous in noir cinema, is discussed throughout.

In historical context, certain developments must be noted in noir filmmaking. First of all, the emergence of noir cinema was a challenge to the Motion Picture Production Code, which, with a film such as *Double Indemnity*, was forced to revise its interpretation of acceptable film fare because "of the considerable changes in American morals, mores, and educational standards" since the code was written in 1934.[1] Other films with relatively ambiguous characters or endings—John Stahl's *Leave Her to Heaven* and Robert Aldrich's *Kiss Me Deadly*—also influenced the relaxation of the code's restrictions. Second, the hard-boiled school of writing, including Hammett and Chandler but also Cain, McCoy (*Kiss Tomorrow Goodbye*), and Woolrich, opened the door to an invigorating and morally complex universe that gave new subject matter to Hollywood studios and helped build the careers of some of its finest screenwriters: Abraham Polonsky, Ben Hecht (*Kiss of Death, Ride the Pink Horse, Where the Sidewalk Ends*), Jay Dratler (*Laura, The Dark Corner, Pitfall* [based on his novel]), Philip Yordan (*The Chase, Suspense, House of Strangers, Detective Story, The Big Combo, The Harder They Fall*), Daniel Mainwaring (*Out of the Past* [as Geoffrey Homes, and based on his novel], *The Phenix City Story*), David Goodis (*Dark Passage* [based on his novel], *Nightfall*), Dorothy B. Hughes (*Ride the Pink Horse*, *In a Lonely Place* [based on her novels]), and A.I. Bezzerides (*Thieves' Highway* [based on his novel], *On Dangerous Ground*, *Kiss Me Deadly*). The third significant result was the first popular use of the documentary technique in Hollywood dramatic film, defining the "second" phase of the film noir.

Among the producers who distinguished themselves in noir production were Hal B. Wallis (*The Maltese Falcon*; *The Strange Love of Martha Ivers*; *Dark City*; *I Walk Alone*; *Sorry, Wrong Number*), Mark Hellinger (*The Killers* [1946], *Brute Force*, *The Naked City*), Joan Harrison (*Phantom Lady*, *Nocturne*, *They Won't Believe Me*, *Ride the Pink Horse*), Edward Small (*T-Men*, *Raw Deal*, *Scandal Sheet*, *Kansas City Confidential*, *99 River Street*), Bob Roberts (*Body and Soul*, *Force of Evil*, *He Ran All the Way*), and Dore Schary, who, as production head at RKO, allowed, from 1947 to 1949, the biggest concentration of noir filmmaking to be done.

Finally, no one can deny the beauty of some of the finest black-and-white cinematography of the American screen in the work of Woody Bredell (*Phantom Lady*, *Christmas Holiday*, *The Killers*), Franz Planer (*The Chase*, *Criss Cross*, *99 River Street*), Nicholas Musuraca (*Stranger on the Third Floor*, *Deadline at Dawn*, *Out of the Past*, *The Hitch-Hiker*, *The Blue Gardenia*), Joseph La Shelle (*Laura*, *Fallen Angel*, *Road House*, *Where the Sidewalk Ends*), George E. Diskant (*Desperate*, *They Live by Night*, *On Dangerous Ground*, *Kansas City Confidential*, *The Narrow Margin* [1952]), and John Alton (*T-Men*, *Raw Deal*, *Hollow Triumph* [*The Scar*], *Mystery Street*, *The People against O'Hara*, *The Big Combo*). Discussed throughout, it is their visual stamp of a noir world that lingers most evocatively—most potently—in our imagination.

NOIR ICONOGRAPHY

Certain images of set pieces and objects recur in the film noir with such familiarity that their visual prominence in the narrative defines their importance in any discussion of the genre. The acknowledged settings of lamp-lit streets at night just after rainfall; tastefully appointed apartments and bungalows where violent acts occur or have just occurred, again, at night; and rays of neon-lighted signs streaming through the venetian blinds of windows in empty offices held hostage by menace outside—all have fed the popular imagination of noir cinema. Other images just as familiar, of shiny cigarette cases—indeed, of cigarettes themselves smoked in profusion—watches, keys, distressingly ringing telephones, lipstick, furs, trench coats (undoubtedly), the bent-brimmed hats of men and the modish couture of women; and, of course, a variety of guns, nightclubs and supper clubs, lounges, and cars have become the paraphernalia of the nighttime noir milieu to the extent that few such films can exist without a requisite assortment of these. At times crucial linchpins of the noir narrative, they radiate the texture and mood and often symbolize the motivations and incriminations of the characters who possess and use them. Among the most significant iconography of the noir are the lounge or nightclub (or its variants, the supper club or jazz club) and the automobile. Although not every film noir has a bar setting, almost every one has an important use for the car.

The bar or nightclub setting here often contains images of the aforementioned objects and attire, but its importance lies in the almost discrete world it creates, within the film noir, of chance, fate, and the complications or revelations that come from unexpected encounters with those who mean trouble with every seductive move they make. In *Nocturne* (Edwin L. Marin, 1946), it is the piano composition played in a supper club that gives away the killer who plays it. In *Road House*, Lily's

Road House (1948). Lily (Ida Lupino) at the lounge piano. ("She does more without a voice than anyone I ever heard.")

sultry singing of "Ten Cents a Dance" at the piano in Jefty's supper club arouses his deranged obsession with her. Vince Stone crushes a cigarette in a barfly's hand in *The Big Heat*, and Philip Marlowe and Vivian Sternwood discuss the relative merits of his sexual prowess in a casino in *The Big Sleep*. The Blue Dahlia in *The Blue Dahlia* is the supper club where Johnny Morrison and Joyce Harwood contrive to keep him from being arrested for his wife's murder while her husband, the owner, jealously observes. It is the strip club that lures policeman Johnny Kelly into a destructive liaison with the stripper Angel Face in *City That Never Sleeps* (John H. Auer, 1953); and it is Rita Moreno's Dolores Gonzales, performing a dazzlingly erotic striptease in *Marlowe*, whose coded gyrations reveal to the detective that she killed Orrin Quest.

The illicit implications from contacts made, directly or indirectly, in this setting, and the unspoken dangers therein, come from the combination of selling hard liquor (originally an illegal enterprise from Prohibition times) and those attracted to the freedom represented by the habitués of such smoke-filled establishments. It is not that lounges in themselves are iniquitous, but that they have gained cinematic currency as the sophisticated and often sleek images of modern excitement, as the appropriate setting for those who seek—or seek escape from—danger and violence and are drawn here to the proximity of both. They exist, too, for those who seek escape from the mundane in reflection and in the possibility of finding life-enhancing encounters. In *Pitfall*, Mona Stevens meets John Forbes for a drink in such a lounge and muses over the experience: "If, for some reason, you want to feel completely out of step with the rest of the world, the only thing to do is sit around a cocktail lounge in the afternoon. . . . You sit around the gloom and have a few quiet, meditative drinks, get everything figured out. Then you go out and the sun hits you. And you feel like something that's been drinking in a gopher hole." The lounge setting is particularly hospitable to the concept of darkness as a sensorium and lubricant of the noir mood. As an escape from the routine obligations of conventional and family life, bars, lounges, and nightclubs emerge as the seductive venues of that which is unknown and unmapped; they become places to discover the capacity to feel the very vitality that is sapped by the deadening conformity of the responsible social contract. Providing such temptation, the neon signs of the clubs and jazz spots (in *Phantom Lady*, for example) that lure their patrons become road markers for a headier and more pulsing exploration of the passionate nature. If clubs serve to lure people to the world of illicit possibilities, then the car serves as the escape vehicle from their entrapment and numerous missteps taken that threaten both body and soul.

The car in the film noir is a complex symbol expressing the various kinds of escape its protagonists attempt. It is also a tool of death. Cars bring troublesome people to town who inquire about one's past (*Out of the Past*). They take people away from trouble (*Dead Reckoning, They Live by Night, Quicksand* [Irving Pichel, 1950], *On Dangerous Ground*). And they mark people for death (Nick, Frank, and Cora in *The Postman Always Rings Twice*, Katie Bannion in *The Big Heat*, Nick in *Kiss Me Deadly*). An interesting irony in several films noirs is that those who meet bad ends also work on cars professionally—they drive them, service them, tinker with them. Playing Don Brady, a mechanic in *Quicksand*, and Eddie Shannon, a mechanic and racer in *Drive a Crooked Road* [Richard Quine, 1954], Mickey Rooney finds himself in hot water because of their automotive skills and easy seduction by *femmes fatales*. Nick, the garage mechanic, is blown up in *Kiss Me Deadly*, and Johnny North, a professional race-car driver, is killed by hit men in Siegel's *Killers*. Indeed, it may be argued that the automobile is the real guiding force of fate in Ulmer's *Detour*, for nothing of consequence happens to Al and Vera without this necessary object.

But as a symbol of the modern urban landscape, the car comes to mean much more: it functions as the symbol of all that has brought America to this ambiguous state of spiritual anxiety. Taunting us as the apex of industrial achievement with its commercial appeal and status, the car in the film noir has been transformed into an object of dubious distinction, like a desperado of sorts, an accomplice. Whether noir characters use it to escape their pursuers (legal or criminal) or their past, the automobile symbolizes that dangerous flight into the unknown that contrasts with its other importance as a symbol of established success in modern American culture. Desperate people steal perfectly reputable vehicles, transforming them into getaway cars, and in the act they sully the very status of material success that these object represent (*The Asphalt Jungle, Odds against Tomorrow*). As an abettor here, the car now becomes an unwilling ally promoting escape from danger, courting violence with the very speed with which it is driven, and contributing to an ever-distorted illusion of successful flight. One thinks of Lewis's *Gun Crazy* and its ultimate eroticizing of speed and violence behind the wheel of a car. Never before or since have the gun and the car in tandem achieved such sensuous power. In its transformation into an escape device, the car carries out one of the narrative goals of noir cinema: to bring the illusion of freedom for its characters up to its dead end—right up to the place from which they can no longer escape, and where they usually die.

THE USE OF VOICE-OVER NARRATION

Voice-over narration has been an important device in defining narrative voice and point of view, and it has certainly not been unique to noir cinema in such importance. In the opening scene of George Stevens's *I Remember Mama* (1948), Katrin reminisces about her mother, now gone but forever living in her daughter's consciousness and behavior. Through voice-over, we know that the modifications of time and experience have changed the girl who is now this woman. *Citizen Kane* uses the voice-over, and Welles's *Magnificent Ambersons*, released a year later, in 1942, uses it even more prominently. In both films it functions as an aural "remembrance of things past" in search of answers to an inscrutable present, and it lingers hauntingly, as though the voices heard in voice-over hover somewhere between timeless consciousness and the present. It was in 1944 that the voice-over narration appeared in the new noir films of the studio period, most spectacularly in Billy Wilder's *Double Indemnity* and Edward Dmytryk's *Murder, My Sweet*.

Double Indemnity is quite daring in its use of voice-over. As every student of the noir knows, Walter Neff reveals himself as a killer at the start of the story and then continues in voice-over to narrate the beginning of his involvement with Phyllis Dietrichson. What Walter Neff records on his Dictaphone is nothing less than his mortal transformation at the point of approaching death. It is his confession for the sins of his blind attraction to Phyllis and the total abnegation of his responsibility to Keyes and to himself. Wilder uses the confessional function of this voice-over to narrate—almost by bleak liturgical chant—the process of Walter's entrapment; and although it certainly underscores the misogyny behind the creation of the prototypical *femme fatale*, Phyllis Dietrichson, she becomes less the object here than Walter does the subject. His confession to Keyes is that privileged analysis that strikes the noir consciousness at the moment of hopeless resignation to doom, and Walter simply wants to speak of *how* he has come to understand where he finally finds himself.

The strategy is similar to Philip Marlowe's description of his beat-

ings and drugging, the constant deceits, and the L.A. locales in *Murder,
My Sweet*, where, compelled by a diarist's need to speak of an ongoing
experience, a noir mystery, he refuses to relinquish a totally engaged
consciousness that will bring him—as it brings Walter Neff, as it brings
Michael O'Hara in *The Lady from Shanghai*—to the point of helplessness. Although the story may certainly inform without voice-over introspection, it rarely reveals the unbridled human voice speaking in
privileged form and often with fear and anxiety. The voice-over narration of, among others, Al Roberts in *Detour*, Frank Chambers in *The
Postman Always Rings Twice*, Rip Murdock in *Dead Reckoning*, Joe
Morse in *Force of Evil*, Pat Regan in *Raw Deal*, Celia Lamphere in *Secret beyond the Door . . .,* Frank Bigelow in *D.O.A.* (Rudolph Maté,
1950), and more recently, Bree Daniels in *Klute*, offers this.

Quite apart from this function, the voice-over narration sometimes
paraphrases or parodies the seriousness of the narrative. In the detective
noir, it did both—exploratively in *Murder, My Sweet*, adventuresomely
and almost to comic effect in *The Brasher Doubloon*, and quite formally
(and irritably) in Robert Montgomery's subjective-camera experiment,
punctuated with moments of voiced-over sarcasm, *The Lady in the Lake*.

It also became an indispensable stylistic in the semidocumentary
noirs of the immediate postwar years. *The Naked City* would not be so
"naked" were it not for Mark Hellinger's voice-over commentary extol-
ling the exceptional civil responsibility displayed in the face of grim
reality by all those who swear by the badge of the law. Bogart's voice as
Martin Ferguson introduces the crime-busting story of *The Enforcer*.
The Street with No Name (William Keighley, 1948) and *Port of New
York* (Laslo Benedek, 1949) have voice-of-God narrations inject the
proper tone of gravity by telling us how federal enforcers go about their
tasks of fighting organized crime and drug smuggling. The voice-of-
God narration sounds as ominous as it finally does hokey and, taken out
of the context of its popularity—from 1947 to the early fifties—dated.
Its aims were to give the story topic an objective raison d'être for the
account that followed, one that would straddle between unauthorial,
unmitigated and authentic "truth,"[2] seemingly unimpeachable in its veracity, and the requirement that such voiced-over truth serve the dramatic development of the story. However, the strategy could hardly be
made to serve anything other than a bracketed truth, and it would have
been naive to expect anything more. Now, the voice-of-God narrations
punctuating the aforementioned films and others of the period, such as

Boomerang! Call Northside 777 (Henry Hathaway, 1948), *City That Never Sleeps*—even *Private Hell 36*—speak in a far less convincing voice than they did in their own time. Or than Walter Neff's speaks yet today, disembodied but quite essential in revealing the interior terrain of one man's noir suffering.

THE FLASHBACK DEVICE

Apart from the voice-over, no other device claims as much importance in the film noir with quite the aesthetic, psychological, and moral value as the flashback does. With several narrative functions that express the fear and betrayal characteristic of noir cinema, the flashback allows the noir protagonist to revisit the past and square the record with his or her perception of the truth in an attempt to make the present clear. The perception may be false—or may spur confrontations, violence, and death before it proves false—but that is a narrative prerogative it can assume. Like the voice-over, the flashback gains privileged access to the perspective of each troubled character whose episode it presents. Not quite in "Roshomon" style but similar, the difference in the film noir is that one account, more than the others, substantially supports the conclusion and the guilt assigned. In this sense the flashback gives each consciousness, often accompanied by voice-over narration, a visual articulation, scrutinized and placed within the larger narrative to be considered.

As mentioned, *Double Indemnity* illustrates this in tandem with the voice-over narration of Walter Neff's consciousness. But in the same year (1944) Otto Preminger also gave us his classic example of the voice-over flashback in *Laura*, where each character's flashback of Laura Hunt becomes a mininarrative all its own. The film achieves an objectivity in flashback use by exposing no particular suspect but simply complicating the consciousness of one Detective MacPherson, who is obsessed with creating a woman from a phantom. It is a fascinating use of the flashback and one rarely repeated with equal justification since.

The multiple point of view in *Sorry, Wrong Number* comes closer to its more common dramatic use of creating suspense and a sense of doom. As Leona Stevenson attempts to piece together the flashback episodes triggered by a series of ominous telephone calls—particularly one from her old rival, Sally Lord—the disturbing mysterious accounts force her to replay her own history with her husband, Henry, and, with revelatory disbelief, to see not only that it is he who is arranging her murder but also, more importantly, that she has provoked it. The flashbacks here serve as codes to decipher a terrible fate. In the 1949 *D.O.A.*, Frank Bigelow's flashbacks serve the same purpose, but with the difference that Frank seeks answers to the arbitrary end of his life. Fear is less the motivation than the need to know the tragic "why" behind his fatal poisoning.

They Won't Believe Me uses the flashback to encompass the scope of a man's life in the project of self-assessment before a trial jury. Larry Ballentine, the *homme fatal* here, elicits an unexpected sympathy from us precisely because each of his voice-over flashbacks illustrating callous and deceitful behavior exposes such perspicacity that we half expect the jury's mercy in sparing him a guilty verdict for the murder of his ex-wife (of which, belying appearances, he is truly innocent). In *Dead Reckoning*, returning vet Rip Murdock tells a priest his story of a

Out of the Past (1947). The past present: how Kathie Moffet (Jane Greer) ensnared Jeff Bailey (Robert Mitchum).

murdered army buddy; the flashbacks in voice-over show his attempt to uncover the truth behind the incident, truth tangled in a web of deceit and derailed by his attraction to Coral Chandler. Memory functions as a tool of enlightenment here, with the flashback as a device of remembrance of an unpleasant past. Murdock tells his story to recall the lesson of his noir experience: that betrayal regrettably can assume a seductive and deadly allure.

Another variation of the personal recollection in flashback occurs in *The Dark Past*, when Dr. Collins asks Betty about gangster Al Walker's violent dreams. A surreal Freudian flashback of a boy's entrapment and fear is shot to her voice-over description of Al's nightmare, which brings to light his childhood abuse by his father. This dream account, by third person, is as distinctive as the flashbacks within Martin Ferguson's flashback of his breakup of Murder Inc. in *The Enforcer*. Each person sought in his investigation recalls his involvement, provides his piece of the puzzle, in the murder-for-hire ring.

The flashback in noir cinema uses subjective perspective to seek answers, to weave together various, often contradictory, accounts in search of an elusive truth in the past. Certainly Leona Stevenson undertakes this project, as does Strom in Siegel's *Killers*, where the flashbacks attempt to answer the question of why a man (racer Johnny North) passively awaits his executioners. In the Siodmak version the same quest takes place, but the difference, of course, is that the same inquiry made by the insurance investigator here is made by the killer in the later version. In Siodmak's *Christmas Holiday*, the flashback functions as a self-interrogation—indeed, as the vindicator of presumed guilt—in the review of a young woman's past, which is too familiar to her; there is also the need to replay its detailed chronology to make a difficult closure at the very least less saddening. Abigail Mannette can resurface from "Jackie Lamont" only by undergoing this process; only then can she be spiritually prepared to free herself of the guilt of not having loved Robert enough as he lay shot and dying.

As a vehicle of inquiry and psychic disburdenment, the flashback used in noir cinema answers above all why, or how, one finds oneself in this moment in the story. It accounts for the present by reckoning with the past, often through the perspective of heightened consciousness but just as often by having this consciousness challenged with competing images that force us to grapple with the narrative demands of all that is spoken and all that is shown.

AMNESIA AS A STORYTELLING DEVICE

As Freudian psychology and its cultural implications gained popularity during the first half of the twentieth century, it became inevitable that the cinema (almost from its beginning) would exploit it. Psychological manifestations, as well as the subject of psychology, proved to be indispensable dramatic devices to the modern screen melodrama. Such interest coincided with, and was encouraged by, the great influx of European scientists, intellectuals, and artists and writers of all kinds who emigrated to America between the wars, especially after Hitler's rise in Germany made it increasingly troublesome to work, or even remain, in Europe. The intellectual nourishment that American culture subsequently received—in whatever dehydrated popular form—cannot be overestimated and is indeed reflected on the 1940s screen and certainly in the noir cinema that followed. The film noir, from its inception, displayed a particular affinity for this field, perhaps to the very modernness of its inquiry, and linked it to the darker expression of human frustration and motivation. Smith Ohlrig is a bitter megalomaniac in *Caught*. Wilma Tuttle is a frightened and paranoid psychology professor who believes she has killed one of her students in a moment of sexually repressed fear in *The Accused*. In *Hollow Triumph* ([*The Scar*] Steve Sekely, 1948), John Muller evades a mob hit by employing his knowledge of psychology to impersonate a respected look-alike psychologist. *Nightmare Alley* (Edmund Goulding, 1947) deals with the ironies of the occult and charlatanism, as does *Night Has a Thousand Eyes*. Daydreams augur distortions of reality in *The Woman in the Window*, and nightmares provoke psychotic impulses in *The Dark Past*. Robert Siodmak gave us perversely charming noir portraits of mental imbalance: Jack Marlow is an insane sculptor of marble hands that arouse him to strangle in *Phantom Lady*, and Robert Mannette is a sweet psychotic killer obsessively loved by his mother and his wife in *Christmas Holiday*. Nightmares and amnesia, as well as hallucinations and madness, abound in the film noir, particularly in the American noir, to offer the viewer an oblique look at a disordered world with tormented victims. From Lang's *M* to Alan Parker's *Angel Heart*, the noir character's consumption with fear and mystery provided an atmosphere of terror comparable to that in Cornell Woolrich's finest writing.

Nightmares and hallucinations free such anxious humors to mingle with the now-distorted reality of those who can no longer function in narrative separation from their nightmares. Their inability to recall something that they sense is terrible haunts them—something Woolrich understood well in his short fiction. *Black Angel*, based on his novel, is the most compelling example of this in the studio noir period, and Dan Duryea's performance as Martin Blair is a signature characterization of the helpless noir man, tormented without knowing why and incapable of freedom through self-illumination. Such psychic entrapment melds psychology with philosophy in the noir, and the amnesia suffered by Blair finally walks an uneasy path alongside the actions he would rather forget. *Somewhere in the Night*, also made in 1946, is centered on the amnesiac's search for identity that only uncovers unpleasant truths about his past. But the story seems rigged; it exonerates its main character, Martin Cravat, alias George Taylor, from a bad history. *Black Angel* is instead possessed of a powerful passion and delirium, felt by pianist Blair, which become a physical response to that which cannot be properly identified, a creative yet violent dynamic that caused him to murder his wife in a fit of jealous rage and then, blinded by drunkenness, forget the episode. He joins forces with Catherine Bennett, the wife of the man

Black Angel (1946). Martin Blair (Dan Duryea) and the torment of a past unknown. With Catherine Bennett (June Vincent) at his side.

convicted for his wife's murder, to prove her husband's innocence. As Martin pursues likelier murder suspects among his deceased's infidelities, he falls in love with Catherine—so taken is he by her devotion to her jailed husband. When she delicately refuses him, the pain of unrequited love is ignited again, as Martin Blair regains his memory at the sight of a familiar piece of his dead wife's jewelry and realizes that it was he who killed her. Anguished by this capacity to act both passionately and heinously, he turns himself in just in time to save Catherine's husband from execution.

Through expressionistic nightmares and hallucinatory flashbacks, we see amnesiacs trapped in the terror of believing themselves guilty of murder (*Stranger on the Third Floor* [Boris Ingster, 1940], *The Guilty*, *Fear in the Night*, *The Clouded Yellow* [Ralph Thomas, 1951], *The Blue Gardenia*), unsure of their guilt (*Deadline at Dawn*, *The Chase*), unaware of their innocence (*Street of Chance*, *Crack-Up* [Irving Reis, 1946]), and, most interestingly, unaware in all guilelessness of their guilt (*Somewhere in the Night*, *Black Angel*). All these characters live in the dark unknown, in a betrayal of the mind that leaves them easy pawns to those that would exploit them. Their quest for self-identity often fuels this unknown with dread in a narrative of fearful culpability.

THE B NOIR PRODUCTION

As with most screen genres, Hollywood studios made B crime dramas requiring little dollar investment, and consequently several noir films of the 1940s and 1950s achieved a degree of artistic liberation through the very limitations imposed upon their production. Set pieces borrowed from bigger-budgeted A films and lighting that obfuscated back projections of often-imprecise set designs provided for a profitable production of low-budget noir films that satisfied a growing moviegoing audience during the war years and immediately after. Production values were limited; spectacle and crowd scenes, complicated shots involving car chases and shootouts or explosions, and huge casts were eliminated. By 1943 the result of wartime government restrictions of raw film stock to the studios, by as much as 25 percent, was felt first by B-film production units.[3] The Monogram B noir *When Strangers Marry*, directed in 1944 by William Castle, was shot so darkly—almost entirely in available light—that it effectively creates the noir mood of unknown peril eventually consuming Kim Hunter when she fears that her new husband, played by a young Dean Jagger, may be a murderer. The fill lighting of her profile in their hotel room, with the classic noir image of a blinking neon hotel sign through the window, generates a veritable claustrophobia of black terror.

Don Miller noted that "there are really three classifications of movies: the A, the B, and the programmers, sometimes alluded to as a 'nervous A' or a 'gilt-edged B.' This hybrid would often play the top half of a double bill, have one or two fairly high-priced performers and, when a character walked into a room, the walls wouldn't shake as he shut the door; it looked reasonably opulent, but if a studio tried to palm it off as a big or A picture, you knew they were kidding."[4] Such B films noirs as the Monogram *Fear* (1946), *The Guilty* (1947), *Night Editor* (Columbia, 1946), *The Pretender* (Republic, 1947), and *The Devil Thumbs a Ride* (RKO, 1947) and programmers such as *Railroaded!* (directed by Anthony Mann for the Producers' Releasing Corporation in 1947) and *Quicksand* (United Artists, 1950) could reasonably exploit the artistic benefits of "poverty row," usually at a running time of less than seventy-five minutes.

By the time Edgar Ulmer started work for the independent Producers' Releasing Corporation (PRC) in 1942, they had begun diversifying their B film production beyond comedies and westerns through the effort of their new production head, Leon Fromkess. One of the most frequently cited examples of the B noir—one that in many ways stands as a model of the type as well as an exception—remains Ulmer's *Detour*, made in 1945. A more cheaply made noir would be hard to come by, for *Detour*, shot in less than a week on a ridiculous budget of thirty thousand dollars and with no stars, forces our recognition of Edgar Ulmer as a filmmaker capable of displaying a striking noir sensibility in a work that makes palpable the terror of fate and arbitrariness. *Detour* is a cruel portrayal of the philosophical implications of noir fatalism reduced to its simple, clean expression. It is the story of an unhappy composer hitchhiking west to meet up with his girlfriend, a nightclub singer, in Los Angeles. The very act of hitchhiking, fraught with the unexpected and dangerous, connects Al Roberts (Tom Neal) with two people that end up dying in his company and leave him bereft of his true identity, destined to live in a world haunted by suspicion and fear.[5]

En route westward with Charles Haskell, the motorist who picks him up, Al starts an irreversible journey that brings him in contact with Vera, another hitchhiker, after Haskell's freak fatal heart attack. He picks

Detour (1945). The reflection of murder, guilt, and fear: Al Roberts (Tom Neal) unwittingly strangles Vera (Ann Savage).

her up in Haskell's car after assuming his identity out of fear of implication in his death. Unaware that she was Haskell's previous pickup and knows of Al's deception, Al is eventually terrorized by Vera into doing her bidding lest she report him to the police. Like a harridan out of a nightmare, as indeed Ulmer's world becomes here, Ann Savage's Vera emerges as one of the most unrelenting and frightening females in noir cinema. Not completely a *femme fatale*—for her allure is limited and her charms negated by a bitterness that is hard to take—Vera comes into focus more and more as the unsuppressed animus that Al Roberts himself harbors but keeps in check. She is the anonymous, albeit miserable, anywoman in Ulmer's world, destined to draw a cynical anyman like Al Roberts into a web of bizarre circumstances and death. But the circumstances have Al's own tacit compliance, as he submits to Vera's scheme that has him impersonate Haskell in a probate fraud involving Haskell's dying father.

Finally, just as Haskell's own death was a weird accident, Vera's strangulation—unwitting, by a telephone cord caught around her neck and pulled hard from under the closed door of an adjoining room— becomes the improbable event for which no reasonable jury could be expected to exonerate Al Roberts of responsibility. In this nightmare and Vera's death arises not the fact of his guilt so much as the necessity for guilt to be assigned. "[I]t is the very implausibility of the action, juxtaposed with the ordinariness of the milieu—a nightclub, an apart- ment, a used car lot, and, of course, the road—that gives the film much of its force," wrote David Coursen. "Ulmer is actually taking several American fantasies ('going west,' looking to Hollywood for success and happiness, finding freedom and happiness on the open road . . .) and performing unnatural acts on them, with devastating effects."[6]

As Murnau's assistant on *The Last Laugh*, *Sunrise*, *City Girl*, and *Tabu*, Ulmer came to low-budget filmmaking armed with the Germanic heritage of illusional reality created out of mist and fog (the long shot of Al and his girlfriend, Sue, contemplating their future during a walk on New York's Upper West Side, identified only by the numbered street signs they pass in the misty night) and the artful use of the interior long take (as when the telephone cord Al yanks in the living room is followed through to the adjoining bedroom to show it having strangled Vera). Ulmer displayed this style in a no-budget noir feature of such cheapness as to enhance, ironically, its austere moral argument, one that leaves little doubt about the cosmic reckoning Al Roberts speaks of in voice- over when he submits: "That's life . . . Whichever way you turn, fate sticks out a foot to trip you."

DOCUMENTARY REALISM IN THE NOIR

On-location documentary shooting became integrated into the film noir after World War II, in part because of the popularity and influence of Italian neorealism. Evoking the outdoor shooting found in much of the interwar French cinema, Italian neorealism adopted a rawer and more immediate representation of the miseries of postwar Italy. Its purpose was to use film technique to show life as it is found. This influence would certainly seem an odd coupling with the expressionistic stylistics of the studio noir; but the year 1947 saw several films use documentary footage in what would hereafter become a regular feature in many films noirs and police dramas. The idea was to lend urgency and the look of realistic authenticity to the topics filmed and to emphasize the social consciousness behind such film production. By the end of the story, the viewer felt that whatever peril existed was vanquished—and could be vanquished—by the strength and integrity of our democratic institutions. Twentieth Century–Fox was the major studio making most of these movies, under producer Louis de Rochemont, the creator of the *March of Time* newsreel series (1935–1943) and the man nicknamed the Rossellini of the United States.[7] Under De Rochemont, Elia Kazan made *Boomerang!* in 1947, based on a true murder trial in which circumstantial evidence nearly convicted an innocent Connecticut man charged with killing a priest. *Boomerang!* shows the criminal justice system's propensity to be corrupted by politicians and the press, and although it lacks the darker motivations of character that a true noir embodies, it displays many of the salient features of the films noirs of the time: the use of modulated chiaroscuro lighting, the accused (or pursued) returning veteran, Freudian psychoanalysis to account for social maladjustment, plenty of low-angle camera work (especially of the small town at the beginning of the film, giving it a decidedly edgy, urban look), and an alarmist voice-over narration throughout the film—particularly at the beginning—that functions as a cross between Greek chorus and soothsayer. Add to these the outdoor shooting that takes place in Stamford, Connecticut, and we see an amalgam of the noir conventions available then.

Henry Hathaway directed most of the semidocumentaries for De Rochemont, and his films, made from 1945 to 1948, cover the entire cycle. He used a voice-of-God voice-over to introduce a 1945 film that, we are told, could not have been made before the first atom bomb was dropped on Hiroshima. *The House on 92nd Street*, about the breakup of a Nazi spy ring in New York City, was shot on location in Washington and New York with further "documentary authenticity" lent by using actual FBI footage of photographed surveillance and having FBI personnel play themselves. The national anthem opens the film. *13 Rue Madeleine*, a spy thriller about the Office of Strategic Services, followed in 1946, *Kiss of Death* in 1947, and *Call Northside 777* in 1948. All have on-location camera work, a fascination with law enforcement protocol, and the appropriately ominous voice-over that informs us of their grave purpose.

Hathaway's films concern avenging crime and misbegotten justice (*Call Northside 777*), but none approach the dark world of the noir man as much as *Kiss of Death*. The difference is one of tone. Shot in New York City, the film's opening scene of a robbery in progress was filmed

Kiss of Death (1947). Documentary realism: Nick Bianco (Victor Mature) in prison. The scene was actually shot in Sing Sing.

in the Chrysler Building, and because more authentic realism was desired, some of its actors were processed through the penal system at the Tombs. However, the film still incorporates a stylized low-key lighting, both on location and on the sets, that transforms Nick Bianco's old neighborhood locales (at Luigi's at night) into a noir landscape where we feel his ambivalence about turning informant. When cinematographer Norbert Brodine takes his camera inside Nick's home, the lights are out and the shades are pulled. We see a play of thin rays of light outlining Nick's perspiring face as he waits for Tommy Udo to come and kill him. His face is lit only by his burning cigarette. It is a tense moment of noir fear and entrapment.

Incorporating documentary elements in noir cinema achieved the disruptive effect that it often sought to dissolve. By providing on-location camera work, nonprofessional performers, and a reliance on documentary artifacts, these films attempted to fuse the gravity of their subject matter with the legitimacy of technical style. They raise instead the very issue of disruption that, more than fifty years later, provokes a curiosity about their meaning. The semidocumentary noirs retain their noir status

The Naked City (1948). New York's skyline as a panorama of the volatile noir city.

precisely *in spite of* their manipulation of a kind of screen realism. Through a judicious incorporation of documentary shooting within the noir drama, the mood was generated primarily by the choice of setting, lighting design, and characters portrayed. One thinks here of Anthony Mann's *T-Men* (1947), Dassin's *Brute Force*, and, to a lesser extent, *The Naked City*, Keighley's *The Street with No Name*, and Siodmak's *Cry of the City*. J.P. Telotte observed that the semidocumentaries "typically bracketed their disturbing subjects within an unconventionally realistic but reassuring, even melodramatic, format, which has the effect of muting their potentially disquieting voice."[8] The concerns of the troubled, dislocated noir protagonist have most often been based in a sensitivity to the human condition as defined by the anxieties of modern American culture—a thesis always at least implied in noir cinema. The extent to which documentary realism addressed this predicament—in the context of misspent passions and crime and the violence that attends them— was really much more in the desire to express noir truths in a stylistic aberration that muffled the very impact that the film noir, with its sources in expressionistic drama, sought to reveal. As Telotte further observed, "what these works . . . most clearly reveal is less the reality of postwar America than their audiences' *desire* and even deep-felt *need* for a reality that might match their assumptions about their world."[9] The disquietude of noir cinema, however, has always been of another, more intransigent and less reassuring, reality.

Nonetheless, it is only fair to recognize that the documentary influence since the late forties has become more, and more vividly, integrated into noir narrative. Just from 1948 to 1951—a mere three years—the seamless and exciting integration of on-location and documentary footage would be found in Polonsky's *Force of Evil*, Mann's *Undercover Man* (1949) and *Side Street*, Kazan's *Panic in the Streets* (1950), Dassin's *Night and the City*, and Berry's *He Ran All the Way*.

CRITICAL AND POPULAR RECEPTION OF THE FILM NOIR

By the midforties the film noir was beginning to make a significant stylistic impact on Hollywood cinema, and it was being noticed at the box office, by critics and even by writers on culture. But the product—the object, the entity—had yet to be properly named. The terms *thriller, mystery* or *detective film* did not completely distinguish it any more than *melodrama* fully acknowledged its difference. It was the French moviegoing public who, immediately after the war, began to see the glut of previously unreleased American films made during the war and in them discern a different—but for the French not unfamiliar—tone that appeared in the melodramas of those years. Raymond Borde and Étienne Chaumeton described "a new type of American film that was revealed to the French public during the summer of 1946. In several weeks, from mid-July until the end of August, five films followed one another on Parisian screens that had in common a strange and cruel atmosphere, tinted with a peculiar eroticism: *The Maltese Falcon* by John Huston, Otto Preminger's *Laura*, Edward Dmytryk's *Murder, My Sweet*, Billy Wilder's *Double Indemnity*, and Fritz Lang's *The Woman in the Window*."[10] Critics wrote that in these films "the essential question no longer consisted in discovering who commits the crime but in seeing how the protagonist goes on to act."[11] Nino Frank, writing in the August 1946 issue of *L'Écran Français*, finally announced their name: "[T]hese film 'noirs' no longer have anything in common with the usual type of detective film. Distinctly psychological narratives and violent or fast-paced action are less important than the faces, the behavior, the thoughts—consequently, the trueness to life of the characters—of this 'third dimension' that has already arrived here in speech" (14). From 1946 to 1949, French and British film journals were publishing major reviews of such films. *La Revue du Cinéma*, under the editorship of Jean-Georges Auriol, wrote about *Brute Force* and *Gilda*. In 1949 Harry Wilson observed in *Sequence* that Raymond Chandler's "real contribution to the cinema is in a style already hinted at, to be found in the early films of this genre [the "crime-thriller" genre], notably *Farewell, My Lovely* [*Murder, My Sweet*]: the feeling for the squalor and menace of a big city; the poetry of back-street, subway, and bar-parlour; the shine of wet streets after rain. . . . What is certain, at any rate, is that since 1944 his work has done much to form the basis of film making as indigenously American as the Western, the social comedy, the musical, and the gangster film of the 'twenties and 'thirties."[12]

Such observations were amplified by American critics, who indeed saw stylistic changes abound in postwar crime films, and the violence displayed in them reached, as said, grim new expression. Manny Farber wrote in 1950 of a series of "ugly melodramas Hollywood has spawned since 1946 featuring a cruel aesthetic, desperate craftsmanship, and a pessimistic outlook." Carried away by them, he ventured on: "These supertabloid geeklike films (*The Set-up, Act of Violence, Asphalt Jungle*) are revolutionary attempts at turning life inside out to find the specks of horrible oddity that make puzzling, faintly marred kaleidoscopes of a street, face, or gesture. Whatever the cause of these depressing films . . . it has produced striking changes in film technique."[13] Farber's vivid commentary illustrates the idiosyncratic style of a critic who took such filmmaking seriously at a time when Hollywood cinema was largely denied critical inquiry by a cultural establishment that was nonetheless nourished by its images. Surely Edward Hopper's *Nighthawks* (1942), one of the most recognized American paintings, is nothing short of a paean to the noir mood developing in film and fiction during the forties. An urban tableau of isolated patrons collected at a late-night—perhaps an all-night—diner, each is in his own world of circumstance that finds him in this way station to nowhere. No one is outside, just as there is no communion among these customers seated at the counter inside, glassed in and in full view, within a larger chiaroscuro world of stark desolation. Abraham Polonsky recalled Hopper's influence on the cinematography of *Force of Evil* and said, speaking to George

Edward Hopper's *Nighthawks* (1942). Edward Hopper, American, 1882-1967, Nighthawks, 1942, oil on canvas, 84.1 x 152.4 cm. Friends of American Art Collection, 1942.51. © The Art Institute of Chicago. All Rights Reserved.

Barnes ("probably the best cameraman we ever had in this town") about the look he wanted: "I went out and got a book of reproductions of Hopper's paintings—Third Avenue, cafeterias, all that back-lighting, and those empty streets. Even when people are there, you don't see them; somehow the environments dominate the people. . . . I said 'This is kind of what I want.' 'Oh, that!' He knew right away what 'that' was, and we had it all the way through the film."[14]

Hopper is probably the artist most identified with the film noir, but the influence between the general culture and the noir can certainly be found in the tabloid photography of Arthur Fellig, known as Weegee (1899–1968), who captured with harsh realism the underbelly of urban crime, passion murders, and sensational acts of urban chaos and tragedy. Fellig's sensibility—if it may be considered such—made him a suitable "technical adviser" on the production of several films in the late forties and early fifties, including the Hellinger-Dassin *Naked City*. Cartoonist Will Eisner (1917–), whose father painted scenery for the Lower East Side Yiddish theaters, created the comic strip "The Spirit" in 1940. Its hero Denny Colt, an ex–private eye presumed dead, is free to pursue crime and justice beyond the proscriptions of the law and, in the process, to discover the scope of corruption not apparent to the law-abiding citizenry.

Right up to the present, the vestiges of the original noir sensibility can be found inspired, co-opted, distorted, or degenerated in everything from the paintings of James Rosenquist to the darkly exultant strains of Talking Heads's "Take Me to the River" and the pulsing melancholy of the Eurhythmics's "Love Is a Stranger," and on down to countless television detective series and the Dick Tracy paraphernalia that follows a hit summer release. The resilience here finally becomes one of memory over vision; for if the film noir displays nothing else, it displays the proximity of anxiety, violence, and despair in modern life. Few artifacts can truly copy this.

HUAC AND THE BLACKLIST

> We, the undersigned, as American citizens who believe in constitutional democratic government, are disgusted and outraged by the continuing attempt of the House Committee of Un-American Activities to smear the motion picture industry.
>
> We hold that these hearings are morally wrong because:
> Any investigation into the political beliefs of the individual is contrary to the basic principles of our democracy;
>
> Any attempt to curb freedom of expression and to set arbitrary standards of Americanism is in itself disloyal to both the spirit and the letter of our Constitution.
> —Committee for the First Amendment

The conjuncture of several artists, key in the creation of the film noir, and the government's anticommunist inquisition, which focused on Hollywood during the immediate postwar era, remains a compelling illustration of how the theme of pursuit and persecution—a theme repeatedly noted as central to noir cinema—was to find an actual, historical, basis in the several lives and careers ruined at this perilous time. After the war ended—in fact, in 1945, the very year it ended—the fomenting government sentiment against Communist activity in our native institutions stood in striking contrast to the left-wing popularity that had flourished just a decade earlier in the ferment of Rooseveltian reforms. Mississippi congressman John Rankin moved to make the Un-American Activities Committee of the House of Representatives a standing committee, empowering it with the authority to investigate the lives of those Americans suspected of being Communists, former Communists, or Soviet sympathizers. In the spring of 1947, Republican congressman J. Parnell Thomas, chairman of the committee, commissioned an investigation of Communist infiltration in the unions of the motion picture industry, and by the end of October that year, HUAC had begun its investigations. They subpoenaed screenwriter John Howard Lawson and eighteen others, out of whom would emerge the famous Hollywood Ten who refused to name names in defense of their constitutional right and would be blacklisted from working in Hollywood because of it.[15]

Hollywood's initial reaction to all this was indignation. Several artists, including Humphrey Bogart, Lauren Bacall, Edward G. Robinson, Burt Lancaster, and Billy Wilder, joined John Huston in forming the Committee for the First Amendment. The singular action underscoring the committee's outrage was to send a delegation to Washington formally petitioning against the government's harassment of those in their industry. "But by the time the first hearings were held," Abraham Polonsky recalled, "by the time that plane got back with them to Los Angeles, the Committee for the First Amendment was in a state of absolute disillusion. I went to the various meetings of the Committee, of course, but no one was there by the second meeting. I remember Humphrey Bogart walking around the room saying to everybody 'You sold me out!' He said 'The hell with all of you. If you don't want to fight, I'll take care of myself!' and Bogart stormed out of the room."[16] The internecine tensions would grow increasingly tragic in Hollywood as movie people took sides. Many were sold on a government-inspired national hysteria, but many more responded out of self-preservation in the face of it, and betrayals of friends and colleagues and shattered lives were the result.

John Garfield, like Bogart, Huston, Richard Conte, Jane Wyatt, Evelyn Keyes, and others, signed the declaration, but it was Hollywood's screenwriters, particularly, who felt the wrath of HUAC's investigation. The "artists of that time, *especially* the writers of that time—were more significantly left *en masse* in Hollywood than later, and even before," Polonsky noted.[17] Many of these writers, as well as the actors, directors, and producers who suffered lost deals, no work, career dislocations, and uprooted lives, were significant in giving the film noir its expression in the late forties. It is an appropriate and perverse irony—and to the extent to which it may have been *more* than this, a compelling historical thesis—that the narratives created by these artists spoke to the haunted

He Ran All the Way (1951). No exit: Nick Robey (John Garfield) runs in vain.

and hunted outcasts of an American landscape quite at odds with the optimistic image of American life extolled by the greater Hollywood establishment.[18] The darker vision of such life ensconced in noir cinema could now be insinuated into an ideological purge for the national good and, in the process, would lay just cause to the very impetus that gives the film noir its subversive authority to this day.

Among the artists for whom the blacklist period was indeed a defining "noir" moment in their lives were producer and writer Adrian Scott (*Murder, My Sweet; Deadline at Dawn; Boomerang!*); screenwriters Albert Maltz (*This Gun for Hire, The Naked City*) and Dalton Trumbo (*Gun Crazy* [*Deadly Is the* Female], *The Prowler*); screenwriter and director Abraham Polonsky (*Body and Soul, Force of Evil, Odds against Tomorrow, Madigan*); directors Edward Dmytryk (*Murder, My Sweet; Cornered; Crossfire; The Hidden Room* [*Obsession*]), Jules Dassin (*Brute Force, The Naked City, Thieves' Highway, Night and the City, Rififi*), John Berry (*Tension, He Ran All the Way*), and Joseph Losey (*M, The Prowler, The Big Night*); and actors Marsha Hunt (*Raw Deal*) and John Garfield (*Body and Soul, Force of Evil, The Breaking Point, He Ran All the Way*). Garfield, hounded by the FBI after refusing to name colleagues with former Communist sympathies, succumbed to the strain of persecution and died of a heart attack in New York City in 1952. He was only thirty-nine.

FIGHT PICTURES

Because of its formal and philosophical concerns, the film noir has rarely subsumed the genre of professional sports films. So many sports pictures show the success of individual excellence, or the excellence of the individual in a team effort to win, that they imply in the process a cultivation of personal and moral character. The optimism inherent in such human endeavors reserves defeat as a test to be overcome. The professional boxer and his game, however, is a subgenre that appropriately illustrates the darker side of such a gloss. Because the fight game encompasses many key noir features—its urban roots, the corruption of power and money and of the criminal element so often controlling it, and the violence and near-narcotic dynamism intrinsic in its exercise—fighting and the fight racket have served as a paradigm for the misbegotten illusion its contenders strive for—of freedom, fame, and wealth in a life otherwise rendered anonymous or, at the very least, unimportant.

The fight racket as portrayed in Robert Wise's *Set-Up* (1949), Mark Robson's *Champion* (1949) and *The Harder They Fall* (1956), and most especially Robert Rossen's *Body and Soul* presents a world where energy acquires an existential drive, where a fight to the top promises individual identity ("the Champ," "Toro," "Kid So-and-so") and "taking a dive" prostitutes self-respect and acclaim for money made. The noir sensibility infuses the personal turmoil of John Garfield's Charley Davis and Robert Ryan's Stoker Thompson with bitterness about the available choices, and it is precisely because all that remains is the violence, greed, and blood lust of the crowds that the training gyms and boxing rings of fight pictures serve as compelling arenas for the cruelty of broken dreams in a noir world.

Control and corruption in the noir boxing films merely reflect a comparable ruthlessness in general society. When Humphrey Bogart's Eddie Willis, a sports commentator in *The Harder They Fall*, sacrifices his principles to promote the unpromotable Toro, he knows, as we do, exactly what he is doing: he is promoting a spectacle that will lure the crowds for the personal financial security it brings him. When he can no longer sustain the damage to his self-esteem or set up another sucker fight, he turns on his sponsors and exposes them through his own honorable craft, sportswriting. Budd Schulberg—never one to soft-pedal the venality of human nature in his fiction—wrote the novel upon which Philip Yordan based his screenplay; no other sports picture has so clearly identified money as the lucre of ambition and corruption. Nor has any other sport than boxing been able to show its lure for the desperate—those fighters, has-beens and wannabes who crystallize their hopes on future success in the ring.

In *Champion*, Kirk Douglas's Midge Kelley undergoes a perversion of character on his way to the top, as he uses and betrays everyone in his path. *Champion*, a devastatingly dark tale unappeased by any hope for human redemption, does not even suggest, as most boxing films do, that the animus found in this environment was spawned much earlier in an unfair, cruel, and deprived urban childhood. Franz Planer's photography captures Kelley from ringside perspective in scenes of stark white frontal lighting against a darker miasmic background that make him appear as a dissection of how a troubled, festering character can become a "champion" without remorse. His collapse at the end of the film cannot mitigate the pain he has inflicted on others; rather, it serves to reiterate the lesson of a dying winner who never understood the rules of honorable victory. The Ring Lardner story becomes a neurotic noir fable of the hard contract a champion makes with the loser in himself.

Unlike Midge Kelley, Bill "Stoker" Thompson in *The Set-Up* becomes a casualty of his dignity. Deemed too old at thirty-five to win a minor title, his manager does not even tell him that criminal money has been bet on his loss (by himself, no less). Stoker musters the elemental strength to fight for what he recognizes as his salvation: a reputable win with a modest purse to finance a small business. His illusion sustains him in a milieu that feeds on vain hope—something he knows too well. Robert Ryan, himself an amateur boxer before his film career, evokes in Stoker the wisdom and rue of a man who has reckoned with failure long enough but still gauges his hope in a vital resistance against defeat. It is what makes Stoker Thompson a man of moral gravity, and of sadness. When his wife Julie refuses to undergo the agony of watching him become battered in yet another fight that she knows he will lose ("Don't you see, Bill, you'll always be one punch away"), the camera tracks her as she walks through the local neighborhood attempting to relieve the tension of waiting for the match to end. As she walks, lost in her musing

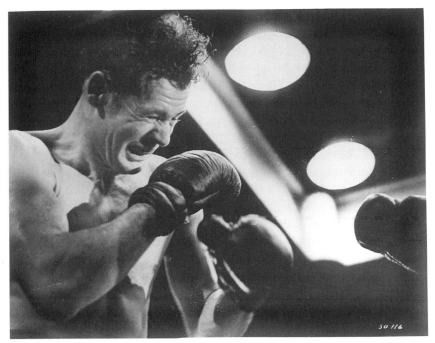

The Set-Up (1949). Robert Ryan as Stoker Thompson: the ring as noir battle-ground.

over their itinerant, misspent life, we see the images of tawdry allure reflecting the pipe dreams of the street's denizens. Blinking neon signs advertise the Paradise City Athletic Club where Stoker is fighting, the cheap Hotel Cozy where they are staying, and the Dreamland Chop Suey restaurant. Her walk ends at a bridge overlooking the noisy subway tracks as the match reaches its finish. The film story is played out in real time—seventy-two minutes—and during the bout, Wise intersperses close-ups of the spectators as they become increasingly hostile by the end of each round. Benign civility gives way to violent passions until Stoker is, finally, declared the victor.

Because Stoker refuses to take a dive, Little Boy's goons crush his hands in a darkened alley. Only Julie can salvage him, and she does so in a display of totally generous love that is rare in the noir cinema. Stoker's enlightened affirmation about the value of his life is born out of her love as he becomes, in James Welsh's words, "an icon for Christ, the 'second Adam,'" having "fall[en] from Paradise into the soiled world of common existence."[19]

A similar salvation occurs in Robert Rossen's *Body and Soul* when Charley Davis finally sees an invitation to spiritual death in the corruption around him. For the sport of boxing in this definitive boxing film delivers much of what the seduction of celebrity promises until personal honor becomes the cost. Corruption and bad money are institutionalized in the fight racket here, and the challenge of violence in the ring undermines the dignity of its combatants. In *Champion*, Midge's promoter notes, "This is the only sport in the world where guys get paid for doing something they'd be arrested for if they got drunk and did it for nothing." In *Body and Soul*, cinematographer James Wong Howe's handheld camera captures fighting as it had never been shown before (and was not seen again until Martin Scorsese's *Raging Bull* [1980]), in a close-up noir boxing ring of fast body punches and bloodied, battered faces. Charley has joined a world of shady maneuvers and accelerating violence, one that has cost him the lives of his best friend and his sparring partner, and he must now face himself and the dilemma he has created: he will not take a dive for the stakes because, after all, he's "no tanker." No other sport has provided the temptation of glory at this steep price and the escalation of moral consequence. Stoker Thompson and Charley Davis become champs in these boxing noirs simply because they have survived to learn this lesson.

CAPER FILMS

As with the boxing films of the late forties, noir cinema found expression in the 1950s through other subgenres particularly sympathetic to its nihilism born of desolation and restlessness. The "wrong (or wronged) man" films of Phil Karlson (*Kansas City Confidential* [1952], *99 River Street*) show the arbitrariness that allows a vulnerable man to suffer for a crime he did not commit but the circumstances of which misrepresent his innocence. It may be his dubious past, a prison term done, or a bad family connection (*The Brothers Rico* [1957]) that destines him to a precarious future increasingly out of his control. It was the flip side of this kind of entrapment that found a striking noir dimension in the caper film, whose stories show instead the meticulous *control* of a group, mostly of men, that schemes to steal money or loot for the freedom it buys. Indeed, the caper film is the most direct expression of the need to have money, money to relieve an intolerable material circumstance or to buy pleasure. Each member of the group, often of disparate viewpoints and appearances, collaborates with other accomplices to form a collective enterprise that functions in this clear defiance of the civil order. The irony is, of course, in the dreams that have driven its members to the point of action, dreams often expressed in the idealized conventional happiness denied them in the very society now threatened by their actions. No film speaks more clearly to such individual motives among the group as Huston's *Asphalt Jungle*, still perhaps the greatest noir caper film, and nothing more clearly expresses the pathos of each member's vision of happiness than Doc Riedenschneider's desire to escape to Mexico, where his share of the loot can buy him the company of attractive Mexican girls. Nor does any film more compellingly express the desperate need for relief from a callous world than this one, in Dix Handley's vain effort to return to the horse farm of his childhood. In Wise's *Odds against Tomorrow*, Johnny Ingram joins forces with, among others, the racist ex-con Earl Slater (beautifully played by Robert Ryan) to heist an upstate New York bank, each person envisioning as his reward a life free from debt and bitterness. The collaboration of misfits, pariahs, and pleasure-seekers often bespeaks the troubled world that

The Killing (1956). Johnny Clay (Sterling Hayden) and company plot a heist.

nurtured them while delineating very disgruntled personalities disruptive to its rules and order.

In *Kansas City Confidential*, the three robbers bound together in anonymous dependence (they wear masks in order not to know each other's identity) are clearly career criminals for whom money is all, but their mastermind is an ex-police detective who seeks this particular revenge against a law enforcement establishment that devalued his commitment to it, forcing his unplanned retirement after a failed robbery investigation. In Kubrick's *Killing*, the cohesiveness of a gang scrupulously assembled to steal racetrack money weakens in suspicions of betrayal and unfulfilled emotional desires (in George and Sherry Peatty) and simply through miscalculation and sheer chance. Johnny Clay loses out precisely because of bad timing, just as Dix Handley fights a losing battle against time and bad luck. (Sterling Hayden plays both roles.) The best-laid plans of such characters crumble by the end of the film, and this defeat is perhaps the harshest judgment of noir nihilism: that the promise and excitement generated by the prospect of successfully pulling one off—against the system, the cops, or the very world that says no to the peripheral social man—is false. The defeat leaves these outsiders with the inevitable negation of their dreams, dreams that money could not buy.

CRIME SYNDICATE EXPOSÉS

Because the film noir is ever so attuned to the criminal milieu, social changes affecting postwar crime found ready expression in many pictures. The gangster portrayed in American cinema had for the most part become an anachronistic and a somewhat romantic figure, one representing an antisocial individualism that clashed with a changing modern world. The Warner Brothers icons James Cagney, Edward G. Robinson, George Raft, and to a lesser extent, Bogart, became cause-and-effect figures, often vicious but just as often vulnerable outsiders who acted against the social order while suggesting that the very cracks within it encouraged their rise to power. The postwar era of crime films challenged this idea of the rebellious criminal personality. The mechanized horrors and destruction of the war modified the home-front consciousness to perceive criminal activity in the starker and more ruthless terms of the modern conglomerate.

It was in 1950 that Humphrey Bogart as Assistant District Attorney Martin Ferguson in *The Enforcer* informed moviegoers that a "syndicate" existed to carry out "contracts." Earlier, in the 1948 *Street with No Name*, the documentary use of FBI files and disclosures foreboded an increasing social menace of criminal activity networked to one mastermind. In late 1948 Mann's *Undercover Man* (released in 1949) fused semidocumentary shooting with expressionistic lighting to tell the story of the Internal Revenue Service's tax-fraud conviction of a murky, Capone-like figure, identified by the press only as "the Big Fellow," who maintains a tight grip over everyone connected with his corrupt enterprise. *The Undercover Man* is one of the earliest films to name the Sicilian Black Hand as the imported heritage behind such social evil. The era of the exposé was inaugurated, and the film noir found in it a sympathetic tool to evoke the ills of modern society at large just as it had dealt with the troubled personal lives within it before. The idea that the film noir is best recognized from the passions and behavior of the individual and that the related philosophical resonances are indicative of a troubled world is understandable and, one may claim, preferable.[20] But the exposés spawned in the fifties claimed a special place in positioning a social change within the accommodating genre of noir cinema—specifically, they announced that organized crime had itself become institutionalized and threatened to undermine the civilized order even as it mimicked it and purchased its respectability through greed and hypocrisy.

In *The Racket*, remade by Howard Hughes's RKO in 1951,[21] gangster Nick Scanlon has it clearly stated by a corporate crime lieutenant that his conduct is brutish and outdated. Their boss (known here simply by the vague appellation "the man"), he is told, does not trade in mayhem and messy rubouts. Such tactics have now been replaced by a more efficient collaboration with the establishment: the right candidates are voted into office, elected officials are bribed, and the police are bought off at the highest level. Murder is clean and untraceable. This film, along with *The Enforcer*, brought the film noir into a changing world, dealing less with personal obsessions than with society's corrupted legal and political institutions.[22] Hopelessness in this context is more than one man's vision of the world; it is a view of modern American life, depersonalized and with its democratic principles undermined.

The Kefauver Crime Hearings

Three events encouraged the American screen's recognition of organized crime as a network infiltrating every avenue of American democracy. In 1949–1950, the murder-for-hire organization infamously known as Murder, Inc. was smashed, thereby providing the subject for Windust's *Enforcer*, filmed later in the summer of 1950.[23] In June 1954 the Democratic candidate for attorney general of Alabama, Albert Patterson, was shot dead when it seemed likely that he would win office and pursue his cleanup of vice in the state, particularly in the town of Phenix City. Phil Karlson's *Phenix City Story*, made the following year, dramatized the public's indulgence of such vice and was intended to serve as a cautionary tale against the growth of other Phenix Citys around the country. During the intervening years, Senator Estes Kefauver of Tennessee had held hearings through the Senate Special Committee to Investigate Organized Crime in Interstate Commerce. Commonly known as the Kefauver Committee, it convened in 1950 to probe the vast criminal enterprise evidenced in operation throughout the country, and it cited the Mafia as its controlling body. The hearings were televised as various mob-connected individuals were questioned. Fifties historian Eric Goldman remembered one Mrs. Virginia Hauser, who "shrugged her mink stole higher on her shoulders, ran a gauntlet of photographers, and left the courthouse yelling at cameramen: 'You bastards, I hope a goddam atom bomb falls on every goddam one of you.' The Kefauver Committee had not exactly proved her role as the bank courier for gangsters. But it had provided quite an education for those thirty million people at TV sets who had known the Virginia Hausers only as a product of Hollywood's imagination."[24] Indeed, for a flip side of this portrait, one need only see Phil Karlson's 1955 *Tight Spot*, where Ginger Rogers, playing a brassy blond of misunderstood reputation, has her prison sentence commuted upon deciding to testify against the Mafia. When asked what her occupation is, Shari Connolly defiantly proclaims to the court and photographers, "Gangbuster!"

Throughout the fifties, organized crime served as the subject matter for a number of exposés, most of them sensationalized and many with lurid undertones. Most of them are not authentic expressions of the film noir; they traded instead on the increasing tabloid popularization of crime in America. Hearst columnist Bob Considine worked on the screenplay for Joseph Kane's *Hoodlum Empire* (1952), which used the Kefauver Hearings as a backdrop.[25] Other films had a "story to tell"—like *The Phenix City Story* but not nearly as resonant—of a particular city, intending to serve up a this-can-happen-in-your-town-too message (*The Las Vegas Story* [1952], *Inside Detroit* [1955], *Chicago Syndicate* [1955],

The Phenix City Story (1955). Noir vision of urban syndicate corruption.

Albert Patterson, Phenix City attorney, received an ultimatum from the under-world.

New Orleans Uncensored [1955], *Miami Exposé* [1956]), or a "confidential" criminal account, implying that certain files exposing the full range of criminal wrongdoing can now, finally, be made known. (*New York Confidential* [1955] and *Chicago Confidential* [1957] have little, if any, of the noir vision of Karlson's *Kansas City Confidential*, which preceded them.) The subject matter was so popular that even a subdivision of New York crime films flourished, among them *Slaughter on Tenth Avenue* (1957), based on Assistant District Attorney William Keating's cleanup of waterfront gangs; *The Case against Brooklyn* (1958); and *The Big Operator* (1959). The best of the exposés—the Karlson films, *The Enforcer*, Lang's *The Big Heat*, Fuller's *Underworld U.S.A.*—retain the isolation characteristic of the noir man trapped in his world, shown through the low-key lighting that expresses its nascent claustrophobia (George Diskant's cinematography in *Kansas City Confidential*, for instance, shows this). Here, characters in despair or fear are often framed in close shot; and despite the incursion in many fifties crime movies of a television photography that dulls the screen with a monochromatic wash, the exceptional works among these films remind us that the film noir could be transmutable without losing its essential style.

ANTHONY MANN (1906–1967)

Desperate (1947)
Railroaded! (1947)
T-Men (1947)
Raw Deal (1948)
Side Street (1950)

Anthony Mann directed a remarkable series of low-budget films noirs between 1947 and 1950 that display a vivacity of atmosphere rarely seen in Hollywood filmmaking. With cinematographers John Alton, George Diskant, and Joseph Ruttenberg, Mann haloed his noir victims, in an atmosphere of darkness and shadows, with dramatic rays of light and pulsing urban scenes accentuating the panic they feel in a misstep taken (*Side Street*) or vengeance encountered (*Desperate*) or the torment of relinquishing love and desire (*Raw Deal*). *Desperate* and *Raw Deal* are two of the most beautifully photographed low-budget movies of the immediate postwar years. Stunningly shot in an almost painterly chiaroscuro, the Eagle-Lion releases (*T-Men* and *Raw Deal*) and *Desperate* constitute a textbook of low- and high-angle and wide-angle shooting and of the use of low-key lighting design to magnify and distort screen space.

Mann's characters, like Lang's, are trapped in a constricting world; but unlike Lang's, they are victims of an internal struggle against the very willfulness that imperils them. The irrevocable course events take in Mann's films forces his protagonists to confront some of the most tension-filled moments in the noir. This kind of fatal reckoning results from the combustion of the human psyche as it clashes with the violence induced by a noir formalism of forever-shifting visual abstraction. However, it becomes more complicated: characters like Patricia Regan, Steve Randall, and especially Joe Norson reckon with moral and emotional crises that, quite uncomplementarily, reinforce the antagonism of the world surrounding them. Beyond simply displaying his characters' fear and dread at the outcome of whatever human frailty caused them to act in jeopardy, Mann created an independent and hostile environment that not only reflects but also feeds their fearful uncertainty. Alton's cinematography is indeed the perfect objective correlative to Mann's vision here, for it becomes the very definition of low-key lighting as the chief component in creating a noir sensibility. Darkness, and the shadows it produces, noted Stephen Neale, "not only signifies concealment, invoking an unknown and unseen presence within it . . . it is also a figure of absence and lack. Darkness is the edge between presence (that which it conceals) and absence (that which it is), and its ambiguity in this respect is reflected in its status *vis à vis* the cinematic signifier on the one hand and the diegesis on the other. It is not fully, completely and unambiguously a property of the narrative world, yet neither is it a property of the cinematic as such. It hovers, oscillates between the two, thereby inscribing scopophilia and epistemophilia in relation to both."[26] It is precisely within this formal code, within this object that is yet not of cinematic design—this darkness—that Mann's characters must seek to reckon with their choices in the noir world that greets them.

In *Raw Deal*, Pat Regan's head is captured in a dark side-lit profile next to a ticking wall clock, and in exquisite juxtaposition to its bright aura, as precious minutes pass before she can bring herself to tell Joe Sullivan that the vicious Rick Coyle is holding Ann Martin hostage. Knowing that Joe truly loves Ann and that he will risk his life to save her—this, moments after his empty marriage proposal to Pat—she is

Raw Deal (1948). Revenge is mine 1: Joe Sullivan (Dennis O'Keefe) confronts Rick Coyle (Raymond Burr).

wrenched with ambivalence between securing her own illusion of happiness with him and losing it by telling him of Ann's distress. The scene intensifies when Mann shows Pat's face within the clock now enlarged as suspense builds and time runs out. When she finally tells him, she knows she has lost him. Pat's struggle, often spoken in voice-over and enshrouded in doom, is remarkable for the introspection that is evident in a deeply romantic interpretation of the *femme fatale*, self-sacrificing and complicated here by her recognition that true love can never be tooled or manipulated solely by desire. Pat Regan emerges as the resurrected *femme fatale* in her sadness, especially as portrayed by Claire Trevor, who invested a subtle melancholy in her portrayal of some of noir cinema's more complex women of the 1940s.[27] Not venal or truly malevolent, Pat instead embodies a tragic anxiety in selfish desire that Mann dissects in the context of an ever-increasing noir tension.

It is a moral tension not unlike Steve Randall's in *Desperate*. Inadvertently caught up in a getaway plan for Walt Radak's heist, Steve resists abetting the gang's escape and faces their wrath. With the life of his pregnant wife threatened, he takes out an insurance policy on his own life, fully prepared to die in his encounter with Radak. Steve has be-

come that resistant challenger, scared but alert and expecting Radak to
hunt him down in revenge for his brother's capture and imminent execution. Early in the film, he sustains a fierce beating by Radak's men, and
his isolation is shown in a brilliant low-key-lighted intimidation scene
where he sits bloodied under a stark, swinging lamplight, shot in slightly
high angle. The light, still swinging back and forth, falls on and off
Radak's face as he watches the brutal moment with satisfaction. Later in
the story, Steve is recaptured by him as the camera closes in on alternating shots of Steve's sweating face and Radak's face. An alarm clock is
shot showing only minutes to go before Radak's brother is executed, at
which time Steve too will be killed. As the minutes pass, the clock becomes a more visually prominent object, shots of which now alternate
between close-ups of Steve's eyes, Radak's eyes, and those of his henchmen. Fear and vengeance and time running out—Mann crystallizes the
essence of these elements. And if the clock motif symbolized internal

Desperate (1947). Revenge is mine 2: Walt Radak (Raymond Burr) determines
to avenge his brother's death as Shorty (Freddie Steele) looks on.

struggle (Pat Regan's) in *Raw Deal*, it does so here, too, in the expectation of a young man's death because of an entanglement he never would have chosen. "Who was it that said 'time flies'?" Radak grimly taunts.

Mann shows violence in these films as the characteristic of a volatile sociopathic temperament often encountered unexpectedly. In *Desperate* and *Raw Deal*, Raymond Burr plays such heavies well. His Radak is obsessed with violence as a tool of control. His Rick Coyle in *Raw Deal* is indiscriminately sadistic, treating one innocent partyer who bumps into him with a flambéed chafing dish thrown in her face (a precursor to Vince Stone's graphic moment in *The Big Heat* when he buries a lighted cigarette in a barfly's hand). In *T-Men*, Mann shoots a particularly cruel moment when Wallace Ford's Schemer is betrayed as an expendable figure in a counterfeiting racket and set up for death in a steam bath. Taking a steam with one of the ring's henchmen, he feels the water temperature rise as the door to the steam bath is closed and locked. He pounds unheard from inside, and we see his terror-stricken face screaming in silent panic through the foggy window as the killer looks away from the outside. Such moments startled precisely because they were new, visceral, and very much the product of a postwar change in the quality and intensity of contemporary violence represented on screen.

T-Men uses a voice-of-God narration to introduce the serious mission of the Treasury Department's law enforcement unit, with a further concession to semidocumentary style that has a Treasury enforcer read a scripted account of the vast responsibilities of his agency. This voice-over is used throughout, as in many semidocumentary noirs, to present historical facts and thereby redeem the mere entertainment value of the film with a sense of gravity.[28] *T-Men* blends this approach with gorgeous Alton cinematography, making Mann one of the few noir directors capable of combining expressionistic lighting with the semidocumentary look indulged in by the studios at the time. But Mann and his cinematographers understood the separate provinces of interior and exterior space and the compositional and lighting demands of each as they may be seamlessly woven into one whole narrative. *Side Street* is an example of this, and the difference between the two films illustrates the changing style of noir filmmaking. *T-Men* has a diffused, darkly lighted scene showing an informant gunned down in a railroad freight yard at the beginning of the film; it establishes the corruption infiltrated in society and the danger involved in uprooting it. Scenes in the Schemer's hotel

Side Street (1950). Joe Norson (Farley Granger) finds an opportunity to escape the anonymity of the noir world.

room are dark, too; the settings have an intoxicating quality, alluding to the mystery of who is masterminding the counterfeiting operation. In *Side Street*, Joe Norson's theft of blackmail money simultaneously underscores his own moment of guilt in having stolen some of it and the impersonality—rather, the depersonalization—of a New York City where his plight is lost among the anonymous crowd. Joe's moment of desperation is highlighted precisely because his is one of many in a city of many stories to be told. Mann's overhead opening shot of New York, with the police captain's voice-over describing the complex panorama of the city and its people, connects us with a real place in time. "Filming in natural settings doubled the scene's veracity," said Mann, "and, consequently, shaped the film by giving it an often unexpected appearance and consistency. I liked the element of chance that could always be introduced."[29] Cinematographer Joseph Ruttenberg shot his famous documentary, *Berlin: Symphony of a City*, in 1929, showing a similar urban grandeur, and here Mann takes the documentary elements of Ruttenberg's shots of New York City life and gradually retreats to the dramatic tension generated in the life of one of its people.

Joe Norson, Steve Randall, and the framed Steve Ryan in *Railroaded!* are all returned veterans—Norson, like Randall, with an expectant wife. Steve Randall is content trying to build a family life but finds himself caught up in something bad. Joe, however, is caught short trying to eke out a survival. The war veteran as a figure in the noir landscape evokes a particular sympathy in his vulnerability as a man lost in a world full of change and dislocations. Joe Norson fights for survival in a harsh urban battleground where military service has transient importance and becomes not so much dishonored as simply unusable. To appease his wife, Ellen, who gives birth in the city clinic that he wanted to spare her from, he tells her that some of the money she has noticed in his possession was advanced from an old army buddy who has a job waiting for him upstate. The relief in her face at the thought of a regular paycheck coming in is shot in a soft-focus aura of serenity found. That Farley Granger and Cathy O'Donnell play these roles just after having made Nicholas Ray's *They Live by Night* allows us to compare images of a dispossessed young couple. In Ray's film, Bowie and Keechie are victims of ignorance, betrayal, and an unheeding society; in *Side Street*, Joe Norson is a victim of something more insidious and disturbing, even though he lives and Bowie is gunned down. He comes back to a noir world that promises little yet excites much. Scenes of commerce, of those who have and those who want or need, surround him. The city in all its images of pleasure and moneyed happiness juxtaposed with those of the hoi polloi of subway riders and office ants—all provoke an anxious loss of self-control that undermines moral resolve. Mann shows Joe's predicament with sympathy. Joe Norson's moment of weakness in theft and the blackmailers who pursue him for their money nearly cost him his life. Mann lets him survive the awkward and perilous course he takes to save it, but there is no promise that the world to which he returns will assuage the hardships that one desperate, seductive moment on a side street promised to do.

Anthony Mann's least interesting noir, *Railroaded!*, lacks the dramatic tension between character and environment generated in his other work, but it has a climax that displays the imaginative use of light and space that we see in his other noirs, and one that makes an argument for Mann as a visual architect of the genre. Here in the last sequence of the story, we are returned to the Club Bombay, owned by gangster Duke Martin, who framed a young Steve Ryan for robbery and the murder of a cop. Ryan's sister, out to prove his innocence, is lured to the club by Martin, in whom she has feigned interest in an attempt to expose him. He intends to kill her because he has learned of her complicity with the police. She has been followed inside by Mickey Ferguson, the detective who believes in her bother's innocence and does not want to see her hurt. As they enter the club after hours, it is dark inside. The camera pans slowly over the chairs upturned on the tables—so darkly lighted that the chair legs alternately suggest cover and entrapment, and their composition achieves a kind of abstract expressionism. Duke fires his gun in their midst, and the camera continues to pan throughout this murky gunplay until we see Martin finally killed. The sequence is remarkable in a well-done but not exceptional programmer. Mann created a distinctive moment here, in a haze of darkness, which with its rare light accompanies his other more memorable work in fear and doubt.

PHIL KARLSON (1908–1985)

Scandal Sheet (1952)
Kansas City Confidential (1952)
99 River Street (1953)
Hell's Island (1955)
Tight Spot (1955)
The Phenix City Story (1955)
The Brothers Rico (1957)

Between 1952 and 1957, Phil Karlson made several films noirs that characterized the changing manner of noir expression in the fifties. Karlson used the evocative lighting of cinematographers Burnett Guffey (*Scandal Sheet*, *Tight Spot*, *The Brothers Rico*), George Diskant (*Kansas City Confidential*), and Franz Planer (*99 River Street*) to display a classical chiaroscuro richness in many sequences while using on-location sets and story themes prevalent in many crime dramas of the decade. His leading noir characters, always men and best portrayed by John Payne, who starred in three Karlson noirs—*Kansas City Confidential*, *99 River Street*, and *Hell's Island*—are invariably trapped by a flawed past in a web of present-day circumstances that generate fear of being caught for a crime they did not do. Indeed, the Karlson-Payne films, particularly *Kansas City Confidential* and *99 River Street*, are among the decade's most compelling cinematic correlatives to the terror evoked in Cornell Woolrich's fiction; yet this interior turmoil is contained in actions governed by a fifties milieu of often brutal criminal activity now seen as intrinsic to America's social foundation.

The Brothers Rico and, to a lesser extent, the exposé *The Phenix City Story* depict a world where, as in Lang's *Big Heat* and Fuller's *Underworld U.S.A.*, the individual becomes indispensable to the purposes of institutionalized corruption. "His movies are remarkable for their endless outlay of scary cheapness in detailing the modern underworld," Manny Farber noted in 1957.[30] But if that were all, Karlson would simply be an interesting cultural sociologist of the screen exposé. What rivets our attention to his films noirs is the recognition of modern postwar America as a landscape that has reduced the individual, left him alone and lonely and in the grasp of these dangerous forces that seek to control him. A twist on this theme is depicted in *Scandal Sheet*, based on Samuel Fuller's novel *The Dark Page*, which revels in presenting the ruthless tactics of tabloid journalism as among the most dehumanizing activities in American urban culture. As a sharp young reporter, Fuller became familiar with the creation of scandal and the exploitation of tragedy, and Karlson explores the topic well, showing the pathos behind the Lonely Hearts Club Dance sponsored by the *New York Express* to boost circulation and offering a bed with built-in television as a grand-prize wedding gift to the lucky couple that meets and marries. It will be editor Mark Chapman's secret, however, that lands his protégé and ace reporter Steve McCleary the story of his career; and it is Chapman's entrapment in murder and deceit that takes *Scandal Sheet* into the realm of noir guilt.

When Chapman returns to a Bowery hock shop to claim his dead wife's pawn ticket, the solid evidence incriminating him as her long-lost husband and murderer, he encounters veteran reporter Charlie Barnes, now an aging alcoholic whom Chapman has derisively dismissed from any possibility of returning to the paper. Charlie mistakenly got the claim ticket in some dollar bills with which Chapman brushed him aside on their previous meeting in the neighborhood and now knows him to be the killer. The scene of Chapman and Charlie in the nearby alley at night, with gleaming cars passing by in the glow of street lights, is typical of many Karlson moments, shot close in low-angle and chiaroscuro lighting as his characters, tense and sweating, face moments of entrapment.

The mythical replay of the Oedipal theme in *Scandal Sheet*, where Chapman is literally smitten by his "son" McCleary (who will presumably inherit the mantle of his power), appeals more to Fuller's imagina-

Scandal Sheet (1952). Mark Chapman (Broderick Crawford) corners Charlie Barnes (Henry O'Neill), who can implicate him in his ex-wife's murder.

tion than to the noir environment that traps Chapman in his office, partially obscured by the light of a desk lamp as he attempts to elude notice by the justice of the peace brought in to identify the man he married to the murdered woman twenty-one years earlier. With no escape, Chapman meets the only real challenge to his heartlessness when he must decide whether to kill Steve McCleary before, finally, being shot dead by the police.

The past that haunts the present, that serves as a component in foreboding a terrible future, is the central nightmare in Karlson's world, and it is most clearly realized in his first two films with John Payne, *Kansas City Confidential* and *99 River Street*. In both films, the Payne characters come into the stories with lives broken in the past that leave them bitter but stronger, and quite without warning they find themselves in a harsh battle with fate. Joe Rolfe's frame-up in *Kansas City Confidential* enrages him as he seeks to exonerate his appearance of guilt in a bank robbery. He did time on a gambling rap, and the suspicion because of this past lands him in jail, where the striking pattern of vertical lines reflected in a low-lit jail cell reinforces the terror of an arbitrary world

Kansas City Confidential (1952). An unwitting Joe Rolfe (John Payne) is framed as an accomplice to robbery.

where you can be picked up for nothing you have done wrong. Released, Rolfe assumes the guise of one of the robbers—unknown, as they are, to each other—and tracks down his cohorts one by one, determined to find the robbery's mastermind. As the Mexican authorities shoot one of them, Rolfe, but feet away, watches as Pete Harris (beautifully played by an early Jack Elam) crumples slowly to his death; Rolfe is dreading the man's last-breath opportunity to betray Rolfe's true identity. When he is beaten by the other two, Kane and Romano, at their rendezvous on a Caribbean island, low-angle shots in low-key lighting maintain the tension of how much physical punishment Rolfe can take without relenting. These moments are tests in Karlson's world, as much of violence as of the psychological resilience his characters need to withstand persecution. And invariably they are shown in close shots. Unlike the close-up, which is inspective, the close shot for filmmakers like Karlson is isolating: men take their punches, as we see in John Payne's battered face, and confront their fear in the image of their battered, sweaty faces—alone.

The final irony here, as in *Tight Spot*, is found in the corruption of policemen who betray their law enforcement role for money and revenge; they are a telling factor in the personal stories of those hunted. Foster, the detective in *Kansas City Confidential*, masterminded the robbery, just as Vince in *Tight Spot* engaged Shari Connolly in the ruse intended to be her setup for murder. Unlike *The Phenix City Story* and *The Brothers Rico*, where law enforcement corruption is cold-bloodedly institutionalized, these policemen are still violable individuals who perhaps bespeak the root of human weakness just as it is about to turn irrevocably bad.

99 River Street is Karlson's best film noir and one that defines well the defeated noir protagonist in the postwar era. Ernie Driscoll is a social representative of a world that encourages success and its rewards. As a frustrated man of lost possibilities, he knows the exhilaration of having "a chance at the top," as he tells Linda. "It's the most important thing in the world." A victim of an eye injury in the boxing ring, he has been reduced to a person without accomplishment in a world that "knows you only if it can exploit you." He drives a taxi now, and his unfaithful wife cannot stand it.

Driscoll, like Rolfe, is no stranger to violence, but unlike him, and poignantly so, he has not learned callousness from his setbacks. Ernie and his actress-friend Linda James, with whom he shares cups of drugstore coffee and sympathy, are characters attenuated by bad breaks in life in the manner that only creative people recognize. Their sensitivity, encouraged by performance—he in the fight ring and she on stage—exempts them from a total submission to noir hell. They function, as dreamers do, in a world all too often out of touch with their needs. It is interesting that Linda deceives Ernie into believing she killed a man in rage and self-defense for an acting audition, but she delivers her greatest "performance" (certainly the best screen time of Evelyn Keyes's career) when she attempts to seduce Pauline Driscoll's killer with what must surely be one of the most erotically charged scenes in American cinema up to then, replete with insinuations of welcome rough sex. Her ruse, filmed in a medium-close panning shot of seemingly endless length, displays a rare moment of the metamorphic noir woman, a creature here who performs against her type to reveal a nonetheless compelling, dark side of her personality.

Linda meets her counterpart in Ernie, who responds with equal passion when he punches her producer for encouraging her "murder" deception. He has been used yet again, and quite unexpectedly, and it has fueled his anger. Similarly, when the police suspect him of Pauline's murder, he knows only to pursue those who are guilty with clever yet indignant rage. As he courses toward the jewel thieves responsible for his predicament, Ernie shows his experience in dealing with violent men; and Karlson subjects him, like Mike Cormack in *Hell's Island*, to several vicious beatings—especially on the ship at the end of the story—that stimulate the very pugilistic impulse that promised Ernie success in the ring. "In a work of art intensity and speed can be creative forces, generating beauty and significance; outside of art, they can be, and often are, destructive," wrote Jack Shadoian of the film. "*99 River Street* uses the American dynamism to condemn it; this is where it and other films of its period differ from similar films of the thirties and forties. Their insistence, often to the point of exaggeration (a valid method in art), is, whether consciously or not, a moral one. . . . Yet films like *99 River Street* have no obvious moral ax to grind—one has to feel their bitterness."[31] That Ernie Driscoll becomes a victim pursued for murder is particularly unkind; our sympathy for him was won early in this story when two lonely people struggle to make themselves heard in a world that has already given them too little cause for notice, too little voice.

The Phenix City Story, *Tight Spot*, and *The Brothers Rico* detail much of what Farber meant in referring to the nastiness in organized crime, and all three were made shortly after the Kefauver hearings impressed the nation with the pernicious magnitude of such activity. In all three films, the main characters must eventually stand alone in battling this force; in the process they discover themselves in the predicament of the noir figure—hunted and scared. In themselves, *The Phenix City Story* and *Tight Spot* do owe as much to the crime dramas of the thirties as to the noirs that followed. (There are parallels in story and character between the 1937 *Marked Woman* with Bette Davis and *Tight Spot* with Ginger Rogers.) The distinguishing mark of these films, however, is the vision of modern American life as a totally corrupt construct that consumes the powerless individual—in striking contradiction to the reformist message of good citizenship in so many Warner Brothers melodramas of an earlier generation.

In *The Phenix City Story*, reformist politics invites deadly consequences; John Patterson discovers this when the assassination of his prosecutor father[32] and the particularly vicious murder of a child scare the citizenry into tacit compliance with the vice overlords' choke hold on the town's economy. Karlson opens the story with a honky-tonk sequence, panning through the interior of a clip joint to show the thriving local corruption. He tracks throughout the club strip, effectively capturing the on-location setting of "Phenix City," with an especially striking track through the street of gaudy, neon-lighted honky-tonks, bars, and casinos at night. Tanner, the vice leader, is caught in dramatic front lighting during a nighttime cleanup rally. The implications are clear, and they are consistent with the Kefauver warning of the time: established family and community values have encountered the urban threats of prostitution and vice and its diversions. The townspeople, Patterson declares, must fight "to clean up the gambling hells of Phenix City!" Everyone is victimized by silence and denial. Karlson is unremitting in his display of grim violence here, including the rather graphic running down of Zeke Ward's little boy. *The Phenix City Story* advances the fifties movement in cinema toward showing African Americans in comparatively uncondescending roles, here by having Zeke admit to a lifetime of facing his own brand of injustice in an attempt to keep Patterson from killing Tanner. (Played by James Edwards of Mark Robson's 1949 *Home of the Brave*, Zeke is a distinctive yet underappreciated variation of the roles that made Sidney Poitier a star.) But John Patterson finds himself crusading essentially alone in this battle, and he comes to understand that the project of fighting institutionalized corruption speaks to his own need for self-definition. As an exposé, *The Phenix City Story* thrives as a cautionary tale about the incursion of volatile urban elements in small-town life and about submission to protected lawlessness. Its message would certainly appeal to any reactionary contingency suspicious of the lures of the big city, but its fight is that of an individual, that of one man devoured in a corrupt world that denies him a decent life. It is the other side of the noir world, an exteriorizing of turmoil from the troubled, interior man to the damaged American landscape.

Like this film, *Tight Spot* and *The Brothers Rico* find their protagonists essentially alone, in a tight spot against the criminal organization. Shari Connolly testifies against the mob because she finally realizes that she can make a difference when Willoughby, her prison escort, is struck by a bullet intended for her. Willoughby had a teenage daughter with a bright future, but now the tragedy that leaves her orphaned speaks to Shari's own experience of adolescent abandonment, which led to her present life. Ginger Rogers plays Shari Connolly with some of the hokiest moll humor heard—even for the time—but with the wisdom of someone who knows the world and the price she will play for testifying. Her civic duty invoked, she replies sarcastically, "Well, if anybody's gotten anything but a kick in the face from society, I don't doubt he might give something back to it." But, of course, she does, and, quite like the John Payne characters, she faces the dilemma shaped by her troubled past as she seeks fair treatment in recognition of having paid for it. She asks of the world, like they ask: "What about me?" Burnett Guffey photographed *Tight Spot* and *The Brothers Rico*, alternating on-location shots with more low-key lighting than that used in other noirs of the period—many increasingly influenced by the look of television. The bathroom scene, where Vince, her cop-on-the-take guard, leaves the small high window open at night for Shari's killer to enter, is shot close, with streaks of outside light revealing his sweaty ambivalence about setting her up after his growing attraction to her. Again, the high tension of Karlson's characters trapped by circumstances or consequences precedes the inevitable reckoning by which, here, Vince will allow himself to take the bullet for Shari.

In *The Brothers Rico*, Karlson made an important contribution to the crime exposé noir. He showed the changing environment and relationships in criminal conduct through characters who span the development of crime from the recent past, when honor was at least a courtesy accorded the individual, to the present, when criminal enterprise has so dehumanized its activities as to annul past family loyalties. Based on the novel *Les Frères Rico* by Georges Simenon, the three brothers in the film provide an extended link through changing criminal behavior over the years. Eddie, portrayed by noir icon Richard Conte, sees his brothers rubbed out by the syndicate for having been in on a job investigated by the district attorney's office. The murders were ordered by organization boss Sid Kubik, a childhood friend of Eddie's, whose life was saved by Eddie's mother when she stepped between him and a bullet and was left crippled. The connection between criminal eras past and present and the attitudes shaping them is reflected in the settings of the film. On-location shots of Miami and New York are used, but a noir photography is seen here more than in other syndicate exposés of the fifties, notably in the trap laid for Eddie's youngest brother, Johnny, who, terrified in a close shot, sweats out in fear his eventual entrapment in a farmhouse hideout before finally being killed. This chiaroscuro effect combines well with the brighter-lit art moderne setting of Eddie and his wife's home and of Kubik's hotel suite—both also in sharp contrast to Mama Rico's apartment behind her candy store in Little Italy, where she thrills over her new "icebox" from Eddie and Grandma is fascinated with the new TV. Eddie and his wife want to live "respectable" lives and adopt a child, but, typical of Karlson's work, Eddie's past involvement with the organization (doing accounting for them) puts him at their mercy—indeed, his respectability as the owner of laundries in southern Florida was probably financed with bad money. The Italian background is established here, and the evolution to a sterile modern world of corruption for the brothers is Karlson's vision of a cold, bloodless, and perhaps more violent world where they finally become expendable.

When Johnny is set up by the paid-off sheriff, he steps out into his trap through the front door of the farmhouse to meet his executioners (frame right) while the sheriff comes out of the hotel room bath wiping his hands in a matching shot following. Eddie's brother is gunned down with the tacit complicity of the law. Mama Rico remarked in her immigrant's voice earlier—"I don't know no more what's right and what's wrong!" Karlson shows us here and in his other exposés a noir landscape of institutionalized corruption in a postwar American society where the distinctions between right and wrong have been similarly effaced; and he shows us the disorientation of his characters, whose noir misfortune it is to revisit the sins of their past as they try to escape them into an uncertain future.

THE NOIR INFLUENCE ON THE FRENCH NEW WAVE

The French romance with American culture extends back to the turn of the previous century and before, but the appeal of American popular art stems from the interwar and immediate postwar attraction to products elusively appealing in their liberating vulgarity. What do we find valuable, even ennobling, in Bogart and Wayne, in Rita Hayworth and Lauren Bacall? Nothing less than the effrontery of a public to insist that they merit serious attention in the face of an expanded commercial film enterprise that generally reduces distinctions, homogenizes heroism, and dilutes genuine tragedy. The images of gangster and western heroes, much more than those of most comic heroes who speak primarily to native temperaments, reward the filmgoer with a satisfaction that the human image, if not always the human conscience, matters in an aesthetically satisfying exercise. The consequences of a century riddled with war on European soil has woven into the fabric of native lives the awareness that life can always diminish one's expectations and hopes; it has made American optimism on the big screen a consumer good more satisfying in its conviction than any local brand could be. Hence, even in the pessimism of the American film noir lies a vitality that belies death, even as such death energizes the forlorn state of its protagonists. Perhaps the great connection between the American film noir and the French nouvelle vague is best thought of in terms of the philosophical implications of life and death as seen in the disruptions and resumed continuity of the French narratives, which never forsake their graceful ritual. The filmmakers who grew up during the war and discovered in adolescence and

À bout de souffle (1959). Play acting: Michel Poiccard's (Jean-Paul Belmondo) insouciance.

young adulthood the effervescence of Hollywood B cinema appreciated the vitality of this moviegoing experience as an honest expression of a screen sensibility unfettered by the forces of premeditation (from the studios, of the marketing and bourgeois conventions that publicized film fare) and lent an excitement by the force of speed and its intuitive grace. For the style of the New Wave cinema most directly inspired by American noir filmmaking, more specifically, crime genre movies, spoke of the nonchalance of the arbitrary act, tinged with a bit of subversiveness.

Of course, not all the New Wave and New Wave–inspired filmmakers referred to American B noirs. Most, in fact, did not. But for Godard (*À bout de souffle, Bande à part, Alphaville, Pierrot le fou*), Truffaut (*Tirez sur le pianiste, La Mariée était en noir, La Sirène du Mississippi, Vivement dimanche!*), Michel Deville (*Lucky Jo*), Alain Corneau (*La Menace, Série Noire*), and even Jean-Pierre Mocky (*La Cité de l'indicible peur, Solo*), among others, the guns and violence of the Monogram cheapies expressed the senselessness, perhaps to be made stylish, hip, to be desensitized in order to be perceived anew, of a continent still troubled by the aftermath of the midcentury's assaults of wars and globalization and the taint they undoubtedly left on the succeeding generation that was coming of age.

No account of the American film noir's influence on the nouvelle vague can begin without recognizing one of the key figures of postwar French cinema, Jean-Pierre Melville. As an acknowledged precursor to the stylistic philosophy of the movement, Melville infused his films noirs with a reverence for the form and manner of noir melancholy and heroism. Without him, Charlie/Édouard in François Truffaut's *Tirez sur le pianiste* (1960) and Michel Poiccard in Jean-Luc Godard's *À bout de souffle* (1959) would fly weightless, without reference or richness, and the laughter of their inside jokes would have quickly expired. *Bob le flambeur* bequeathed elegance to the dubious character of Charlie, the piano player who attempts to maintain asceticism in a most public role, as the purveyor of sad or brassy tunes, a tinkler who wants to exempt himself from the responsibilities of the present because he cannot bear the painful consequences of his past. The Aznavour character achieves the kind of harsh, pathetic glamour that is equally attractive in another mode, that of the amoral play actor and petty criminal, Michel, in Godard's movie.

> Arthur said they'd wait for night to do the job out of respect for second-rate thrillers."
> —Narrator in *Bande à part* (1964)

The influence of American cinema, particularly the American film noir, on the filmmaking consciousness of Jean-Luc Godard has by now become legendary, certainly to the world of film study and to his fans. However, Godard's work isolated in this particular consideration reshapes our perceptions of the contemporary uses of noir cinema. For Godard approached film noir as a modern structure of communication, however failed, in the relationships between men and women and of people to their contemporary society in all its political, humanist, and consumerist dissonances. Most of all, he has deconstructed the mythic illusions of the genre as he has used them to deconstruct the realities of his life. In this Godard disavowed much that he obviously grew up loving about American cinema; but the odyssey of love, disavowal, and then rediscovery only better defines Godard's sensibility from *À bout de souffle* in 1959 to *Détective* in 1985. With a twenty-five-year gap between them, Godard has come to do what he felt necessary back in 1962, when he said about Michel in *À bout de souffle*: "I decided that my avowed ambition was to make ordinary gangster films; I had no business deliberately contradicting the genre: he must die. If the House of Atreus no longer kill each other, they are no longer the House of Atreus."[1] The connection of American noir cinema to the nouvelle vague was efficiently summed up by Alfred Appel twenty-five years ago, when he wrote: "When Jean-Paul Belmondo stands before the icon-like poster of Bogart in *Breathless*, touches his own curled lip, and intones 'Bogey,' director Jean-Luc Godard gives us a deathless image of the degree to which life *does* imitate art, in the most willful and fatal sense of that cliché. Godard himself appears in the film to denounce his hero to the police, a self-consciously symbolic act that articulates the director's ambivalent feelings toward his own creation as well as the manner in which American gangster films may have in turn created *him*, unhappily enough."[2] Long after the contentiousness of politics and aesthetics surrounding 1960s modernist cinema subsided, it is the one image that resonates the awareness that the American film noir had for Godard and Truffaut when it spoke of the possibility of much more than graceful misbehavior: it also signified the capacity for attractive rebellion and the freedom of movement masking a melancholy that the new cinema spoke of in style and technique.

Godard's Belmondo in *À bout de souffle* and *Pierrot le fou* goes from being a criminal desiring escape to Italy to a fugitive needing to get away from the morass of consumerism and contemporary dispiritedness. That both films are about ideas such as betrayal, isolation, and, indeed, a certain aesthetic finesse stems from the rejectable in modern culture. And what effrontery to modern culture could be more rejectable than American B crime films? That the French respected the hard-boiled American fiction of David Goodis and Woolrich made sympathy for B noirs easier to understand. However, what is so peculiarly modern about

Bande à part (1964). Arthur (Claude Brasseur) and Franz (Sami Frey): planning a robbery the way the big boys do.

the New Wave's reference to the American film noir is the French tendency to give screen time to this genre over others. The Italian cinema found the western an easier genre to adopt for commercial purposes and to reflect their national temperament, and the Japanese used the western to allude to their formal past and the science fiction film as a metaphor for the horror of their more modern history (Hiroshima and Nagasaki). But the French have found in the crime drama and its history in literature and film the sensibility so imitative of our own in form and spirit.[3]

In *À bout de souffle*, Godard has taken the form of the B crime drama and in a seemingly perfunctory fashion displayed it in all its truth and contrivance to show the nature of human action, its unknown motivations, and its consequences in terms of life and death, of love and passion, and of an existence devoid of both. The idea develops that psychology gives little philosophical weight to the consequences of our actions. Hence, Patricia's betrayal of Michel makes her a "bitch" because Michel expected her to behave otherwise; she, in contrast, betrays no recognition of pain, remorse, or love. Michel emulates in perhaps the most iconic and philosophically bankable image in popular cinema,that of Humphrey Bogart, here in a poster advertising his last film, *The Harder They Fall*, an elegiac reference to honorable comportment. What a filmmaker like Godard took from American noir cinema, finally, was nothing less than the terrifying glamour of social isolation with its insouciant arrogance, ideological annulment, and rejection of convention, and he attached it to his protagonists, from Michel Poiccard to Arthur to Ferdinand, and, in the distinct inability to connect emotionally, to Natasha Von Braun and her private eye protector, Lemmy Caution, in *Alphaville*. When Godard jailed his characters in his attempt to create a true film noir story, as he did twenty years later with *Détective*, complete with plot complications, sexual liaisons, and cursory psychological motivation, he stumbled. It was as if, for him, respecting the conventions of the genre could no more be achieved than it could be for Truffaut, who, in quite different fashion, took the film noir as a touchstone to explore his themes of romance and love and passion. Truffaut, an ardent admirer of Cornell Woolrich, modeled an affectionate homage to the Woolrich universe in his last film, *Vivement dimanche!* but completely drained it of the terror the unknown brings in Woolrich and substituted instead the comedy of manners that makes Fanny Ardant so incredibly appealing here. It harks back to the days of the Hollywood studio noir, of *Phantom Lady*

Tirez sur le pianiste (1960). Charlie Koller (Charles Aznavour): the poignancy of the loner.

and *The Dark Corner*, and makes us nostalgic in the best sense for the love of cinema that nurtured a generation of postwar French film critics. It is a different appeal from that of the film noir, but it is nonetheless related.

In Truffaut's world, we must return to Charlie Koller, attractive in his isolation in *Tirez sur le pianiste*. His identity is that of an individual, alone. Unlike Godard's characters, Charlie has a past and has not forgotten the pain of remembering it. His connection to the noir world is rooted in such consciousness, from which he tries to escape but which he cannot erase. Lena's death at the end reminds him that he cannot step out of the scenario that is his life, that, alas, the piano player singled out to be shot is doomed to live.

JEAN-PIERRE MELVILLE (1917–1973)

Bob le flambeur (1955)
Le Doulos (1962)
Le Deuxième Souffle (1966)[4]
Le Samouraï (1967)
Le Cercle rouge (1970)

Melville's protagonists form an aesthetic of modern heroism, without sentimentality yet full of muted tenderness and moral grace. Motivated by the exercise of honorable behavior, in a near-symmetry of inexorable actions destined to define such honor, seemingly opaque men form alliances with each other in assertion of criminal activity, or in combat of it, to define the figure of the gangster or the cop. His characters form solemn bonds of friendship and are punished for betraying them. Melville, more than any other French *metteur-en-scène*, has been influenced by the myths of the American screen with its gangsters, cops, and private eyes. In this context his heroes, not always attractive but certainly compelling, thrive in the claustrophobic environment of the only world he recognizes, a world of greed and violence, of justice and violence, and of the dispassionate exercise of criminal ritual. "Tragedy doesn't go at all well with dinner jackets and frilly shirtfronts," Melville pronounced. "It has come down in the world. Tragedy is the immediacy of death that you get in the underworld, or at a particular time such as war."[5]

This is, of course, not the case with Bob, the gambler, a graying swain of a gentleman, impeccably turned out. *Bob le flambeur* is the

Bob le flambeur (1955). That old gang of mine: Bob (Roger Duchesne) and company discuss the possibility of a heist.

most direct appeal to the French filmmaking sensibility of the crime drama as it developed in large part on the American screen. As with *Du Rififi chez les hommes* and *Touchez pas au grisbi*, it uses the caper film as a vehicle to exercise the values of honor, loyalty, and risk-taking and its consequences. And it shows the failure of these in a regretful gesture of disavowal.

The film was produced cheaply and with no current star power, and Melville had total control over his own script. *Bob le flambeur* came to symbolize by example the personal cinema that inspired the nouvelle vague. Melville called *Bob* a comedy of manners rather than a film noir; and to the extent that Bob is a carefree fellow, fettered by no greater despair than a wistful regret of time's passing him by, there is charm in his dignity. Alas, however, in Bob's great tragic moment, the one that undermines his courtliness, he submits to his gambling vice, and it costs Paulo his life. It is a consequence difficult to dismiss, and Melville hu-

Bob le flambeur (1955). Bob (Roger Duchesne): the embodiment of honor among thieves.

miliates his hero's existence here, indeed, robs Bob of his heroic stature at the expense of a young cohort's life, a life that cannot be so cavalierly expunged from the story. Bob, the attractive loner marching to the beat of his own drum, cannot deny his responsibility to a world of others that affords him the privilege to stand alone.

In all of Melville's noirs, there are long sequences of silent activity by his protagonists, scenes of almost ritualistic necessity as we see them prepare to do battle with forces they have met many times before. His camera movements seem never-ending, tortuous takes that, with the vivid cinematography of Henri Decaë, create a noir world of melancholy without sentimentality.[6] The sequences seem tedious at first until we realize that it is in the rhythm of these actions that we begin to see an exercise in destiny, destiny in a universe without which no relationship would have meaning or consequence. In *Bob*, Bob is walking home alone in the early morning after a long night out when he notices Anne, who will ultimately be responsible for divulging the heist scheme to Marc and thus dooming it. Nothing is spoken in those opening shots; they are simply gorgeous snapshots of Montmartre the morning after, as some people prepare to start their day while others end it. In *Le Doulos*, Maurice Faugel wearily tracks down Gilbert Varnove, a former accomplice, upon his release from jail, and he kills him in retribution for his wife's murder. The sequence, over thirteen minutes long, is a near-wordless opening to a film that, like all of Melville's noirs, attests to the psychic drain of upholding honor, revenge, and ritual. In *Le Samouraï*, Jeff Costello prepares to execute a hit by meticulously adjusting his attire, quietly leaving his apartment, and carefully, cautiously, trying each car key on a ring he carries until one of them turns the ignition of a car he has eyed and will steal. Nothing is spoken during these first ten minutes of the film.

Melville's films seek to illustrate what Jacques Zimmer and Chantal de Béchade see as the accidental and the inevitable in his world. Melvillian suspense, if it may be so recognized, is really the dance of inevitability. "The inexorable is the evident and unannounced fate of the hero or heroes, the place of the ceremonial being precisely fixed."[7] In all of Melville's *policiers* and films noirs, the protagonists come full circle (as indeed Zimmer and de Béchade point out of the thieves in *Le Cercle rouge*). In *Bob le flambeur*, Bob goes back to warn the others of their entrapment, even though it is too late. In *Le Doulos*, Maurice attempts to head off his friend Silien, who, he is now convinced, is not a snitch (*un doulos*), but he is too late and Silien is killed. In *Le Samouraï*, Jeff Costello goes back to the bar where he performed his hit (he took another contract from the very employers who wanted him dead) and is

Le Doulos (1962). Shades of Bogart: Belmondo as Silien.

brought face to face with the enigmatic piano player he is to kill. The accidental in these films is the thwarted plan (*Bob le flambeur*, *Le Cercle rouge*), the misunderstood actions (*Le Doulos*), and the unexpected circumstances (*Le Samouraï*). Yet these are really only the complications of fate, since the accidental is but man's folly, the plan missing a crucial detail, those circumstances altering the original details, or the human element that is unreliable and weak and dispenses with the meticulous planning needed to do a job, that brings the protagonist to his death.

The need for the hired gun, the safe cracker, or the gangster to perform this rite of passage unto death in Melville's noirs stems from the central dilemma of his world and of the film noir in general: it speaks to the conflict between an impossible isolation and a world of others. The simplest gestures of his killers are solitary ones, privileged and forlorn moments that bear little resemblance to anything an American gangster outside of Hemingway would do. Melville's films embellish this theme with a stylized reference to the American crime drama's most salient qualities: the need for the appropriate iconography, the spiritual kinship between the pursued and their pursuers, and the often misogynistic treatment of women, less ambiguous here but at least as brutal as anything on the American screen. The striking difference, of course, is that the American structure acquires a decidedly Gallic interpretation. In all of his noirs, Melville presents his protagonists trench-coated, complete with a gun and a smoldering cigarette, prepared to face violence. Jean-Paul Belmondo (Silien), Alain Delon (Jeff Costello, Corey), and Yves Montand (Jansen) are emblematic of all that can reverberate of the American gangster, but as in Godard's work, these figures are opaque; they resonate not with psychology or with a collective national consciousness, but with a mythology, at once alluring and enigmatic. The police, too, function much less as enforcers of the law than as opponents in defense of some sort of reverse honor to be upheld. Commissaire Ledru in *Bob le flambeur*, Clain in *Le Doulos*, and most of all the inspector in *Le Samouraï* understand their role as law enforcers in much the same way as Don Siegel's law enforcers do: as sentinels of a social order the rules of which often exist in striking similarity to those of the underworld they pursue. In Melville's films, however, these policemen face the challenge of a much more cerebral order; in Siegel's of a much more savage one.

Melville's women, so vacant, and treacherous on top of it, bespeak a masculine world where codes exist only to define men. They clearly lack the complexity and fascination of the American screen's *femme fatale*. In *Le Doulos*, Silien slaps Thérèse senseless because she squealed to the cops. We are not given any reason for her betrayal, any more than we can truly understand why Anne gloats to Marc about Bob and Paulo's plan to rob the casino at Deauville in *Bob le flambeur*. Melville, in fact, described Anne as "the kind of girl who has been around all [my] life: very young, very high heels, making no distinction between good and evil, and instantly burning their wings under the impression that they are really living. Beautiful girls who are trapped and ground down by the city of men, because of course a city belongs to its men."[8] What these women have to counterpoint them are supporting women like Yvonne, Bob's loyal friend, whose bar, *Pile ou Face*, he helped finance. Or Fabienne (*Le Doulos*) and Jeanne Lagrange (*Le Samouraï*), chronically disappointed women who have been abandoned by their men too often to hope for any lasting love.

Finally, the ritual act of all Melville noir protagonists is the salutary gaze underscoring their self-awareness, which functions both as an existential gaze and a cinematic referent. Bob looks at himself in the mirror and knows that his best years are behind him. In *Le Doulos*, after he is shot, Silien poses in front of a mirror to adjust his hat and contemplate his image before dropping dead. Jeff Costello strikes a similar pose in his trench coat and hat in *Le Samouraï* before he leaves his flat to pursue his employers. Shades of Michel Poiccard in *À bout de souffle*, one may ask? Perhaps. But then who did Michel attempt to emulate, down to the very utterance of his name, except Bogart?

Epilogue

COMMENTS ON THE CLASSIC FILM NOIR AND THE NEO-NOIR

Like errant children, films noirs have changed, subsumed by their history and turning into self-referential creatures not always beholden to their parents. What is it that makes one film made in the nineties a great noir (*The Grifters*), whereas another made almost twenty years ago (*Body Heat*) is a decided offshoot of the classic film noir? A new variant of an old look with a new, yet not unfamiliar, feel? At the beginning of this millennium, critics and historians are still refiguring the scope and boundaries of the film noir, taking into account the cultural and political changes in the strain as well as its aesthetic modifications. Discussing such a subject—like the topic of the neo-noir itself—is a whole different show, albeit one that cannot stand without reference to the rich mother lode of noir history. However, more than twenty years after a film like Walter Hill's *Driver* (1978), and twenty years since Lawrence Kasdan's *Body Heat* (1981), a number of films have come into existence that have drawn on the stylistics of the film noir as they have been appropriated by mass culture for everything marketable, including film history and scholarship.[1]

The classic noir has been pronounced dead so often that the humor of it equals that of the long-awaited announcement of a terribly aged and mean relative's passing that simply fails to arrive: it just never comes. I maintain that the film noir in its original appeal does not have bracketed self-consciousness and self-referencing. Despite the changes in production (almost always wide-screen color) and exhibition (Dolby sound), filmmaking has achieved a remarkable degree of democracy in style, and what was once considered dated always seems to return anew. The film noir, in its original fascination, still thrives in recent works like Alan Parker's *Angel Heart* (1987), Alan Rudolph's *Mortal Thoughts* (1991), Bryan Singer's *Usual Suspects* (1995), and Carl Franklin's *Devil in a Blue Dress* (1995).

> When people are in trouble, they need to talk.
> —Christina Bailey, *Kiss Me Deadly* (1955)

> People say I talk too much.
> —Verbal Kint, *The Usual Suspects* (1995)

"*Neo noir*, qu'est que c'est?" B. Ruby Rich asked rather flippantly in her 1995 essay on the subject; she then proceeded to answer rather seriously and quite aptly that "its power stems from those end-of-the-line dramas in which nobody could be trusted and not even the final frame held any explanation: films like *Gun Crazy*, *Kiss Me Deadly*, *The Big Combo* and *Touch of Evil* . . . *Neo noir* picks up on the irrational universe embedded in these demonic narratives as fertile ground for the postmodern cultivation of our own *fin-de-siècle* nightmares."[2] Rich is correct in these remarks (albeit questionable in her essay as a whole), for neo-noir arrives very much as the product of a new variant of genre narrative created to speak for us and to us. It is interesting that Rich sees its antecedents as demonic. Nicholas Christopher, in his long meditation on the film noir and the American city, also refers to the "satan" now visible in our mythologized urban landscape, and he illustrates this in his discussions of *Angel Heart* and *The Usual Suspects*.[3] Both of these films are structured as inquiries in the familiar sense of unraveling a noir mystery while exposing the iniquitous characters surrounding it. However, Christopher reiterates the central narrative strategy in all films noirs in his impressive analysis of *The Usual Suspects*; he does so by exposing what he sees of the Devil now visible in noir territory. He writes:

> [O]n its deepest level, *The Usual Suspects* is a story about
> the implication of telling stories, and about the inherent
> ambiguities of the storyteller's role, especially when his
> motives may be a story unto themselves, with myriad roots:
> to convey a putative reality, to refashion events or make
> sense of them, to purge himself, to deceive. As with any

The Usual Suspects (1995). . . . And what of Kaiser Soze?: complex noir storytelling.

narrator, what he amplifies or diminishes, includes or
omits, and the infinite variations therein, are what make the
story what it is. Thus in the best of film, as in literature,
there is always the story behind the story, the word within
the word, the revelations that come not only from content,
but from seeing how and why a story is being told, and
with what particular fusion of those disparate essential
elements: memory and fantasy, truth and lies. (250–51)

Verbal Kint, one of the two survivors who witnessed the mass murder of
a crew on a ship purportedly carrying drugs, weaves a tale of horror and
mystery of the arch criminal Kaiser Soze, and he does so with incredible
finesse—until we realize who Kaiser Soze really is. Christopher speaks
of the Devil, of a previously spiritual manifestation *within* unregenerate
noir characters now being permitted an appearance of his own in the
furthest extension of noir yet. He refers to *Alias Nick Beal* (John Farrow,
1949) with Ray Milland as a sinister Mephistopheles in modern dress as
a precedent. But now there is no doubt that Louis Cyphre (Lucifer) in
Angel Heart, in the person of Robert De Niro, who crushes a hard-cooked
egg with his hand and then devours it, is the Devil incarnate. Or that
Kaiser Soze is an invisible devil around us. The Devil, so concrete be-

fore us visually in these contemporary noirs, emerges as the symbol for the very horror of our capacity to unwittingly be his servant, to be complicit in the corruption around us. In *Angel Heart*, private eye Harold Love learns that his soul was fatefully bartered in a transaction of evil. Verbal Kint in *Suspects* says with mocking innocence, "The greatest trick the Devil ever pulled was convincing the world he didn't exist."

But the "story behind the story, the word within the word" is—regrettably perhaps—that there is no Devil. The unsettling narratives of Alan Parker and Bryan Singer provoke us because these filmmakers have found new escape hatches through which to cunningly reveal—or shall we say speak?—their noir tales and in the process implicate us in their noir vision. True films noirs invariably confront this idea of the need to communicate visually and verbally the inchoate, the helpless, the terror-stricken, just as they need to confess, lie, and reveal. Neo-noirs often mimic these qualities. Yet like, but very much unlike, the aesthetic self-consciousness of the French New Wave–inspired cinema of the 1960s and 1970s, the neo-noir exists alongside the classic film noir in mutated form and has among others these four prominent characteristics:

1. The neo-noir is generally more violent, and more graphically violent at that, than the classic film noir ever was. Such violence is almost always stylized and often less disturbing, but it is also shown more. David Fincher's *Seven* (1995) literally extracts a pound of flesh carved from one of the victims as his serial murderer attempts to illustrate the punishment to be paid for each of the "seven deadly sins." Ridley Scott's *Blade Runner* (1982), one of the first films to lay claim to the title of "future-*noir*," spatters blood like cherry pie filling throughout the fog-filled gloomy alleyways of this unfortunate new world. Certainly none of the Quentin Tarantino films—*Reservoir Dogs* (1992), *Pulp Fiction* (1994), or even his greatest appeal to the traditional noir, *Jackie Brown* (1997)—could have been made before the midseventies. How audiences respond to this violence is really incalculable, but it is violence that appears more suddenly and often inflected by comedy and brutal wit. In *Pulp Fiction*, Jules Winfield delivers an eloquent sermon on the nature of fate as a taunt to the three young men—all seemingly middle-class and all but one white—who stole drugs from Marcellus. He turns to leave, then turns around again, and with his partner Vincent showers the room with bullets.

Martin Scorsese's *GoodFellas* (1990), a bitter homage to the classic gangster noir as well as a meditation on the cultural use of the mob-

Jackie Brown (1997). Mordant and violent Tarantino: Louis (Robert De Niro) and Ordell (Samuel L. Jackson) catch up.

ster figure, has two scenes of violence that show how the filmmaker straddles the neo-noir and the classic noir. In the scene where all the wise guys end up at the home of Tommy De Vito's mother (played by Scorsese's mother, Catherine) for a late-night dinner, Tommy nervously admires one of her kitchen knives and asks to borrow it, ostensibly to cut off the appendage of a deer that ran into his vehicle. He excuses himself for a moment to go out back and open the trunk door of this car; it seems that the muffled banging from inside the trunk has become annoying. He raises the trunk door and quickly stabs Billy Batts three or four times to make certain that he is good and dead and then closes the trunk door. Murder here is abstracted into a comic moment, perhaps horrible to contemplate but palatable—even amusing—to watch, since we see only De Vito's difficulty in silencing a troublesome rival who has been beaten to within an inch of his life and stuffed in the trunk for future disposal but who refuses to shut up and die. However, in a later scene, a young neighborhood bar boy whom Tommy harassed and carelessly shot in the foot now hobbles past him in his cast and tells Tommy to go fuck himself. Kidded by a fellow wise guy for being soft in taking such backtalk, Tommy shoots the boy dead this time. It is a silencing moment—no one can laugh here—and it is essentially what Scorsese's film is finally about.

Violence in the film noir has always been predicated upon the entrapment that engendered it, its sociopathology part of the larger scheme of spiritual and cultural ills. A work like Lewis's 1950 *Gun Crazy* is a singularly fascinating exception to watch precisely because it appeals to the possibility of the irrational overtaking us, of violence providing an excitement that no substitute can. But killing for the most part satisfied the narrative requirement to eliminate someone, often impulsively and sometimes brutally, in tangent with the killer's or killers' other, selfish, goals. After all, in the noir world, maiming and killing are rarely intelligent and expedient actions, but detours taken out of necessity. In the neo-noir, one glories in the aesthetics of violence, pirouettes killing with a canny grin, and this necessitates a new recognition of such violence and its value.

2. The period accoutrements of classic noir cinema are almost always contemporary. Any deviation from this modifies the spatial/historical style (urban/contemporary) essential to this modern genre. However, a film like Curtis Hanson's *L.A. Confidential* that glories in postwar forties period style to the inevitable expectation of human rottenness nonetheless loses its noir authority. James Cromwell's crooked police chief is hardly a surprising villain in a story that awaits his exposure. Its atmosphere, unlike, say, that of Polanski's *Chinatown*, comes bracketed in the audience's knowledge of what has been clearly marketed in 1997 as a film noir. *Chinatown*, in contrast, is a period film—given the time in which it is set, the late 1930s—and strongly evokes the Chandlerian world it comments on, but it does so with the truth of genuine horror over Noah Cross's monstrous incest, the shooting of Evelyn Mulwray, and—and this is most important—the creepiness of Cross's benevolence. Neo-noirs, which may certainly address an array of cinematic and cultural concerns, do so around quotation marks and from the position of premeditated sensationalism. Hence, Cromwell is expectedly corrupt, but in Noah Cross John Huston is taking corruption to a new and unexpected depth of evil in familiar terrain.

3. The neo-noir, in keeping with its time, has become racially variegated and sexually complex. The Don Cheadles, Ving Rhameses, and Samuel L. Jacksons of the contemporary crime scene would not only have been invisible in the 1940s and for most of the 1950s but also

would not have been convincingly utilized in the 1960s either. Tokenism would have prevented any such viciousness from being shown by any of the very few black screen actors of that time. The very presence of Samuel L. Jackson in any crime film today induces uneasiness in the thought of the pain he may inflict; he wields menace much like a cross between Lawrence Tierney and Richard Widmark of the 1940s. Likewise, Morgan Freeman (*Seven*) and Denzel Washington (Phillip Noyce's *Bone Collector* [1999]) exercise the kind of sage authority as police detectives that would not have been possible in an earlier era when African Americans and non-European Americans were not seen in positions of power.

The film noir has always suggested a sexual democracy between the lines. Sexual arousal stimulated by the various taboos of the studio system had been hinted at, suggested, punished, and, indeed, persecuted in characters who stood apart from the rest because of their desires. A film like Larry and Andy Wachowski's *Bound* (1996) would have been impossible to make a generation earlier, not only because the thieves in it become instantly attracted to each other in a lesbian bar but also because they get away with stealing money from the husband of one of them, *and* do so with the audience's sympathy. Moreover, their independence from conformity and conventional ties puts them in a kind of noir fantasy that allows them the freedom to direct the story's action: together they are the brainpower and the force that execute the scam. No men allowed. Corky (Gina Gershon) and Violet (Jennifer Tilly), a fascinating duo, mirror the two sides of the *femme fatale*, a figure here that has been melded of two protagonists to become a summation of all that she could possibly represent—the independent and resourceful woman who is attractive (Gershon) and the sexually alluring female who is shrewd (Tilly).

4. However, *Bound* is an exceptional film. The arousal of the *femme fatale* in the film noir was a radical departure from the suffering or glorification of women traditionally seen in screen melodrama. She startled precisely because she exercised an independent spirit—however culturally defined her rapacious image may have been—to the discomfort of a conventional patriarchal society. She existed in a position of defiance and was most often punished for it. In the neo-noir, wickedness achieves emancipation (one might even say, celebration) and with it, ironically, a subjugation of character and purpose. In *Body Heat*, Kathleen Turner is calculatingly evil, and Linda Fiorentino is determinedly so in *The Last Seduction*, but there is very little in either role that allows these actresses

Bound (1996). Corky (Gina Gershon) and Violet (Jennifer Tilly): neo-noir's answer to the *femme fatale*.

to discover their position as *femmes fatales* with the daring of an Anjelica Huston playing Lily Dillon in *The Grifters*.[4] In an unexpected yet decisive gesture of brutal infanticide, we are taken into new territory, found having to settle a new score over what female wickedness in a screen genre can be.

In this family context, both *Chinatown* and *The Grifters*, like James Foley's 1986 *At Close Range*, emerge as true films noirs in the originality with which they restate or expand the boundaries of the genre. There is a silencing moment of grim family perversion in *At Close Range*, when Brad Whitewood stares at his drunken, killer dad in astonished rage at the suggestion that he kill his younger brother for money. Having wrested his father's weapon, he shouts plaintively, "What is this?! *The family gun?!*" Interestingly, these three films take evil and cleave it to the family; it is almost as if, incapable of arousing pity and horror in the social world, these conflicts are best left contained within the ancient arena of family agony.

Neo-noirs such as *Body Heat*, *Blood Simple* (Joel Coen, 1984), *Blue Velvet* (David Lynch, 1986), *Stormy Monday* (Mike Figgis, 1988), *Basic*

Instinct (Paul Verhoeven, 1992), *Lost Highway* (David Lynch, 1997), and others claim a historical reference to noir cinema in ways that mutate the genre to reveal it more culturally ingrained than we may have recognized. And these changes are not just in the conventions of the genre or these movies' mimicry of them; the stylistics of noir filmmaking may all be present, but at one remove from the narrative authenticity of true noir cinema. Rather, it is a matter of tone and mood, of the very ineffable qualities that emanated from technique more than sixty years ago when the film noir first appeared in this country. The reinvention of the film noir necessarily becomes neo because it has become something else. The historicity of noir cinema is challenged here, and the whole idea of screen genres and their evolution and exhaustion is revived yet again for consideration in the context of a largely commercial filmmaking enterprise. The new émigré influence of the neo-noir will not be central Europe, but perhaps central L.A. or film school (Richard Rodriguez, the Coen brothers). The misogyny of the neo-noir will no

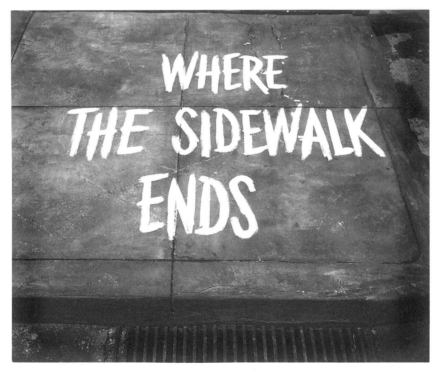

Where the Sidewalk Ends, title credit

longer be the exclusive product of a male sensibility but now of a female mind as well (as in Kathryn Bigelow's vicious *Blue Steel* [1990]). Such films may no longer speak to familiar taboos and fears, now recognized and even dramatized on nightly television, but to new unseen forces that will require their own images to inflict their own terrors.

CREDITS OF SELECTED FILMS NOIRS

The following are the credits for those American films most frequently discussed in the text that I believe have attained particular importance in the noir canon. These credits are taken directly from the screen, with some of the names of bit characters and players in the cast listings taken from Alain Silver and Elizabeth Ward's *Film Noir: An Encyclopedic Reference to the American Style*. The *Motion Picture Guide*, compiled by Jay Robert Nash and Stanley Ralph Ross, was also consulted. Running times, always a contentious issue, were taken mostly from the prerelease reviews that appeared in *Variety*. Silver and Ward, *Film Noir*; and Leonard Maltin's *Movie Video Guide* were also consulted for running times.

99 River Street (United Artists, 1953)
Director: Phil Karlson
Producer: Edward Small (World Films, Inc.)
Screenplay: Robert Smith, based upon an unpublished story by George Zuckerman
Cinematography: Franz Planer
Editing: Buddy Small
Sound: Lambert Day
Music Score: Emil Newman, Arthur Lange
Art Direction: Frank Sylos
Assistant Director: Ralph Black
Cast: John Payne (*Ernie Driscoll*), Evelyn Keyes (*Linda James*), Brad Dexter (*Victor Rawlins*), Frank Faylen (*Stan Hogan*), Peggie Castle (*Pauline Driscoll*), Jay Adler (*Christopher*), Jack Lambert (*Mickey*), Eddie Waller (*Pop Dudkee*), Glen Langan (*Lloyd Morgan*), John Day (*Bud*), Ian Wolfe (*Waldo Daggett*), Peter Leeds (*Nat Finley*), William Tannen (*Director*), Gene Reynolds (*Chuck*)
Running time: 83 minutes

The Asphalt Jungle (MGM, 1950)
Director: John Huston
Producer: Arthur Hornblow Jr.
Screenplay: Ben Maddow and John Huston, based upon the novel by W.R.
    Burnett
Cinematography: Harold Rosson
Editing: George Boemler
Sound: Douglas Shearer, Robert Lee
Music Score: Miklos Rozsa
Art Direction: Cedric Gibbons, Randall Duell
Set Decoration: Edwin B. Willis, Jack D. Moore (associate)
Makeup: Jack Dawn
Hair Styling: Sydney Guilaroff
Cast: Sterling Hayden (*Dix Handley*), Louis Calhern (*Alonzo D. Emmerich*),
    Jean Hagen (*Doll Conovan*), James Whitmore (*Gus Minissi*), Sam Jaffe
    (*Doc Erwin Riedenschneider*), Anthony Caruso (*Louis Ciavelli*), John
    McIntire (*Police Commissioner Hardy*), Marc Lawrence (*Cobby*), Barry
    Kelley (*Lieutenant Dietrich*), Marilyn Monroe (*Angela Phinlay*), Teresa
    Celli (*Maria Ciavelli*)
Running time: 112 minutes

The Big Heat (Columbia, 1953)
Director: Fritz Lang
Producer: Robert Arthur
Screenplay: Sydney Boehm, based upon the *Saturday Evening Post* serial by
    William P. McGivern
Cinematography: Charles Lang
Editing: Charles Nelson
Sound: George Cooper
Musical Director: Mischa Bakaleinikoff
Art Direction: Robert Peterson
Set Decoration: William Kiernan
Costumes: Jean Louis
Makeup: Clay Campbell
Hair Styling: Helen Hunt
Assistant Director: Milton Feldman
Cast: Glenn Ford (*Dave Bannion*), Gloria Grahame (*Debbie Marsh*), Jocelyn
    Brando (*Katie Bannion*), Alexander Scourby (*Mike Lagana*), Lee Marvin
    (*Vince Stone*), Jeanette Nolan (*Bertha Duncan*), Peter Whitney (*Tierney*),
    Willis Bouchey (*Lieutenant Wilkes*), Robert Burton (*Gus Burke*), Adam
    Williams (*Larry Gordon*), Howard Wendell (*Commissioner Higgins*),

Dorothy Green (*Lucy Chapman*), Carolyn Jones (*Doris*), Dan Seymour
(*Atkins*), Edith Evanson (*Selma Parker*)
Running time: 90 minutes

The Big Sleep (Warner Brothers, 1946)
Director: Howard Hawks
Producer: Howard Hawks
Screenplay: William Faulkner, Leigh Brackett, and Jules Furthman, based
    upon the novel by Raymond Chandler
Cinematography: Sid Hickox
Special Effects: E. Roy Davidson (Director), Warren E. Lynch
Editing: Christian Nyby
Sound: Robert B. Lee
Music Score: Max Steiner
Musical Direction: Leo F. Forbstein
Art Direction: Carl Jules Weyl
Set Decoration: Fred M. MacLean
Costumes: Leah Rhodes
Makeup: Perc Westmore
Cast: Humphrey Bogart (*Philip Marlowe*), Lauren Bacall (*Vivian Sternwood*),
    John Ridgely (*Eddie Mars*), Martha Vickers (*Carmen Sternwood*),
    Dorothy Malone (*Bookstore Clerk*), Peggy Knudsen (*Mona Mars*), Regis
    Toomey (*Bernie Ohls*), Charles Waldron (*General Sternwood*), Charles D.
    Brown (*Norris*), Elisha Cook Jr. (*Harry Jones*), Bob Steele (*Canino*),
    Louis Jean Heydt (*Joe Brody*), Sonia Darrin (*Agnes*), James Flavin
    (*Captain Cronjager*), Thomas Rafferty (*Carol Lundgren*), Theodore Von
    Eltz (*Arthur Gwynne Geiger*), Dan Wallace (*Owen Taylor*), Joy Barlowe
    (*Taxi Driver*)
Running time: 114 minutes

Black Angel (Universal, 1946)
Director: Roy William Neill
Producer: Roy William Neill, Tom McKnight
Screenplay: Ray Chanslor, based upon the novel by Cornell Woolrich
Cinematography: Paul Ivano
Special Effects: David S. Horsley
Editing: Saul A. Goodkind
Sound: Bernard B. Brown
Music Score: Frank Skinner; songs by Jack Brooks and Edgar Fairchild
Art Direction: Jack Otterson, Martin Obzina
Set Decoration: Russell A. Gausman, E.R. Robinson
Gowns: Vera West

Makeup: Jack P. Pierce
Hair Styling: Carmen Dirigo
Assistant Director: Charles S. Gould
Cast: Dan Duryea (*Martin Blair*), June Vincent (*Catherine Bennett*), Peter
   Lorre (*Marko*), Broderick Crawford (*Captain Flood*), Constance Dowling
   (*Mavis Marlowe*), Wallace Ford (*Joe*), Hobart Cavanaugh (*Jake*), Freddie
   Steele (*Lucky*), John Phillips (*Kirk Bennett*), Ben Bard (*Bartender*), Junius
   Matthews (*Dr. Courtney*), Marion Martin (*Flo*), Michael Branden
   (*Mitchell*), St. Clair and Vilova (*Dance Team*), Robert Williams (*2nd
   Detective*)
Running time: 81 minutes

Body and Soul (United Artists, 1947)
Director: Robert Rossen
Producer: Bob Roberts (Enterprise Studios)
Screenplay: Abraham Polonsky
Cinematography: James Wong Howe
Special Effects: "Special Montages" directed by Guenther Fritsch
Editing: Robert Parrish
Sound: Frank Webster
Music Score: Hugo Friedhofer; "Body and Soul," music by Johnny Green
   and lyrics by Edward Newman, Robert Sour, and Frank Eyton
Music Direction: Rudolph Polk
Art Direction: Natan Juran
Set Decoration: Edward J. Boyle
Costumes: Marion Herwood Keyes
Makeup: Gustaf M. Norin
Production Manager: Joseph Gilpin
Assistant Director: Robert Aldrich
Cast: John Garfield (*Charley Davis*), Lilli Palmer (*Peg Born*), Hazel Brooks
   (*Alice*), Anne Revere (*Anna Davis*), William Conrad (*Quinn*), Joseph
   Pevney (*Shorty Polaski*), Canada Lee (*Ben Chaplin*), Lloyd Goff
   (*Roberts*), Art Smith (*David Davis*), James Burke (*Arnold*), Virginia Gregg
   (*Irma*), Peter Virgo (*Drummer*), Joe Devlin (*Prince*)
Running time: 104 minutes

Brute Force (Universal-International, 1947)
Director: Jules Dassin
Producer: Mark Hellinger (Mark Hellinger Productions)
Associate Producer: Jules Buck
Screenplay: Richard Brooks, based upon a story by Robert Patterson
Cinematography: William Daniels

Special Photography: David S. Horsley
Technical Adviser: Jacques Gordon
Editing: Edward Curtiss
Sound: Charles Felstead, Robert Pritchard
Music Score: Miklos Rozsa
Art Direction: Bernard Herzbrun, John F. DeCuir
Set Decoration: Russell A. Gausman, Charles Wyrick
Gowns: Rosemary Odell
Makeup: Bud Westmore
Hair Styling: Carmen Dirigo
Assistant Director: Fred Frank
Cast: Burt Lancaster (*Joe Collins*), Hume Cronyn (*Captain Munsey*), Charles
    Bickford (*Gallagher*), Yvonne De Carlo (*Gina*), Ann Blyth (*Ruth*), Ella
    Raines (*Cora*), Anita Colby (*Flossie*), Sam Levene (*Louie*), Howard Duff
    (*Soldier*), Art Smith (*Dr. Walters*), Whit Bissell (*Tom Lister*), Jeff Corey
    (*Freshman*), John Hoyt (*Spencer*), Jack Overman (*Kid Coy*), Roman
    Bohnen (*Warden Barnes*), Sir Lancelot (*Calypso*), Vince Barnett (*Mugsy*),
    Jay C. Flippen (*Hodges*), Richard Gaines (*McCollum*), Frank Puglia
    (*Ferrara*), James Bell (*Crenshaw*), Ray Teal (*Jackson*), Howland
    Chamberlin (*Gaines*), Charles McGraw (*Andy*)
Running time: 98 minutes

Chinatown (Paramount, 1974)

Director: Roman Polanski
Producer: Robert Evans
Associate Producer: C.O. Erickson
Screenplay: Robert Towne
Cinematography: John A. Alonzo
Special Effects: Logan Frazee
Editing: Sam O'Steen
Sound: Larry Jost
Music Score: Jerry Goldsmith
Art Direction: W. Stewart Campbell
Set Design: Gabe Resh, Robert Resh
Set Decoration: Ruby Levitt
Costumes: Anthea Sylbert
Wardrobe Direction: Richard Bruno, Jean Merrick
Makeup: Hank Edds, Lee Harmon
Hair Styling: Susan Germaine, Vivienne Walker
Unit Production Manager: C.O. Erickson
Assistant Director: Howard W. Koch Jr.
Cast: Jack Nicholson (*J.J. Gittes*), Faye Dunaway (*Evelyn Mulwray*), John

Huston (*Noah Cross*), Perry Lopez (*Escobar*), John Hillerman (*Yelburton*), Darrell Zwerling (*Hollis Mulwray*), Diane Ladd (*Ida Sessions*), Roy Jenson (*Mulvihill*), Roman Polanski (*Man with knife*), Dick Bakalyan (*Loach*), Joe Mantell (*Walsh*), Bruce Glover (*Duffy*), Nandu Hinds (*Sophie*), Roy Roberts (*Mayor Bagby*), Noble Willingham, Elliott Montgomery (*Councilmen*), Rance Howard (*Irate Farmer*), Burt Young (*Curly*)
Running time: 130 minutes

Christmas Holiday (Universal, 1944)

Director: Robert Siodmak
Producer: Felix Jackson
Associate Producer: Frank Shaw
Screenplay: Herman J. Mankiewicz, based upon the novel by W. Somerset Maugham
Cinematography: Elwood Bredell
Special Photography: John P. Fulton
Editing: Ted Kent
Sound: Bernard B. Brown, Joe Lapis
Music Score: Hans J. Salter; "Spring Will Be a Little Late This Year," music and lyrics by Frank Loesser; "Always," music and lyrics by Irving Berlin
Musical Direction: Hans J. Salter
Art Direction: John B. Goodman, Robert Clatworthy
Set Decoration: Russell A. Gausman, E.R. Robinson
Costumes: Vera West. Deanna Durbin's gowns by Muriel King and Howard Greer
Assistant Director: William Holland
Cast: Deanna Durbin (*Jackie Lamont/Abigail Mannette*), Gene Kelly (*Robert Mannette*), Richard Whorf (*Simon Fenimore*), Dean Harens (*Charles Mason*), Gladys George (*Valerie de Merode*), Gale Sondergaard (*Mrs. Mannette*), David Bruce (*Gerald Tyler*), Minor Watson (*Townsend*)
Running time: 93 minutes

Criss Cross (Universal-International, 1949)

Director: Robert Siodmak
Producer: Michel Kraike
Screenplay: Daniel Fuchs, based upon the novel by Don Tracy
Cinematography: Frank(z) Planer
Special Photography: David S. Horsley
Editing: Ted J. Kent
Sound: Leslie I. Carey, Richard DeWeese
Music Score: Miklos Rozsa

Art Direction: Bernard Herzbrun, Boris Leven
Set Decoration: Russell A. Gausman, Oliver Emert
Gowns: Yvonne Wood
Makeup: Bud Westmore
Hair Styling: Carmen Dirigo
Cast: Burt Lancaster (*Steve Thompson*), Yvonne De Carlo (*Anna*), Dan
  Duryea (*Slim Dundee*), Stephen McNally (*Pete Ramirez*), Richard Long
  (*Slade Thompson*), Meg Randall (*Helen*), Tom Pedi (*Vincent*), Percy
  Helton (*Frank*), Alan Napier (*Finchley*), Griff Barnett (*Pop*), Joan Miller
  (*the Lush*), Edna M. Holland (*Mrs. Thompson*), John Doucette (*Walt*),
  Marc Krath (*Mort*), James O'Rear (*Waxie*), John Skins Miller (*Midget*),
  Robert Osterloh (*Mr. Nelson*), Tony Curtis (*the Gigolo*), Esy Morales and
  His Rhumba Band
Running time: 87 minutes

Cry of the City (20th Century–Fox, 1948)

Director: Robert Siodmak
Producer: Sol C. Siegel
Screenplay: Richard Murphy, based on the novel *The Chair for Martin Rome*,
  by Henry Edward Helseth
Cinematography: Lloyd Ahern
Special Effects: Fred Sersen
Editing: Harmon Jones
Sound: Eugene Grossman, Roger Heman
Music Score: Alfred Newman
Musical Direction: Lionel Newman
Art Direction: Lyle Wheeler, Albert Hogsett
Set Decoration: Thomas Little, Ernest Lansing
Costumes: Bonnie Cashin
Wardrobe Direction: Charles LeMaire
Makeup: Ben Nye
Cast: Victor Mature (*Lieutenant Candella*), Robert Conte (*Martin Rome*),
  Fred Clark (*Lieutenant Collins*), Shelley Winters (*Brenda*), Betty Garde
  (*Mrs. Pruett*), Barry Kroeger (*Niles*), Tommy Cook (*Tony*), Debra Paget
  (*Tina Riconti*), Hope Emerson (*Rose Given*), Tito Vuola (*Papa Roma*),
  Mimi Aguglia (*Mama Roma*), Konstantin Shayne (*Dr. Veroff*), Howard
  Freeman (*Sullivan*), Dolores Castle (*Rosa*), Claudette Ross (*Rosa's
  Daughter*)
Running time: 96 minutes

The Dark Corner (20th Century–Fox, 1946)

Director: Henry Hathaway

Producer: Fred Kohlmar
Screenplay: Jay Dratler and Bernard Schoenfeld, based upon a short story by
    Leo Rosten
Cinematography: Joe MacDonald
Special Effects: Fred Sersen
Editing: J. Watson Webb
Sound: W.D. Dick, Harry M. Leonard
Music Score: Cyril Mockridge
Musical Direction: Emil Newman
Art Direction: James Basevi, Leland Fuller
Set Decoration: Thomas Little, Paul S. Fox
Costumes: Kay Nelson
Makeup: Ben Nye
Cast: Mark Stevens (*Bradford Galt*), Lucille Ball (*Kathleen*), Clifton Webb
    (*Hardy Cathcart*), William Bendix (*"White Suit"*), Kurt Kreuger (*Tony
    Jardine*), Cathy Downs (*Mary Cathcart*), Reed Hadley (*Lieutenant Frank
    Reeves*), Constance Collier (*Mrs. Kingsley*), Molly Lamont (*Lucy
    Wilding*), Eddie Heywood and His Orchestra
Running time: 99 minutes

Desperate (RKO, 1947)
Director: Anthony Mann
Producer: Michel Kraike
Screenplay: Harry Essex, with additional dialogue by Martin Rackin, based
    upon an unpublished story by Dorothy Atlas and Anthony Mann
Cinematography: George E. Diskant
Special Effects: Russell A. Cully
Editing: Marston Fay
Sound: Earl A. Wolcott, Roy Granville
Music Score: Paul Sawtell
Musical Direction: Constantin Bakaleinikoff
Art Direction: Albert S. D'Agostino, Walter E. Keller
Set Decoration: Darrell Silver
Cast: Steve Brodie (*Steve Randall*), Audrey Long (*Anne Randall*), Raymond
    Burr (*Walt Radak*), Douglas Fowley (*Pete*), William Challee (*Reynolds*),
    Jason Robards Sr. (*Ferrari*), Freddie Steele (*Shorty*), Lee Frederick (*Joe*),
    Paul E. Burns (*Uncle Jan*), Ilka Gruning (*Aunt Clara*), Larry Nunn (*Al
    Radak*), Carol Forman (*Mrs. Roberts*), Erville Alderson (*Simon Pringle*)
Running time: 73 minutes

Detour (Producers Releasing Corporation, 1945)
Director: Edgar G. Ulmer

Producer: Leon Fromkess
Associate Producer: Martin Mooney
Screenplay: Martin Goldsmith
Cinematography: Benjamin H. Kline
Editing: George McGuire
Sound: Max Hutchinson
Music Score: Leo Erdody
Art Direction: Edward C. Jewell
Set Decoration: Glenn P. Thompson
Costumes: Mona Barry
Makeup: Bud Westmore
Production Manager: Raoul Pagel
Assistant Director: William A. Calihan Jr.
Cast: Tom Neal (*Al Roberts*), Ann Savage (*Vera*), Claudia Drake (*Sue*),
    Edmund MacDonald (*Charles Haskell Jr.*), Tim Ryan (*Diner Proprietor*),
    Esther Howard (*Hedy*), Donald Brodie (*Used Car Salesman*), Roger Clark
    (*Dillon*)
Running time: 67 minutes

Double Indemnity (Paramount, 1944)

Director: Billy Wilder
Producer: Joseph Sistrom
Screenplay: Billy Wilder and Raymond Chandler, based upon the novel by
    James M. Cain
Cinematography: John F. Seitz
Process Photography: Farciot Edouart
Editing: Doane Harrison
Sound: Stanley Cooley, Walter Oberst
Music Score: Miklos Rozsa; the *D Minor Symphony* by César Franck
Art Direction: Hans Dreier, Hal Pereira
Set Decoration: Bertram Granger
Costumes: Edith Head
Makeup: Wally Westmore
Cast: Fred MacMurray (*Walter Neff*), Barbara Stanwyck (*Phyllis
    Dietrichson*), Edward G. Robinson (*Barton Keyes*), Jean Heather (*Lola
    Dietrichson*), Tom Powers (*Mr. Dietrichson*), Byron Barr (*Nino Zachette*),
    Porter Hall (*Mr. Jackson*), Richard Gaines (*Mr. Norton*), Fortunio
    Bonanova (*Sam Gorlopis*), John Philliber (*Joe Pete*)
Running time: 106 minutes

Fallen Angel (20th Century–Fox, 1946)

Director: Otto Preminger

Producer: Otto Preminger
Screenplay: Harry Kleiner, based upon the novel by Marty Holland
Cinematography: Joseph La Shelle
Special Effects: Fred Sersen
Editing: Harry Reynolds
Sound: Bernard Freericks, Harry M. Leonard
Music Score: David Raksin; "Slowly," music by David Raksin and Kermit
    Goell
Musical Direction: Emil Newman
Art Direction: Lyle Wheeler, Leland Fuller
Set Decoration: Thomas Little, Helen Hansard
Costumes: Bonnie Cashin
Makeup: Ben Nye
Cast: Alice Faye (*June Mills*), Dana Andrews (*Eric Stanton*), Linda Darnell
    (*Stella*), Charles Bickford (*Mark Judd*), Anne Revere (*Clara Mills*), Bruce
    Cabot (*Dave Atkins*), John Carradine (*Madley*), Percy Kilbride (*Pop*), Olin
    Howlin (*Joe Ellis*), Hal Taliaferro (*Johnson*), Mira McKinney (*Mrs. Judd*),
    Jimmy Conlin (*Hotel Clerk*)
Running time: 97 minutes

Force of Evil (MGM/Enterprise, 1948)

Director: Abraham Polonsky
Producer: Bob Roberts
Screenplay: Abraham Polonsky and Ira Wolfert, based upon the novel
    Tucker's People, by Ira Wolfert
Cinematography: George Barnes
Editing: Art Seid
Sound: Frank Webster
Music Score: David Raksin
Musical Direction: Rudolph Polk
Art Direction: Richard Day
Set Decoration: Edward G. Boyle
Wardrobe Direction: Louise Wilson
Makeup: Gus Norin
Hair Styling: Lillian Lashin
Production Manager: Joseph C. Gilpin
Assistant Director: Robert Aldrich
Cast: John Garfield (*Joe Morse*), Beatrice Pearson (*Doris Lowry*), Thomas
    Gomez (*Leo Morse*), Howland Chamberlin (*Freddy Bauer*), Roy Roberts
    (*Ben Tucker*), Marie Windsor (*Edna Tucker*), Paul McVey (*Hobe
    Wheelock*), Tim Ryan (*Johnson*), Sid Tomack (*"Two & Two" Taylor*),
    Georgia Backus (*Sylvia Morse*), Sheldon Leonard (*Ficco*), Jan Dennis

(*Mrs. Bauer*), Stanley Prager (*Wally*), Beau Bridges (*Frankie Tucker*), Perry Ivans (*Mr. Middleton*), Cliff Clark (*Police Lieutenant*), Jimmy Dundee (*Dineen*)
Running time: 78 minutes

The Grifters (Scorsese/Miramax, 1990)
Director: Stephen Frears
Producer: Martin Scorsese, Robert A. Harris, and James Painten
Coproducer: Peggy Rajski
Screenplay: Donald E. Westlake, based upon the novel by Jim Thompson
Cinematography: Oliver Stapleton
Editing: Mick Audsley
Sound Mixer: John Sutton
Music Score: Elmer Bernstein
Art Direction: Leslie McDonald
Production Design: Dennis Gassner
Set Decoration: Nancy Haigh
Costumes: Richard Hornung
Makeup: Juliet Hewett
Hair Styling: Sidney Cornell
Assistant Director: Stephen Buck (First), Joe Camp (Second)
Cast: Anjelica Huston (*Lilly Dillon*), John Cusack (*Roy Dillon*), Annette Bening (*Myra Langtry*), Pat Hingle (*Bobo*), J.T. Walsh (*Cole*), Charles Napier (*Hebbing*), Henry Jones (*Simms*), Gailard Sartain (*Joe*), Stephen Tobolowsky (*Jeweler*)
Running time: 113 minutes

Gun Crazy ([*Deadly Is the Female*] United Artists, 1950)
Director: Joseph H. Lewis
Producers: Frank and Maurice King (King Brothers)
Screenplay: MacKinlay Kantor and Millard Kaufman, based upon the *Saturday Evening Post* story "Gun Crazy," by MacKinlay Kantor. Dalton Trumbo worked on the screenplay uncredited.
Cinematography: Russell Harlan
Editing: Harry Gerstad
Sound: Tom Lambert
Music Score: Victor Young; "Mad about You," music by Victor Young and lyrics by Ned Washington
Musical Orchestration: Leo Shuken, Sidney Cutner
Production Design: Gordon Wiles
Set Decoration: Raymond Boltz Jr.
Costumes: Norma for Peggy Cummins

Production Manager: Allen K. Wood

Assistant Director: Frank Heath

Cast: Peggy Cummins (*Annie Laurie Starr*), John Dall (*Barton Tare*), Barry Kroeger (*Packett*), Morris Carnovsky (*Judge Willoughby*), Anabel Shaw (*Ruby Tare*), Harry Lewis (*Clyde Boston*), Nedrick Young (*Dave Allister*), Rusty Tamblyn (*Bart Tare, age 14*), Trevor Bardette (*Sheriff Boston*), Mickey Little (*Bart Tare, age 7*), Paul Frison (*Clyde Boston, age 14*), Dave Bair (*Dave Allister, age 14*), Stanley Prager (*Bluey-Bluey*), Virginia Farmer (*Miss Wynn*), Anne O'Neal (*Miss Seifert*)

The film was released as *Deadly Is the Female* on January 26, 1950; it was rereleased as *Gun Crazy* on August 24, 1950 at a running time of 87 minutes.

In a Lonely Place (Columbia, 1950)

Director: Nicholas Ray

Producer: Robert Lord (Santana Productions)

Associate Producer: Henry S. Kesler

Screenplay: Andrew Solt, based upon the novel by Dorothy B. Hughes, adapted by Edmund H. North

Cinematography: Burnett Guffey

Technical Adviser: Rodney Amateau

Editing: Viola Lawrence

Sound: Howard Fogetti

Music Score: George Antheil

Musical Direction: Morris Stoloff

Art Direction: Robert Peterson

Set Decoration: William Kiernan

Costumes: Jean Louis

Makeup: Clay Campbell

Hair Styling: Helen Hunt

Assistant Director: Earl Bellamy

Cast: Humphrey Bogart (*Dixon Steele*), Gloria Grahame (*Laurel Gray*), Frank Lovejoy (*Brub Nicolai*), Carl Benton Reid (*Captain Lochner*), Art Smith (*Mel Lippman*), Jeff Donnell (*Sylvia Nicolai*), Martha Stewart (*Mildred Atkinson*), Robert Warwick (*Charlie Waterman*), Morris Ankrum (*Lloyd Barnes*), William Ching (*Ted Barton*), Steven Geray (*Paul*), Hadda Brooks (*Night Club Singer*), Alice Talton (*Frances Randolph*), Jack Reynolds (*Henry Kessler*), Ruth Warren (*Effie*), Ruth Gillette (*Martha*), Guy Beach (*Swan*), Lewis Howard (*Junior*), Mike Romanoff as himself

Running time: 92 minutes

The Killers (Universal, 1946)

Director: Robert Siodmak
Producer: Mark Hellinger (Mark Hellinger Productions)
Assistant Producer: Jules Buck
Screenplay: Anthony Veiller, based upon the short story by Ernest
    Hemingway. John Huston worked on a version of the screenplay
    uncredited.
Cinematography: Elwood Bredell
Special Photography: David S. Horsley
Editing: Arthur Hilton
Sound: Bernard B. Brown, William Hedgecock
Music Score: Miklos Rozsa; "The More I Know of Love," music by Miklos
    Rozsa and lyrics by Jack Brooks
Art Direction: Jack Otterson, Martin Obzina
Set Decoration: Russell A. Gausman, E.R. Robinson
Costumes: Vera West
Makeup: Jack P. Pierce
Hair Styling: Carmen Dirigo
Assistant Director: Melville Shyer
Cast: Burt Lancaster (*Swede*), Ava Gardner (*Kitty Collins*), Edmond O'Brien
    (*Riordan*), Albert Dekker (*Colfax*), Sam Levene (*Lubinsky*), Vince Barnett
    (*Charleston*), Virginia Christine (*Lilly*), Jack Lambert (*Dum Dum*),
    Charles D. Brown (*Packy*), Donald MacBride (*Kenyon*), Charles McGraw
    (*Al*), William Conrad (*Max*), Phil Brown (*Nick*), Queenie Smith (*Queenie*),
    Garry Owen (*Joe*), Harry Hayden (*George*), Bill Walker (*Sam*), Jeff Corey
    (*Blinky*), Wally Scott (*Charlie*), Gabrielle Windsor (*Ginny*), Charles
    Middleton (*Farmer Brown*)
Running time: 103 minutes

Kiss Me Deadly (United Artists, 1955)

Director: Robert Aldrich
Producer: Robert Aldrich
Screenplay: A.I. Bezzerides, based upon the novel by Mickey Spillane
Cinematography: Ernest Laszlo
Editing: Michael Luciano
Sound: Jack Solomon
Music Score: Frank DeVol; "Rather Have the Blues," music and lyrics by
    Frank DeVol, sung by Nat "King" Cole
Art Direction: William Glasgow
Set Decoration: Howard Bristol
Makeup: Bob Schiffer
Production Supervisor: Jack R. Berne

Assistant Director: Robert Justman

Cast: Ralph Meeker (*Mike Hammer*), Maxine Cooper (*Velda*), Albert Dekker (*Dr. Soberin*), Gaby Rogers (*Gabrielle/Lily Carver*), Paul Stewart (*Carl Evello*), Wesley Addy (*Pat*), Juano Hernandez (*Eddie Yeager*), Nick Dennis (*Nick*), Cloris Leachman (*Christina*), Fortunio Bonanova (*Carmen Trivago*), Marion Carr (*Friday*), Jack Lambert (*Sugar Smallhouse*), Jack Elam (*Charlie Max*), Jerry Zinneman (*Sammy*), Percy Helton (*Morgue Doctor*)

Running time: 105 minutes

The Lady from Shanghai (Columbia, 1948)

Director: Orson Welles
Producer: Orson Welles
Associate Producers: Richard Wilson, William Castle
Screenplay: Orson Welles, based upon the novel *Before I Die*, by Sherwood King
Cinematography: Charles Lawton Jr.
Special Mirror Effects: Lawrence Butler
Editing: Viola Lawrence
Sound: Lodge Cunningham
Music Score: Heinz Roemheld; "Please Don't Kiss Me," music and lyrics by Allan Roberts and Doris Fisher
Musical Direction: M.W. Stoloff
Art Direction: Stephen Goosson, Sturges Carne
Set Decoration: Wilbur Menefee, Herman Schoenbrun
Gowns: Jean Louis
Hair Styling: Helen Hunt
Assistant Director: Sam Nelson
Cast: Orson Welles (*Michael O'Hara*), Rita Hayworth (*Elsa Bannister*), Everett Sloane (*Arthur Bannister*), Glenn Anders (*George Grisby*), Ted de Corsia (*Sidney Broome*), Erskine Sanford (*Judge*), Gus Schilling (*Goldie*), Carl Frank (*District Attorney*), Louis Merrill (*Jake*), Evelyn Ellis (*Bessie*), Wong Show Chong (*Li*), Harry Shannon (*Cab Driver*), Sam Nelson (*Yacht Captain*)

Running time: 87 minutes

Laura (20th Century–Fox, 1944)

Director: Otto Preminger
Producer: Otto Preminger
Screenplay: Jay Dratler, Samuel Hoffenstein, and Betty Reinhardt, based upon the novel by Very Caspary
Cinematography: Joseph La Shelle

Special Effects: Fred Sersen
Editing: Louis Loeffler
Sound: E. Clayton Ward, Harry M. Leonard
Music Score: David Raksin
Musical Direction: Emil Newman
Art Direction: Lyle Wheeler, Leland Fuller
Set Decoration: Thomas Little, Paul S. Fox
Costumes: Bonnie Cashin
Costumes for Gene Tierney: Oleg Cassini
Makeup: Guy Pearce
Cast: Gene Tierney (*Laura Hunt*), Dana Andrews (*Mark McPherson*), Clifton
    Webb (*Waldo Lydecker*), Vincent Price (*Shelby Carpenter*), Judith
    Anderson (*Ann Treadwell*), Dorothy Adams (*Bessie Clary*), James Flavin
    (*McAvity*), Clyde Fillmore (*Bullitt*), Ralph Dunn (*Fred Callahan*), Grant
    Mitchell (*Corey*), Kathleen Howard (*Louise*)
Running time: 88 minutes

The Maltese Falcon (Warner Brothers, 1941)
Director: John Huston
Producer: Hal B. Wallis
Associate Producer: Henry Blanke
Screenplay: John Huston, based upon the novel by Dashiell Hammett
Cinematography: Arthur Edeson
Editing: Thomas Richards
Sound: Oliver Garretson
Music Score: Adolph Deutsch
Musical Direction: Leo F. Forbstein
Art Direction: Robert Haas
Costumes: Orry-Kelly
Makeup: Perc Westmore
Assistant Directors: Jack Sullivan, Claude Archer
Cast: Humphrey Bogart (*Sam Spade*), Mary Astor (*Brigid O'Shaughnessy*),
    Peter Lorre (*Joel Cairo*), Sydney Greenstreet (*Kasper Gutman*), Lee
    Patrick (*Effie Perine*), Ward Bond (*Detective Tom Polhaus*), Barton
    MacLane (*Lieutenant Detective Dundy*), Elisha Cook Jr. (*Wilmer Cook*),
    Gladys George (*Iva Archer*), Jerome Cowan (*Miles Archer*), James Burke
    (*Luke*), Murray Alper (*Frank Richman*), John Hamilton (*Bryan*), Emory
    Parnell (*Sailor on the* La Paloma), Walter Huston (*Man delivering the
    falcon*)
Running time: 100 minutes

Mildred Pierce (Warners Brothers, 1945)

Director: Michael Curtiz
Producer: Jerry Wald
Screenplay: Ranald MacDougall, based upon the novel by James M. Cain
Cinematography: Ernest Haller
Montages: James Leicester
Special Effects: Willard Van Enger
Editing: David Weisbart
Sound: Oliver S. Garretson
Music Score: Max Steiner
Musical Direction: Leo F. Forbstein
Art Direction: Anton Grot
Set Decoration: George James Hopkins
Wardrobe Direction: Milo Anderson
Makeup: Perc Westmore
Cast: Joan Crawford (*Mildred Pierce*), Ann Blyth (*Veda Pierce*), Zachary
    Scott (*Monty Beragon*), Jack Carson (*Wally Fay*), Eve Arden (*Ida*), Bruce
    Bennett (*Bert Pierce*), George Tobian (*Mr. Chris*), Lee Patrick (*Maggie
    Binderhof*), Moroni Olsen (*Inspector Peterson*), Jo Anne Marlowe (*Kay
    Pierce*), Butterfly McQueen (*Lottie*), Barbara Brown (*Mrs. Forrester*),
    Charles Trowbridge (*Mr. Williams*), John Compton (*Ted Forrester*)
Running time: 109 minutes

Murder, My Sweet (RKO, 1945)

Director: Edward Dmytryk
Producer: Adrian Scott
Screenplay: John Paxton, based on the novel *Farewell, My Lovely*, by
    Raymond Chandler
Cinematography: Harry J. Wild
Special Effects: Vernon L. Walker
Editing: Joseph Noreiga
Sound: Bailey Fesler, James E. Stewart
Music Score: Roy Webb
Musical Direction: Constantin Bakaleinikoff
Art Direction: Albert S. D'Agostino, Carroll Clark
Set Decoration: Darrell Silvera, Michael Ohrenbach
Costumes: Edward Stevenson
Assistant Director: William Dorfman
Cast: Dick Powell (*Philip Marlowe*), Claire Trevor (*Velma/Mrs. Grayle*), Ann
    Shirley (*Ann Grayle*), Otto Kruger (*Jules Amthor*), Mike Mazurki (*Moose
    Malloy*), Esther Howard (*Jessie Florian*), Miles Mander (*Mr. Grayle*),

Douglas Walton (*Marriott*), Don Douglas (*Lieutenant Randall*), Ralf
Harolde (*Doctor Sonderborg*)
The film was originally released as *Farewell, My Lovely* in December 1944
and as *Murder, My Sweet* in 1945 at a running time of 95 minutes.

Night and the City (20th Century–Fox, 1950)

Director: Jules Dassin
Producer: Samuel J. Engel
Screenplay: Jo Eisinger, based upon the novel by Gerald Kersh
Cinematography: Max Greene
Editing: Nick De Maggio, Sidney Stone
Sound: Peter Handford, Roger Heman
Music Score: Franz Waxman
Musical Orchestration: Edward Powell
Art Direction: C. P. Norman
Costumes: Oleg Cassini for Gene Tierney, Margaret Furse for Googie Withers
Assistant Directors: George Mills, Percy Hermes
Cast: Richard Widmark (*Harry Fabian*), Gene Tierney (*Mary Bristol*),
    Googie Withers (*Helen Nosseros*), Hugh Marlowe (*Adam Dunn*), Francis
    L. Sullivan (*Phil Nosseros*), Herbert Lom (*Kristo*), Stanislaus Zbyszko
    (*Gregorius*), Mike Mazurki (*"Strangler"*), Charles Farrell (*Beer*), Ada
    Reeve (*Molly*), Ken Richmond (*Nikolas*), Maureen Delaney (*Anna*), James
    Hayter (*Figler*), Elliott Makeham (*Pinkney*), Betty Shale (*Mrs. Pinkney*)
Running time: 96 minutes

On Dangerous Ground (RKO, 1952)

Director: Nicholas Ray
Producer: John Houseman
Screenplay: A.I. Bezzerides, based upon an adaptation by Bezzerides and
    Nicholas Ray of the novel *Mad with Much Heart*, by Gerald Butler
Cinematography: George E. Diskant
Editing: Roland Gross
Sound: Phil Brigandi, Clem Portman
Music Score: Bernard Herrmann
Musical Direction: Constantin Bakaleinikoff; *Viola d'amour* played by
    Virginia Majewski
Art Direction: Albert S. D'Agostino, Ralph Berger
Set Decoration: Darrell Silvera, Harley Miller
Makeup: Mel Burns
Hair Styling: Larry Germain
Assistant Director: Roland Gross
Cast: Ida Lupino (*Mary Malden*), Robert Ryan (*Detective Jim Wilson*), Ward

Bond (*Walter Brent*), Charles Kemper (*Bob Daley*), Anthony Ross (*Pete Santos*), Ed Begley (*Captain Brawley*), Ian Wolfe (*Carrey*), Sumner Williams (*Danny Malden*), Gus Schilling (*Lucky*), Frank Ferguson (*Willows*), Cleo Moore (*Myrna*), Olive Carey (*Mrs. Brent*), Richard Irving (*Bernie*), Pat Prest (*Julie*)
Running time: 82 minutes

Out of the Past (RKO, 1947)

Director: Jacques Tourneur
Producer: Warren Duff
Screenplay: Geoffrey Homes [Daniel Mainwaring, pseud.], based upon his novel *Build My Gallows High*. Frank Fenton worked on a version of the screenplay uncredited.
Cinematography: Nicholas Musuraca
Special Effects: Russell A. Cully
Editing: Samuel E. Beetley
Sound: Francis M. Sarver, Clem Portman
Music Score: Roy Webb
Musical Conductor: Constantin Bakaleinikoff
Art Direction: Albert S. D'Agostino, Jack Okey
Set Decoration: Darrell Silvera
Gowns: Edward Stevenson
Makeup: Gordon Bau
Assistant Director: Harry Mancke
Cast: Robert Mitchum (*Jeff Bailey*), Jane Greer (*Kathie Moffet*), Kirk Douglas (*Whit Sterling*), Rhonda Fleming (*Meta Carson*), Richard Webb (*Jim*), Steve Brodie (*Fisher*), Virginia Huston (*Ann*), Paul Valentine (*Joe*), Ken Niles (*Eels*), Dickie Moore (*the Child*), Frank Wilcox (*Sheriff Douglas*), Mary Field (*Marny*)
Running time: 97 minutes

Phantom Lady (Universal, 1944)

Director: Robert Siodmak
Associate Producer: Joan Harrison
Screenplay: Bernard C. Schoenfeld, based upon the novel by Cornell Woolrich [William Irish, pseud.]
Cinematography: Elwood Bredell
Editing: Arthur Hilton
Sound: Bernard B. Brown
Musical Direction: Hans J. Salter; "Chick-ee-Chick," music by Jacques Press and lyrics by Eddie Cherkose
Art Direction: John B. Goodman, Robert Clatworthy

Set Decoration: Russell Gausman, L.R. Smith
Costumes: Vera West; the "phantom hat" created by Kenneth Hopkins
Assistant Director: Seward Webb
Cast: Franchot Tone (*Jack Marlow*), Ella Raines (*Carol "Kansas" Richman*), Alan Curtis (*Scott Henderson*), Aurora (*Estela Monteiro*), Thomas Gomez (*Inspector Burgess*), Fay Helm (*Ann Terry*), Elisha Cook Jr. (*Cliff March*), Andrew Tombes Jr. (*Bartender*), Regis Toomey (*Detective*), Joseph Crehan (*Detective*), Doris Lloyd (*Kettisha*), Virginia Brissac (*Dr. Chase*), Milburn Stone (*District Attorney*)
Running time: 87 minutes

Pickup on South Street (20th Century–Fox, 1953)
Director: Samuel Fuller
Producer: Jules Schermer (Jules Schermer Productions)
Screenplay: Samuel Fuller, based on a story by Dwight Taylor
Cinematography: Joe Macdonald
Special Effects: Ray Kellogg
Editing: Nick De Maggio
Sound: Winston H. Leverett, Harry M. Leonard
Music Score: Leigh Harline
Musical Direction: Lionel Newman
Art Direction: Lyle Wheeler, George Patrick
Set Decoration: Al Orenbach
Costumes: Travilla
Wardrobe Direction: Charles LeMaire
Makeup: Ben Nye
Assistant Director: Ad Schaumer
Cast: Richard Widmark (*Skip McCoy*), Jean Peters (*Candy*), Thelma Ritter (*Moe*), Murvyn Vye (*Captain Dan Tiger*), Richard Kiley (*Joey*), Willis B. Bouchey (*Zara*), Milburn Stone (*Winoki*), Harry Slate (*MacGregor*), Jerry O'Sullivan (*Enyart*), Harry Carter (*Dietrich*), George Eldredge (*Fenton*), Stuart Randall (*Police Commissioner*)
Running time: 81 minutes

Pitfall (United Artists, 1948)
Director: André de Toth
Producer: Samuel Bischoff (Regal Films)
Screenplay: Karl Lamb, based upon the novel *The Pitfall*, by Jay Dratler
Cinematography: Harry Wild
Editing: Walter Thompson
Sound: Frank Webster
Musical Direction: Louis Forbes

Art Direction: Arthur Lonergan
Set Decoration: Robert Priestley
Makeup: Robert Cowan, Kiva Hoffman
Hair Styling: Hedvig Mjorud
Production Supervisor: Ben Hersh
Assistant Director: Joseph Depew
Cast: Dick Powell (*John Forbes*), Lizabeth Scott (*Mona Stevens*), Jane Wyatt
    (*Sue Forbes*), Raymond Burr (*MacDonald*), John Litel (*District Attorney*),
    Byron Barr (*Bill Smiley*), Jimmy Hunt (*Tommy Forbes*), Ann Doran
    (*Maggie*), Selmer Jackson (*Ed Brawley*), Margaret Wells (*Terry*), Dick
    Wassel (*Desk Sergeant*)
Running time: 86 minutes

Raw Deal (Eagle-Lion, 1948)

Director: Anthony Mann
Producer: Edward Small (Reliance Pictures)
Screenplay: Leopold Atlas and John C. Higgins, based upon a story by
    Arnold B. Armstrong and Audrey Ashley
Cinematography: John Alton
Special Effects: George J. Teague, Jack R. Rabin
Editing: Alfred DeGaetano
Sound: Leon S. Becker, Earl Sitar
Music Score: Paul Sawtell
Musical Direction: Irving Friedman
Art Direction: Edward L. Ilou
Set Decoration: Armor Marlowe, Clarence Steenson
Costumes: France Ehren
Makeup: Ern Westmore, Ted Larsen
Hair Styling: Joan St. Oegger, Anna Malin
Production Manager: James T. Vaughn
Assistant Director: Ridgeway Callow
Cast: Dennis O'Keefe (*Joe Sullivan*), Claire Trevor (*Pat*), Marsha Hunt (*Ann
    Martin*), John Ireland (*Fantail*), Raymond Burr (*Rick Coyle*), Curt Conway
    (*Spider*), Chili Williams (*Marcy*), with Richard Fraser, Whit Bissell, and
    Cliff Clark
Running time: 79 minutes

The Reckless Moment (Columbia, 1949)

Director: Max Ophüls
Producer: Walter Wanger (Walter Wanger Productions)
Screenplay: Henry Garson and Robert W. Soderberg, adapted by Mel Dinelli

and Robert E. Kent from the short story "The Blank Wall," by Elisabeth
Sanxay Holding
Cinematography: Burnett Guffey
Editing: Gene Havlick
Sound: Russell Malmgren
Music Score: Hans Salter
Musical Direction: Morris Stoloff
Art Direction: Cary Odell
Set Decoration: Frank Tuttle
Gowns: Jean Louis
Makeup: Newt Jones
Hair Styling: Carmen Dirigo
Assistant Director: Earl Bellamy
Cast: James Mason (*Martin Donnelly*), Joan Bennett (*Lucia Harper*),
    Geraldine Brooks (*Bea Harper*), Henry O'Neil (*Mr. Harper*), Shepperd
    Strudwick (*Ted Darby*), David Bair (*David Harper*), Roy Roberts (*Nagle*),
    Francis Williams (*Sybill*), Danny Jackson (*Drummer*), Paul E. Burns (*Desk
    Clerk*)
Running time: 81 minutes

Ride the Pink Horse (Universal-International, 1947)

Director: Robert Montgomery
Producer: Joan Harrison
Screenplay: Ben Hecht and Charles Lederer, based upon the novel by
    Dorothy B. Hughes
Cinematography: Russell Metty
Editing: Ralph Dawson
Sound: Leslie I. Carey, Jack A. Bolger Jr.
Music Score: Frank Skinner
Musical Orchestration: David Tamkin
Art Direction: Bernard Herzbrun, Robert Boyle
Set Decoration: Russell A. Gausman, Oliver Emert
Costumes: Yvonne Wood
Makeup: Bud Westmore
Hair Styling: Carmen Dirigo
Assistant Director: John F. Sherwood
Cast: Robert Montgomery (*Lucky Gagin*), Wanda Hendrix (*Pila*), Andrea King
    (*Marjorie*), Thomas Gomez (*Pancho*), Fred Clark (*Frank Hugo*), Art Smith
    (*Bill Retz*), Richard Gaines (*Jonathan*), Rita Conde (*Carla*), Iris Flores
    (*Maria*), Grandon Rhodes (*Mr. Edison*), Edward Earle (*Locke*), Harold
    Goodwin (*Red*), Tito Renaldo (*Bellboy*), Martin Garralaga (Barkeeper)
Running time: 101 minutes

Scarlet Street (Universal, 1945)
Director: Fritz Lang
Producer: Fritz Lang
Executive Producer: Walter Wanger (Diana Productions)
Screenplay: Dudley Nichols, based upon the novel and play *La Chienne*, by
    Georges de la Fouchardière in collaboration with Mouezy-Eon
Cinematography: Milton Krasner
Special Photography: John P. Fulton
Editing: Arthur Hilton
Sound: Bernard B. Brown, Glenn E. Anderson
Music Score: Hans J. Salter
Art Direction: Alexander Golitzen
Set Decoration: Russell A. Gausman, Carl Lawrence
Costumes: Travis Banton
Makeup: Jack P. Pierce
Hair Styling: Carmen Dirigo
Assistant Director: Melville Shyer
Cast: Edward G. Robinson (*Christopher Cross*), Joan Bennett (*Kitty March*),
    Dan Duryea (*Johnny Prince*), Jess Barker (*Janeway*), Margaret Lindsay
    (*Millie*), Rosalind Ivan (*Adele*), Samuel S. Hinds (*Charles Pringle*), Arthur
    Loft (*Dellarowe*), Vladimir Sokoloff (*Pop Lejon*), Charles Kemper
    (*Patcheye*), Russell Hicks (*Hogarth*), Anita Bolster (*Mrs. Michaels*), Cyrus
    W. Kendall (*Nick*), Fred Essler (*Marchetti*)
Running time: 103 minutes

The Set-Up (RKO, 1949)
Director: Robert Wise
Producer: Richard Goldston
Screenplay: Art Cohn, based upon the poem by Joseph Moncure March
Cinematography: Milton Krasner
Fight Sequences: John Indrisano
Editing: Roland Gross
Sound: Phil Brigandi, Clem Portman
Musical Director: Constantin Bakaleinikoff
Art Direction: Albert S. D'Agostino, Jack Okey
Set Decoration: Darrell Silvera, James Altweis
Makeup: Gordon Bau
Assistant Director: Edward Killy
Cast: Rober Ryan (*Stoker*), Audrey Totter (*Julie*), George Tobias (*Tiny*),
    Wallace Ford (*Gus*), Alan Baxter (*Little Boy*), Percy Helton (*Red*), Hal
    Fieberling (*Tiger Nelson*), Darryl Hickman (*Shanley*), Kenny O'Morrison

(*Moore*), James Edwards (*Luther Hawkins*), David Clark (*Gunboat Johnson*), Philip Pine (*Souza*), Edwin Max (*Danny*)
Running time: 72 minutes

Side Street (MGM, 1950)
Director: Anthony Mann
Producer: Sam Zimbalist
Screenplay: Sydney Boehm, based upon his original story
Cinematography: Joseph Ruttenberg
Special Effects: A. Arnold Gillespie
Editing: Conrad A. Nervig
Sound: Douglas Shearer
Music Score: Lenny Hayton
Art Direction: Cedric Gibbons, Daniel B. Cathcart
Set Decoration: Edwin B. Willis, Charles de Crof
Makeup: Jack Dawn
Hair Styling: Sydney Guilaroff
Cast: Farley Granger (*Joe Norson*), Cathy O'Donnell (*Ellen Norson*), James Craig (*Georgie Garsell*), Jean Hagen (*Harriet Sinton*), Paul Kelly (*Captain Walter Anderson*), Charles McGraw (*Stanley Simon*), Edmon Ryan (*Victor Backett*), Paul Harvey (*Emil Lorrison*), Ed Max (*Nick Drummon*), Adele Jergens (*Lucille "Lucky" Colner*), Harry Bellaver (*Larry Giff*), Whit Bissell (*Harold Simpson*), John Gallaudet (*Gus Heldon*), Esther Somers (*Mrs. Malby*), Harry Antrim (*Mr. Malby*), George Tyne (*Detective Roffman*), Kathryn Givney (*Miss Carter*), King Donovan (*Gottschalk*), Norman Leavitt (*Pete Stanton*), Sid Tomack (*Louie*)
Running time: 83 minutes

Touch of Evil (Universal-International, 1958)
Director: Orson Welles
Producer: Albert Zugsmith
Screenplay: Orson Welles, based upon the novel *Badge of Evil*, by Whit Masterson
Cinematography: Russell Metty
Editing: Virgil M. Vogel, Aaron Stell
Sound: Leslie I. Carey, Frank Wilkinson
Music Score: Henry Mancini
Musical Supervisor: Joseph Gershenson
Art Direction: Alexander Golitzen, Robert Clatworthy
Set Decoration: Russell A. Gausman, John P. Austin
Gowns: Bill Thomas
Makeup: Bud Westmore

Assistant Director: Phil Bowles

Cast: Orson Welles (*Hank Quinlan*), Charlton Heston (*Ramon Miguel
"Mike" Vargas*), Janet Leigh (*Susan Vargas*), Joseph Calleia (*Pete
Menzies*), Akim Tamiroff (*Uncle Joe Grandi*), Marlene Dietrich (*Tanya*),
Joanna Moore (*Marcia Linnekar*), Ray Collins (*Adair*), Dennis Weaver
(*Motel Manager*), Victor Millan (*Manolo Sanchez*), Lalo Rios (*Risto*),
Valentin de Vargas (*Pancho*), Mercedes McCambridge (*Gang Moll*), Mort
Mills (*Schwartz*), Michael Sargent (*Pretty Boy*), Phil Harvey (*Blaine*), with
Joseph Cotton, Keenan Wynn, and Zsa Zsa Gabor

Shooting was completed in April 1957, and the film was released in May
1958 at a running time of 95 minutes. The University of California at Los
Angeles Film Archive discovered a 105–minute version of the film, which
was released in 1977.

Underworld U.S.A. (Columbia, 1961)

Director: Samuel Fuller

Producer: Samuel Fuller (Globe Enterprises)

Screenplay: Samuel Fuller, based upon the *Saturday Evening Post* articles by
Joseph F. Dinneen

Cinematography: Hal Mohr

Editing: Jerome Thoms

Sound: Josh Westmoreland, Charles J. Rice

Music Score: Harry Sukman

Musical Orchestration: Leo Shuken, Jack Hayes

Art Direction: Robert Peterson

Set Decoration: Bill Calvert

Costumes: Bernice Pontrelli

Makeup: Ben Lane

Hair Styling: Helen Hunt

Assistant Director: Floyd Joyer

Cast: Cliff Robertson (*Tolly Devlin*), Dolores Dorn (*Cuddles*), Beatice Kay
(*Sandy*), Paul Dubov (*Gela*), Robert Emhardt (*Conners*), Larry Gates
(*Driscoll*), Richard Rust (*Gus*), Gerald Milton (*Gunther*), Allan Gruener
(*Smith*), David Kent (*Tolly at age 12*), Sally Mills (*Connie*), Neyle Morrow
(*Barney*), Henry Norell (*Prison Doctor*)

Running time: 99 minutes

The Usual Suspects (Polygram/Spelling Films International/Blue Parrot/Bad Hat Harry, 1995)

Director: Bryan Singer

Producer: Michael McDonnell, Bryan Singer

Coproducer: Kenneth Kokin

Screenplay: Christopher McQuarrie
Cinematography: Newton Thomas Sigel
Special Effects: Roy L. Downey
Editing: John Ottman
Music Score: John Ottman
Art Direction: David Lazan
Production Design: Howard Cummings
Set Decoration: Sara Andrews
Costumes: Louise Mingenbach
Makeup: Michelle Bühler
Hair Styling: Barbara Olvera
Cast: Kevin Spacey (*Verbal Kint*), Gabriel Byrne (*Dean Keaton*), Chazz
     Palminteri (*Dave Kujan*), Stephen Baldwin (*Michael McManus*), Benicio
     Del Toro (*Fred Fenster*), Kevin Pollak (*Todd Hockney*), Pete Postlethwaite
     (*Kobayashi*), Suzy Amis (*Edie Finnerman*), Giancarlo Esposito (*Jack
     Baer*), Dan Hedaya (*Jeff Rabin*), Paul Bartel (*Smuggler*), Carl Bressler
     (*Saul Berg*), Phillip Simon (*Fortier*), Jack Shearer (*Renault*), Christine
     Estabrook (*Dr. Plummer*)
Running time: 106 minutes

Where the Sidewalk Ends (20th Century–Fox, 1950)
Director: Otto Preminger
Producer: Otto Preminger
Associate Producer: Frank P. Rosenberg
Screenplay: Ben Hecht, based upon an adaptation by Victor Trivas, Frank P.
     Rosenberg, and Robert E. Kent of the novel *Night Cry*, by William L.
     Stuart
Cinematography: Joseph La Shelle
Special Effects: Fred Sersen
Editing: Louis Loeffler
Sound: Alfred Bruzlin, Harry M. Leonard
Music Score: Cyril Mockridge
Musical Director: Lionel Newman
Musical Orchestration: Edward Powell
Art Direction: Lyle Wheeler, J. Russell Spencer
Set Decoration: Thomas Little, Walter M. Scott
Costumes: Oleg Cassini
Wardrobe Direction: Charles LeMaire
Makeup: Ben Nye
Cast: Dana Andrews (*Mark Dixon*), Gene Tierney (*Morgan Taylor*), Karl
     Malden (*Lieutenant Thomas*), Gary Merrill (*Scalise*), Tom Tully (*Jiggs
     Taylor*), Bert Freed (*Klein*), Ruth Donnelly (*Martha*), Craig Stevens (*Ken

Paine), Robert Simon (*Inspector Foley*), Harry Von Zell (*Ted Morrison*), Neville Brand (*Steve*), Don Appell (*Willie*), Grace Mills (*Mrs. Tribaum*), Lou Krugman (*Mike Williams*), David Wolfe (*Sid Kramer*), David McMahon (*Harrington*)
Running time: 95 minutes

The Woman in the Window (RKO, 1944)

Director: Fritz Lang
Producer: Nunnally Johnson (International Pictures)
Screenplay: Nunnally Johnson, based upon the novel *Once Off Guard*, by J.H. Wallis
Cinematography: Milton Krasner
Special Effects: Paul Lerpae
Editing: Marjorie Johnson
Sound: Frank McWhorter
Music Score: Arthur Lange
Art Direction: Duncan Cramer
Set Decoration: Julia Heron
Costumes: Muriel King
Makeup: Jack P. Pierce
Cast: Edward G. Robinson (*Professor Richard Wanley*), Joan Bennett (*Alice Reed*), Dan Duryea (*Heidt*), Raymond Massey (*Frank Lalor*), Edmond Breon (*Dr. Barkstone*), Thomas E. Jackson (*Inspector Jackson*), Arthur Loft (*Claude Mazard*), Dorothy Peterson (*Mrs. Wanley*), Frank Dawson (*Steward*), Carol Cameron (*Elsie*), Bobby Blake (*Dickie*)
Running time: 99 minutes

NOTES

PREFACE

1. Foster Hirsch also uses such a list of films noirs to make a similar point in his book *Dark Side of the Screen*, p. 10.
2. Barrett, *Irrational Man*, pp. 226–27.

INTRODUCTION

1. Sobchack, "Genre Film," p. 196.
2. Durgnat, "Genre Populism and Social Realism," p. 21.
3. Whitney, "A Filmography of *Film Noir*," p. 321.
4. Appel, "End of the Road," p. 25.
5. Porfirio, "Dark Age of American Film," p. 9.
6. Todorov, *Genres in Discourse*, pp.17–18.
7. Wellek and Warren, *Theory of Literature*, p. 231.
8. Todorov, *Genres in Discourse*, p. 19.
9. Ibid.
10. Tudor, *Theories of Film*, pp. 139, 149.
11. Porfirio, "Dark Age of American Film," p. 17.
12. Borde and Chaumeton, *Panorama du film noir américain*, p. 177, my translation.
13. The most evocative films noirs were shot in black and white. The confluence of aesthetics and the history of the time account for this, I believe. However, the film noir, properly discussed, speaks to the "dark" anxiety and passions that the French recognized in the American cinema of the wartime years. Such a vision may certainly be infused with color. Darkness, as a state of lacking clarity, being lost and helpless, has been the literal device and the metaphor in color of at least one great noir of the last generation, *Chinatown* (1974). Color has been similarly used in other impressive noirs, such as *Point Blank* (1967), *Tightrope* (1984), and *Angel Heart* (1987).
14. Schrader, "Notes on *Film Noir*," pp. 10–11.
15. Harvey, "Woman's Place," pp. 22–23.
16. See Eisner, *Haunted Screen*, pp. 47–48. Throughout her seminal text, Eisner

describes the convergent influences of expressionism and Reinhardt in the staging and lighting of many German films of the period.

17. Eisner writes:

> In any German film the preoccupation with rendering *stimmung* ("mood") by suggesting the "vibrations of the soul" is linked to the use of light. In fact this *stimmung* hovers around objects as well as people: it is a "metaphysical" accord, a mystical and singular harmony among the chaos of things, a kind of sorrowful nostalgia which, for the German, is mixed with well-being, an imprecise nuance of nostalgia, languor colored with desire, lust of body and soul.
> . . . This *stimmung* is most often diffused by a "veiled," melancholy landscape, or by an interior in which the etoliated glow of a hanging lamp, an oil lamp, a chandelier, or even a sunbeam shining through a window creates penumbra. (Ibid., pp. 199–200)

On a further technical note, which can apply to *stimmung* as well as *umwelt*, Barry Salt notes that smudges were painted onto the sets to create a chiaroscuro effect "intensified by soft-edged ellipses and circles of bright light cast on them in the actual shot in the later films. This was not the case in 1921, because the spotlights to do this were not then readily available in Germany" ("From *Caligari* to Who?" p. 122).

18. Kracauer, *From Caligari to Hitler*, p. 33.

19. Erich Pommer, in a previously unpublished interview with George Huaco (in Huaco, *Sociology of Film Art*, pp. 35–36). For sources on the birth and development of the German film industry, see (in addition to Eisner, *Haunted Screen*; and Kracauer, *From Caligari to Hitler*), Manville and Fraenkel, *German Cinema*; and Murray, *Film and the German Left*.

20. Furness, *Expressionism*, pp. 3–4.

21. Sokel, *Writer in Extremis*, p. 50. A clear explanation of the anti-intellectualism behind the expressionist project is found in Geoffrey Perkins's *Contemporary Theory of Expressionism*, in which he writes: "The 'expressionist situation' may therefore be summed up as a situation in which man becomes aware of his God or of a higher spiritual order in the universe, the knowledge of which is not, and can never be, exhausted by man's own efforts at comprehension and intellectual mastery of that universe. It is a situation, consequently, in which he recognizes, or more precisely, begins to feel, that the higher spiritual order is susceptible only to instinct and intuition and that appearances in the natural world are necessarily deceptive. From this proceeds an uncertain and undefined fear in the face of a 'reality' that appears to be preventing a union between man and this higher spiritual order or God" (pp. 97–98).

22. Gordon, *Expressionism*, p. 175. Gordon notes that Matějček "explicitly labeled his thesis 'Expressionism.'"

23. Perkins, *Contemporary Theory of Expressionism*, p. 119.

24. Cardinal, *Expressionism*, pp. 92–93.

25. Mitry, "Cinema," pp. 220–21.

26. Durgnat, *Films and Feelings*, p. 103. Edschmidt held that the visionary expressionist transformed—abstracted—the real world through his visceral encounter with its essence. For a concise description of his fevered ambition, see Eisner, *Haunted Screen*, pp. 10–11.

27. Furness, *Expressionism*, p. 35.

28. Eisner, *Haunted Screen*, p, 23.

29. Murray, *Film and the German Left*, p. 81.

30. Eisner, *Haunted Screen*, p. 251.

31. Monaco, *Cinema & Society*, pp. 137–38.

32. Appel, "The Director," p. 16.

33. Bogdanovich, *Fritz Lang in America*, pp. 87–88.

34. Flinn, "*The Big Heat* and *The Big Combo*," p. 25.

35. Siodmak, "Hoodlums," p. 10.

36. "I think it's not widely known that the script [for *The Killers*] was in fact by [John] Huston," Robert Siodmak said. "His name didn't appear on the credits because he was under contract to another studio [Warner Brothers] at the time, but he wrote the script for us in his spare afternoons (with Tony Veiller cracking the whip occasionally)" (in Taylor, "Encounter with Siodmak," p. 182).

37. McArthur, *Underworld USA*, p. 112.

38. Clarens, *Crime Films*, p. 201.

39. Renoir, *My Life and My Films*, pp. 106, 58.

40. Godard, *Godard on Godard*, p. 254.

41. Borde and Chaumeton, *Panorama du film noir américain*, pp. 155–56. Borde and Chaumeton recognize the first period of "films noirs," from 1935 to 1939, distinguished by the Carné films and Duvivier's *Pépé le Moko*, as one of social study at its best and of facile melodrama at its worst, and the second period, in the middle and late 1940s, as one linked to the naturalism of Zola and to Freud (e.g., Allégret's *Une si jolie petite plage* and *Manèges*). In a rather sordid realism, they believe French producers exploited the postwar cycle in popular response to the American films noirs of the time. They note that, interestingly, none of these films are deliberately situated in an underworld milieu.

42. Courtade, *Cinéma expressioniste*, p. 193, my translation.

43. Borde, "'Golden Age' French Cinema," p. 79.

44. For an excellent historical essay on the birth of this movement, see Andrew, "Poetic Realism," pp. 115–19. Andrew refers to Jean Mitry, whose *Histoire du cinéma*, vol. 4, may be usefully consulted, esp. pp. 291, 325–28, 338–52.

45. Andrew, "Poetic Realism," p. 117.

46. Ibid., p. 118.

47. Jeancolas, *15 ans d'années trente*, p. 270. Also, the title of MacOrlan's book includes the article *Le*, which is popularly omitted from reference to the film title.

48. Raymond Borde, interview published in *Les Cahiers de la Cinémathèque*, no. 5, Perpignan (1972), as quoted in Jeancolas, *15 ans d'années trente*; my translation.

49. See Barsacq, *Caligari's Cabinet and Other Grand Illusions*, p. 82.

50. Guérif, *Le Cinéma policier français*, p. 67, my translation.

51. André Bazin, "The Destiny of Jean Gabin," in *What Is Cinema?* 2:77.

52. Bazin et al., "Six Characters in Search of *auteurs*," p. 37.

53. Borde and Chaumeton, "The Sources of Film Noir," p. 62. From Borde and Chaumeton's *Panorama du film noir américain*, p. 28.

54. "One editor," according to François Guérif, "[Georges Ventillard,] demands that his writers supply French readers, deprived of American novels for political reasons, some 'American' adventures. Léo Malet writes like this of the exploits of Johnny Métal under the pseudonym of Frank Harding" (in Guérif, *Le Cinéma policier français*, p. 19, my translation).

55. Ibid.

56. Bazin, *Jean Renoir*, p. 116.

57. Simsolo, "Notes sur le film noir," p. 29, my translation.

58. In Clouzot's *Quai des Orfèvres*, a weary police detective formerly of the colonies works to solve a city murder and derives his sole satisfaction from seeing his job honorably done. A cynical loner, his only solace in a world that brings him into contact with all elements of humanity in their least flattering circumstances is the little Arab orphan he has adopted. *Quai des Orfèvres* is a rather creaky narrative alongside its American counterparts. Obvious and weak in construction, the story puts its detective through frustrations and obstacles in solving his case similar to those that Don Siegel showed with the much more violent *Madigan* and Harry Callahan tales a generation later on the American screen. The residual sentimentality of the story here detracts from a totally noir vision.

59. Houston, *Contemporary Cinema*, p. 83.

60. *Panique* is based on the novel *Les Fiançailles de M. Hire* by Georges Simenon, who worked on the screenplay and dialogue for the film with Charles Spaak. It was remade as *Monsieur Hire* in 1989 by Patrice Leconte and starred Michel Blanc and Sandrine Bonnaire.

61. Chartier, "Les Américains aussi font des films 'noirs,'" p. 70, my translation.

62. A similar view was expressed by Garbicz and Klimowski in *Cinema, the Magic Vehicle*, 1:482–83.

63. Allégret's noirs featured many of the same actors, who, like the supporting actors of the American noir cinema, achieved a certain familiarity with their audience: Signoret and Bernard Blier (*Dédée d'Anvers, Manèges*) and Jane Marken (*Dédée d'Anvers, Une si jolie petite plage, Manèges*).

64. Borde and Chaumeton, *Panorama du film noir américain*, p. 160.

65. Taken from Ford, *Histoire du cinéma français contemporain*, pp. 246–47.

66. Borde and Chaumeton, *Panorama du film noir américain*, p. 160.

67. Guérif, *Le Cinéma policier français*, p. 99.

68. Borde and Chaumeton, *Panorama du film noir américain*, p. 168.

CHAPTER 1. THE NOIR IN AMERICA

1. Porfirio, "Dark Age of American Film," p. 77.

2. Gurko, *Heroes, Highbrows and the Popular Mind*, p. 279.

3. Robert Warshow, "The Gangster as Tragic Hero," in Warshow, *Immediate Experience*, p. 131.

4. On August 11, 1996, Polonsky took questions after a screening of *Odds against Tomorrow* at Lincoln Center's Walter Reade Theater in New York. He remarked that he wrote the script for the film while working with Tyrone Guthrie on a stage production of *Oedipus Rex* in Canada. He never met the cast or production people of the movie. The story, based on William McGivern's book, was essentially "rewritten" by Polonsky. "I changed the book and wrote the screenplay from the new book," he said. The occasion of the screening, as part of the theater's John Garfield retrospective, was the formal acknowledgment by the Screenwriters Guild thirty-seven years later of his screenwriting contribution to the film.

5. Sherman and Rubin, *Director's Event*, p. 16.

6. It is ironic, of course, that Dassin would find himself the victim of the McCarthy era inquisitions and end up in England and France during the fifties for most of his remaining film career.

7. Undoubtedly the source material of novelist Auguste Le Breton (*Rififi, Bob le flambeur, Razzia*) and his screenwriting participation (*Rififi, Bob le flambeur*) generated an audience attraction for the seamier Parisian criminal milieu.

8. François Truffaut and Claude Chabrol asked Dassin about Harry Fabian's death scene, and he recounted: "The entire scene was shot at dawn. We had the light for less than a half hour. I took twenty-two shots in eighteen minutes with the aid of six cameras. Widmark left the shot from one camera only to enter in one from another. We repeated this several mornings. Widmark played that magnificently" ("Entretien avec Jules Dassin," p. 1, my translation).

9. Alberto Cavalcanti's British noir, *They Made Me a Fugitive*, with Trevor Howard and Sally Gray, was also made in 1947 and has a remarkably similar story with a less tragic ending. Beautifully photographed by Otto Heller, this film shows how the noir lighting stylistics of the studio period were evocatively used in the English cinema.

10. Wilmington, "Nicholas Ray," p. 38.

11. Perkins, "Cinema of Nicholas Ray," p. 8.

12. Telotte, *Voices in the Dark*, p. 69.

13. Alloway, *Violent America*, p. 45.

14. Bazin, *Orson Welles*, p. 119.

15. McBride, *Orson Welles*, p. 11.

16. The final editing of *Touch of Evil* has been a contentious issue "in light of the wholesale re-editing of the film by the executive producer, a process of re-hashing in which I [Welles] was forbidden to participate. Confusion was further confounded by several added scenes which I did not write and was not invited to direct" (Welles, Letter to the editor, p. 666).

17. Agel, *Romance Américaine*, p. 134, my translation.

18. Bessy, *Orson Welles*, pp. 54–55.

CHAPTER 2. THE HARD-BOILED FICTION INFLUENCE

1. Chandler wrote to Blanche Knopf on October 22, 1942, "He is every kind of writer I detest . . . a Proust in greasy overalls" (MacShane, *Selected Letters of Raymond Chandler*, p. 23).

2. Hoopes, *Cain,* pp. 232–33.

3. Harper, *World of the Thriller*, p. 51.

4. See crime fiction critic and historian Julian Symons's "An Aesthete Discovers the Pulps," p. 21.

The private eye thriller is to be distinguished, but not necessarily separated, from the "tough-guy" novel, David Madden wrote in his book on James M. Cain, *Cain's Craft*: "[T]he pure tough novel . . . is a separate type which presents a hard-boiled picture of life for its own sake, without the justification of either an ideology or a conventional form, whether strictly adhered to or consciously violated" (p. 7).

5. Symons, "An Aesthete Discovers the Pulps," p. 21.

6. Rosenbaum, "Black Window," pp. 36, 38. See also the detailed biography by Francis M. Nevins Jr., aptly titled *Cornell Woolrich: First You Dream, Then You Die*, esp. chaps. 5, 21, 23. Woolrich also wrote under the pseudonyms of William Irish and George Hopley.

7. Horace McCoy's *No Pockets in a Shroud* (*Un Linceul n'a pas de poches*) was the fourth entry in this series.

8. Cornell Woolrich, "Hot Water," in Woolrich, *Darkness at Dawn,* p. 282.

9. Cornell Woolrich, "Kiss of the Cobra," in Woolrich, *Darkness at Dawn*, p. 112.

10. Cornell Woolrich, "Momentum," in Woolrich, *'Rear Window' and Other Stories*, p. 143.

11. Woolrich, *I Married a Dead Man,* pp. 7–8.

12. Cornell Woolrich, "Three O'Clock," in Woolrich, *'Rear Window' and Other Stories*, pp. 103, 107, 108.

13. Lacassin, *Mythologie du roman policier*, 2:123, my translation.

14. Deleuze, *Cinema,* p. 164.

15. Certainly Raymond Chandler honored such a man of his own creation when he wrote: "[D]own these mean streets a man must go who is not himself mean, who is neither tarnished nor afraid. The detective in this kind of story must be such a man. He is the hero; he is everything. He must be a complete man and a common man and yet an unusual man. He must be, to use a rather weathered phrase, a man of honor—by instinct, by inevitability, without thought of it, and certainly without saying it. He must be the best man in his world and a good enough man for any world. . . . If there were enough like him, the world would be a safe place to live in, without becoming too dull to be worth living in" (Chandler, "Simple Art of Murder," p. 59).

16. Lattimore, *Story Patterns in Greek Tragedy*, p. 10.

17. Obstfeld, "Opus in G Minor for Blunt Instrument," p. 11, my emphasis.

18. Chandler, *Little Sister*, p. 81.

19. Michael Walker speaks of the private eye as a seeker-hero in his article "Hawks and *Film Noir*," p. 30.

20. I do not include as films noirs here *Time to Kill*, loosely based on *The High Window* and an entry in actor Lloyd Nolan's Mike Shayne series, or *The Falcon Takes Over*, a comedy-mystery loosely based on *Farewell, My Lovely*. Both were released in 1942. Nor do I include the retro-noirs *Farewell, My Lovely* (Dick Richards, 1975) and *The Big Sleep* (Michael Winner, 1978), the former a nostalgic curio of the period and the latter a 1970s-style schematic remake. Both starred Robert Mitchum as a weary but not unattractive Marlowe, and both significantly distorted the novels upon which they were based. Richards's *Farewell, My Lovely*, for instance, does away completely with the character of Anne Riordan and changes the character of Jules Amthor, a man and a psychic, to Frances Amthor, an intimidatingly large madam of an exclusive brothel. The Winner film sets all the action around London rather than southern California.

21. George Grella traced the lineage of the private detective in fiction concisely, when he noted: "Raymond Chandler embellishes the toughness of his Philip Marlowe with compassion, honesty, and wit, and a dimension of nobility that Spade and the laconic Op lack. Lew Archer, named for Spade's partner and modeled on Marlowe, is distinguished beyond the others, for natural goodness. Perhaps the most sympathetic of the hard-boiled dicks, his forte is neither cynicism nor toughness, but a limitless capacity for pity" (Grella, "Murder and the Mean Streets," p. 415). The same parameters apply to the screen adaptations of these characters.

22. Cavell, *The World Viewed*, p. 28. Cavell is speaking about Bogart's films from *The Maltese Falcon* on.

23. Quoted in Pratley, *Cinema of John Huston*, p. 40.

24. *The Big Sleep*, scripted by Jules Furthman, Leigh Brackett, and William Faulkner, was completed in 1945 and sent overseas to be shown to servicemen before commercial release here. In the interim, Bacall's overnight stardom in her first film, Hawks's *To Have and Have Not*, prompted Warner Brothers to reshoot and reedit the film to include more scenes between her and Bogart, thus expanding the role of Vivian Sternwood beyond its status in Chandler's novel. The master of the original version was rediscovered by the Film and Television Archive at the University of California in Los Angeles in 1995. It includes more expository scenes between Marlowe and Bernie Ohls, none of which add to the artistic value of the film as we know it.

   There has been much comment on which screen actor Chandler regarded as the definitive Marlowe. He was obviously pleased with Bogart's interpretation of the character and Hawks's direction of the movie. He wrote to his friend and British publisher Hamish Hamilton, on May 30, 1946: "When and if you see *The Big Sleep* (the first half of it anyhow), you will realize what can be done with this sort of story by a director with the gift of atmosphere and the requisite touch of hidden sadism. Bogart, of course, is also so much better than any other tough-guy actor that he makes bums of the Ladds and the Powells. As we say here, Bogart can be tough without a gun. Also he has a sense of humor that contains that grating undertone of contempt. Ladd is hard, bitter and occasionally charming, but he is after all a small boy's idea of a tough guy, Bogart is the genuine article" (MacShane, *Selected Letters of Raymond Chandler*, p. 75).

25. Bazin, "Death of Humphrey Bogart," pp. 98, 99.

26. Agel, *Romance Américaine*, pp. 168, 170, my translation.

27. Schumach, *Face on the Cutting Room Floor*, p. 21. See also Walsh, *Sin and Censorship*, esp. pp. 100–103, for a particularly disturbing anti-Semitism that infected the formation of the Legion.

28. Schumach, *Face on the Cutting Room Floor*, p. 173.

29. Warshow, "The Gangster as Tragic Hero," p. 130.

30. Cawelti, *Adventure, Mystery, and Romance*, p. 77.

31. Robert Warshow, "Movie Chronicle: The Westerner," in Warshow, *Immediate Experience*, p. 152.

32. Cavell, *The World Viewed*, p. 33.

33. Jacob, "La Tragédie," p. 17, my translation.

34. Madsen, *John Huston*, p. 100.

35. Tuska, *Dark Cinema*, p. 155.

36. Appel, "The Director," p. 17.

37. Shadoian, "America the Ugly," p. 288.

38. McArthur, *Underworld USA*, p. 139.

39. Lourié, who also designed the sets for *The Naked Kiss*, designed the sets for eight of Renoir's films, including *La Grande Illusion* and *La Règle du jeu*.

40. Hardy, *Samuel Fuller*, p. 86.

41. Ibid., p. 36.

42. The more ludicrous examples of these films are his *What Ever Happened to Baby Jane?* (1962); *Hush . . . Hush, Sweet Charlotte* (1964); *The Legend of Lylah Clare* (1968); and *The Killing of Sister George* (1968).

43. Although directed by Rossen, the remarkably poetic *Body and Soul* provokes the viewer to ask whether the beauty and power of this film could have been achieved without Polonsky's screenplay.

44. Aldrich's original plan was to have Callahan learn that Frennessey is a lesbian. See Aldrich's remarks in Combs, *Robert Aldrich*.

45. Ibid., p. 7.

46. In this, Hammer resembles the private investigator, Bradford Galt, in Henry Hathaway's 1946 *The Dark Corner*.

47. Telotte, *Voices in the Dark*, pp. 209–10, quotation on 199. "[T]o speak 'so as not to die'" refers to a related line in philosopher Michel Foucault's *Language, Counter-Memory, Practice*, p. 53. Foucault's line is in turn a riff on literary critic, theorist, and novelist Maurice Blanchot's line that speaks of the need to *write* "so as not to die."

48. Holden, "A Brash Outsider inside Hollywood," p. C1; " . . . looks terminally irradiated" is from the same article.

49. Silver, "Old Hollywood," p. 24.

50. Ida Lupino was one of the very few women directors in Hollywood during the studio era and virtually the only woman directing films noirs. In 1953 she directed *The Hitch-Hiker*, with William Talman, Edmond O'Brien, and Frank Lovejoy. Collier Young was a producer and scenarist who married Lupino (1948–1951) and collaborated with her on these projects. He produced *Beware, My Lovely* (Harry Horner, 1952), starring Lupino and Robert Ryan; *The Hitch-Hiker*; and *Private Hell 36*. Young also wrote the story upon which Fred Zinnemann's *Act of Violence* (1949) is based.

51. Janey Place recognized this in her essay "Women in *Film Noir*," when she wrote: "[I]n *film noir*, it is clear that men need to control women's sexuality in order not to be destroyed by it. The dark woman of *film noir* had something her innocent sister lacked: access to her own sexuality (and thus to men's) and the power that this access unlocked" (p. 36).

52. Shadoian, *Dreams and Dead Ends*, pp. 8–9.

53. Doane, *Desire to Desire*, p. 93.

54. Mingo and Fante share an unfortunately depicted homosexual relationship clearly bound by a sociopathic romanticism.

Chapter 3. Women as Seen in the Film Noir

1. See Kaplan's excellent collection of essays *Women in Film Noir*.

2. Gledhill, "*Klute* 1," p. 17.

3. See Harvey, "Woman's Place"; and Cook, "Duplicity in *Mildred Pierce*." See also Leibman, "Piercing the Truth"; and Boozer, "Entrepreneurs and 'Family Values.'"

4. "For *Mildred Pierce* is one woman's struggle against a great social injustice—which is the mother's necessity to support her children even though husband and community give her not the slightest assistance," wrote Cain to Jerry Wald, the film's producer, in a November 10, 1944, letter (in Hoopes, *Cain*, p. 349).

5. Archer, "*Laura*," p. 13.

6. Tierney's husband at the time, Oleg Cassini, did the costumes for all her Preminger films of the period and was largely responsible for that look of casual chic that Tierney sported throughout the 1940s and early 1950s.

Chapter 4. Noir Production

1. Madden, "Cain and the Movies of the Thirties and Forties," p. 18. See also Schumach, *Face on the Cutting Room Floor*, pp. 63–70.

2. Its disclaimer was often that the story is "based on an actual incident the names and places of which have been changed to protect the innocent."

3. Kerr, "Out of What Past?" p. 52.

4. Miller, "American B Film," p. 31.

5. Ann Savage, who plays Vera, appeared in programmers at the time such as *The Spider*, a 1945 Fox mystery with an early Richard Conte. Tom Neal, after

appearing in numerous B films, was found guilty of involuntary manslaughter after killing his third wife in 1964. He served six years in prison and died in 1972, shortly after his release.

6. Coursen, "Closing Down the Open Road," p. 19.

7. Dumont, *Robert Siodmak*, p. 212.

8. Telotte, *Voices in the Dark*, p. 151.

9. Ibid., pp. 151–52.

10. Borde and Chaumaton, *Panorama du film noir américain*, p. 1, my translation. The revelation of Howard Hawks's *Big Sleep* to French cineasts cannot be overestimated; it provoked the following declaration from Borde and Chaumeton: "[T]out cela fait de *The Big Sleep* une date dans l'histoire du cinéma américain. Jamais le film noir, n'ira plus loin dans la description d'un univers cynique, sensuel et féroce." [That all makes *The Big Sleep* a key moment in the history of the American cinema. The film noir will never go farther in describing a cynical universe, sensual and fierce.] (pp. 70–71).

11. Frank, "Un Nouveau Genre 'policier,'" p. 9, my translation.

12. Wilson, "Dark Mirror," pp. 21, 22.

13. Farber, *Negative Space*, p. 61.

14. Sherman and Rubin, *Director's Event*, pp. 19, 20.

15. The Hollywood "Unfriendly" Ten included Lawson; screenwriters Alvah Bessie, Lester Cole, Ring Lardner Jr., Albert Maltz, Samuel Ornitz, and Dalton Trumbo; producer-writer Adrian Scott; director-writer Herbert Biberman; and director Edward Dmytryk. For an incisive account of the blacklist era and those called to testify, see Navasky, *Naming Names*, esp. pp. 78–155. Lauren Bacall describes the creation of, and her involvement with, the Committee for the First Amendment in her memoir, *By Myself*, pp. 158–64.

16. Polonsky, "How the Blacklist Worked in Hollywood," pp. 45–46.

17. Quoted in Jensen, "Return of Dr. Caligari," p. 38.

18. For a particularly cogent view of the political and social ironies of HUAC, Hollywood, and noir cinema, see Kemp, "From the Nightmare Factory," pp. 268–70.

19. Welsh, "Knockout in Paradise," p. 16.

20. See Hirsch, *Dark Side of the Screen*, p. 200, for a substantive argument on this position.

21. Hughes first acquired and produced the Bartlett Cormack play in 1928 for his newly formed Caddo Company, and Lewis Milestone directed it. This later refilming reflects a decidedly post–World War II environment.

22. William Dieterle also directed *The Turning Point* for Paramount in 1951, starring William Holden, Edmond O'Brien, and Alexis Smith. A reformist-minded film about a crime commission convening to clean up a midwestern city, *Turning Point* was clearly capitalizing on the Kefauver hearings, but it lacked a noir perspective, in which crime as a social study is shown to be motivated by darker human forces. The picture redeems the corrupted democratic institutions and ends on a hopeful note.

23. Raoul Walsh also worked uncredited on this film.

24. Goldman, *Crucial Decade—and After*, p. 196.

25. Stanford, "Joseph Kane," p. 167.

26. Neale, *Genre*, p. 43.

27. Trevor played some of the more interesting women in the forties noirs precisely because she was able to suggest a melancholy acceptance of life's inequities, yet without relinquishing her willfulness and intelligence in pursuit of goals often murderous and venal but just as often romantic. Her 1948 Oscar-winning role in *Key Largo* as the alcoholic lounge singer, Gaye Dawn, is a heartrending depiction of what happens to such a figure when she becomes helpless and remains unloved. Claire Trevor played vulnerable yet tough-exteriored women in their glory—such as Ruth Dillon in *Street of Chance* (1942), Mrs. Grayle in *Murder, My Sweet* (1944), Lilah Gustafson in *Johnny Angel* (1945), Terry Cordeau in *Crack-Up* (1946), and Helen Trent in *Born to Kill* (1947).

28. Mann uses the same style to emphasize the gravity of the exploitation of illegal aliens from Mexico in his later, quasi-noir, law enforcement procedural, *Border Incident* (1950).

29. Missiaen, "A Lesson in Cinema," p. 46.

30. Farber, *Negative Space*, p. 23.

31. Shadoian, "America the Ugly," p. 290.

32. Based on Albert A. Patterson, the Democratic candidate for attorney general of Alabama, who was killed on June 17, 1954.

Chapter 5. The Noir Influence on the French New Wave

1. Godard, *Godard on Godard*, p. 174. This comment originally appeared in the December 1962 interview conducted by the contributing editors of *Cahiers du Cinéma*.

2. Appel, *Nabokov's Dark Cinema*, p. 4.

3. Strangely, the British screen did not find a noir spirit to quite the same degree that the French did.

4. *Le Deuxième Souffle* has been unavailable in the United States for years. An altered version was shown in the French film noir series at the Walter Reade Theater in 1997. Therefore, I have refrained from commenting on a film that Melville himself remarked was a film noir (see Nogueira, *Melville on Melville*, p. 113). *Deux hommes dans Manhattan* (1958) and *L'Aîné des ferchaux* (1962) also claimed to display a noir vision; however, they too have been unavailable to American audiences.

5. Nogueira, *Melville on Melville*, p. 99.

6. Decaë's color cinematography in *Le Samouraï* and *Le Cercle rouge* beautifully illustrates how vivid color, especially in the day for night shooting in Paris and its environs, can evoke the noir mood.

7. Zimmer and Béchade, *Jean-Pierre Melville*, p. 26, my translation.

8. Nogueira, *Melville on Melville*, p. 61.

EPILOGUE:
COMMENTS ON THE CLASSIC FILM NOIR AND THE NEO-NOIR

1. In *More Than Night*, James Naremore discusses these concerns at length and offers what must surely be the most exhaustive applications of the term *noir* collected in book form. Admittedly troublesome, the concepts of film noir are explained here to the extent that one may almost be forgiven for forgetting to recognize the film noir as, above all else, a screen genre.

2. Rich, "Dumb Lugs and Femmes Fatales," p. 8. Rich's piece attempts to draw parallels between the political and ideological preoccupations of America a few years ago—the Oklahoma City bombing, the right-wing Congress of Newt Gingrich, and the O.J. Simpson trial—and the production of a neo-noir cinema.

3. Christopher, *Somewhere in the Night*, pp. 247–62.

4. Likewise, the *homme fatal* has become more malicious in his psychopathic inclination than he was a half century ago. In Curtis Hanson's *Bad Influence* (1990), murderer Alex (Rob Lowe) lends a pornographic element to his intimidation of Michael (James Spader) by videotaping him having sex with another woman and then playing the tape at a party attended by Michael's fiancée and her parents.

BIBLIOGRAPHY

BOOKS

Agel, Henri. *Romance Américaine*. Paris: Éditions du Cerf, 1963.

Alloway, Lawrence. *Violent America: The Movies 1946–64*. New York: Museum of Modern Art, 1971.

Andrew, Dudley. "Poetic Realism." In *Rediscovering French Film*, ed. Mary Lea Bandy, pp. 115–19. New York: Museum of Modern Art, 1983.

Appel, Alfred, Jr. *Nabokov's Dark Cinema*. New York: Oxford Univ. Press, 1974.

Bacall, Lauren. *By Myself*. New York: Knopf, 1979.

Barrett, William. *Irrational Man: A Study in Existential Philosophy*. New York: Doubleday, 1958.

Barsacq, Léon. *Caligari's Cabinet and Other Grand Illusions: A History of Film Design*. Trans. Michael Bullock. Ed. Elliot Stein. Boston: Little, Brown, 1976.

Bazin, André. *What Is Cinema?* Vol. 2. Ed. and trans. Hugh Gray. Berkeley: Univ. of California Press, 1971.

———. *Jean Renoir*. Trans. W.W. Halsey II and William H. Simon. Ed. François Truffaut. New York: Simon and Schuster, 1973.

———. *Orson Welles: A Critical View*. Trans. Jonathan Rosenbaum. Foreword by François Truffaut. New York: Harper and Row, 1978.

———. "The Death of Humphrey Bogart." Trans. Phillip Drummond. In *Cahiers du Cinéma, the 1950s: Neo-Realism, Hollywood, New Wave*, ed. Jim Hillier, pp. 98–101. Cambridge: Harvard Univ. Press, 1985. Originally appeared in *Cahiers du Cinéma*, no. 68 (Feb. 1957).

Bazin, André, Jacques Doniol-Valcroze, Pierre Kast, Roger Leenhardt, Jacques Rivette, and Eric Rohmer. "Six Characters in Search of *auteurs*: A Discussion about the French Cinema." Trans. Liz Heron. In *Cahiers du Cinéma, the 1950s: Neo-Realism, Hollywood, New Wave*, ed. Jim Hillier, pp. 31–46. Cambridge: Harvard Univ. Press, 1985. Originally appeared in *Cahiers du Cinéma*, no. 71 (May 1957).

Bessy, Maurice. *Orson Welles*. Trans. Ciba Vaughan. New York: Crown,

1971. Originally published in the *Cinéma d'Aujourd'hui* series by Éditions Seghers, 1963.

Bogdanovich, Peter. *Fritz Lang in America*. New York: Praeger, 1967.

Boozer, Jack, Jr. "Entrepreneurs and 'Family Values' in the Postwar Film." In *Authority and Transgression in Literature and Film*, ed. Bonnie Braendlin and Hans Braendlin, pp. 89–101. Gainesville: Univ. Press of Florida, 1996.

Borde, Raymond. "'The Golden Age' French Cinema of the '30s." In *Rediscovering French Film*, ed. Mary Lea Bandy, pp. 67–81. New York: Museum of Modern Art, 1983.

Borde, Raymond, and Étienne Chaumeton. *Panorama du film noir américain (1941–1953)*. Paris: Éditions de Minuit, 1955.

———. "The Sources of *Film Noir*." Trans. Bill Horrigan. In *Film Reader 3*, ed. Bruce Jenkins, pp. 58–66. Evanston, Ill.: Northwestern Univ. Press, 1978. Originally published in French in Borde and Chaumeton, *Panorama du film noir américain*.

Cain, James M. *The Postman Always Rings Twice*. 1934. Reprint, New York: Vintage, 1989.

———. *Double Indemnity*. 1936. Reprint, New York: Vintage, 1989.

———. *Mildred Pierce*. 1941. Reprint, New York: Vintage, 1989.

Cardinal, Roger. *Expressionism*. London: Paladin, 1984.

Cavell, Stanley. *The World Viewed: Reflections on the Ontology of Film*. Cambridge: Harvard Univ. Press, 1979.

Cawelti, John G. *Adventure, Mystery, and Romance*. Chicago: Univ. of Chicago Press, 1976.

Chandler, Raymond. *Pickup on Noon Street*. New York: Ballantine, 1973.

———. *The Big Sleep*. 1939. Reprint, New York: Ballantine, 1975.

———. *Farewell, My Lovely*. 1940. Reprint, New York: Ballantine, 1975.

———. *The Little Sister*. 1949. Reprint, New York: Vintage, 1988.

Christopher, Nicholas. *Somewhere in the Night: Film Noir and the American City*. New York: Free Press, 1997.

Clarens, Carlos. *Crime Films: From Griffith to* The Godfather *and Beyond*. New York: Norton, 1980.

Combs, Richard, ed. *Robert Aldrich*. London: British Film Institute, 1978.

Cook, Pam. "Duplicity in *Mildred Pierce*." In Kaplan, *Women in Film Noir*, pp. 68–82.

Courtade, Francis. *Cinéma expressioniste*. Paris: Henri Veyrier, 1984.

Deleuze, Gilles. *Cinema: The Movement-Image*. Trans. Hugh Tomlinson and Barbara Habberjam. Minneapolis: Univ. of Minnesota Press, 1986.

Doane, Mary Ann. *The Desire to Desire: The Woman's Film of the 1940s*. Bloomington: Indiana Univ. Press, 1987.

Dumont, Hervé. *Robert Siodmak: Le Maître du film noir*. Lausanne: L'Age d'Homme, 1981.

Durgnat, Raymond. *Films and Feelings*. London: Faber and Faber, 1967.

Eisner, Lotte H. *The Haunted Screen.* Berkeley: Univ. of California Press, 1973.

Farber, Manny. *Negative Space.* New York: Praeger, 1971.

Ford, Charles. *Histoire du cinéma français contemporain, 1945–1977.* Paris: Éditions France-Empire, 1977.

Foucault, Michel. *Language, Counter-Memory, Practice: Selected Essays and Interviews.* Ed. Donald F. Bouchard. Ithaca, N.Y.: Cornell Univ. Press, 1977.

Furness, R.S. *Expressionism.* London: Methuen, 1973.

Garbicz, Adam, and Jacck Klinowski. *Cinema, the Magic Vehicle: A Guide to Its Achievement.* Vol. 1. Metuchen, N.J.: Scarecrow, 1975.

Gledhill, Christine. "*Klute* 1: A Contemporary *Film Noir* and Feminist Criticism." In Kaplan, *Women in Film Noir*, pp. 6–21.

Godard, Jean-Luc. *Godard on Godard.* Trans. Tom Milne. New York: Viking, 1972.

Goldman, Eric F. *The Crucial Decade—and After: America, 1945–1960.* New York: Vintage, 1960.

Gordon, Donald E. *Expressionism: Art and Idea.* New Haven, Conn.: Yale Univ. Press, 1987.

Grella, George. "Murder and the Mean Streets: The Hard-Boiled Detective Novel." In *Detective Fiction: Crime and Compromise,* ed. Dick Allen and David Chacko, pp. 411–29. New York: Harcourt, 1974.

Guérif, François. *Le Cinéma policier français.* Paris: Éditions Henri Veyrier, 1981.

Gurko, Leo. *Heroes, Highbrows and the Popular Mind.* Indianapolis: Bobbs-Merrill, 1953.

Hammett, Dashiell. *The Big Knockover: Selected Stories and Short Novels.* Ed. Lillian Hellman. New York: Viking, 1972.

———. *The Glass Key.* 1931. Reprint, New York: Vintage, 1972.

———. *The Maltese Falcon.* 1929. Reprint, New York: Vintage, 1972.

———. *The Continental Op.* Ed. Steven Marcus. New York: Vintage, 1974.

Hardy, Phil. *Samuel Fuller.* New York: Praeger, 1970.

Harper, Ralph. *The World of the Thriller.* Cleveland: Press of Case Western Reserve Univ., 1969.

Harvey, Sylvia. "Woman's Place: The Absent Family of *Film Noir.*" In Kaplan, *Women in Film Noir*, pp. 22–34.

Hirsch, Foster. *The Dark Side of the Screen: Film Noir.* New York: A.S. Barnes, 1981.

Hoopes, Roy. *Cain: The Biography of James M. Cain.* New York: Holt, 1982.

Houston, Penelope. *The Contemporary Cinema.* 1963. Reprint, Baltimore: Penguin, 1968.

Huaco, George A. *The Sociology of Film Art.* New York: Basic Books, 1965.

Jeancolas, Jean-Pierre. *15 ans d'années trente: Le Cinéma des français, 1929–1944*. Paris: Éditions Stock, 1983.

Johnston, Claire. *"Double Indemnity."* In Kaplan, *Women in Film Noir,* pp. 100–111.

Kaplan, E. Ann, ed. *Women in Film Noir*. London: British Film Institute, 1980.

Kracauer, Siegfried. *From Caligari to Hitler: A Psychological History of the German Film*. Princeton, N.J.: Princeton Univ. Press, 1947.

Lacassin, Francis. *Mythologie du roman policier*. Vol. 2. 1974. Reprint, Paris: Union Générale d'Éditions, 1987.

Lattimore, Richmond. *Story Patterns in Greek Tragedy*. Ann Arbor: Univ. of Michigan Press, 1964.

Macdonald, Ross. *The Moving Target*. 1949. Reprint, New York: Warner Books, 1990.

———. *The Drowning Pool*. 1950. Reprint, New York: Warner Books, 1993.

MacShane, Frank, ed. *Selected Letters of Raymond Chandler*. New York: Columbia Univ. Press, 1981.

Madden, David. *Cain's Craft*. Metuchen, N.J.: Scarecrow, 1985.

Madsen, Axel. *John Huston*. Garden City, N.Y.: Doubleday, 1978.

Manville, Roger, and Heinrich Fraenkel. *The German Cinema*. London: Dent, 1971.

McArthur, Colin. *Underworld USA*. New York: Viking, 1972.

McBride, Joseph. *Orson Welles*. New York: Viking, 1972.

Mitry, Jean. *"Cinema."* In *Phaidon Encyclopedia of Expressionism*. Oxford: Phaidon, 1978.

———. *Histoire du cinéma: Art et industrie*. Vols. 4, 5. Paris: Éditions Universitaires, 1980.

Monaco, Paul. *Cinema & Society: France and Germany during the Twenties*. New York: Elsevier, 1976.

Murray, Bruce. *Film and the German Left in the Weimar Republic: From Caligari to Kuhle Wampe*. Austin: Univ. of Texas Press, 1990.

Naremore, James. *More than Night: Film Noir in Its Contexts*. Berkeley: Univ. of California Press, 1998.

Navasky, Victor S. *Naming Names*. New York: Viking, 1980.

Neale, Stephen. *Genre*. London: British Film Institute, 1980.

Nevins, Francis M., Jr. *Cornell Woolrich: First You Dream, Then You Die*. New York: Mysterious Press, 1988.

Nogueira, Rui. *Melville on Melville*. New York: Viking, 1972.

Perkins, Geoffrey. *Contemporary Theory of Expressionism*. Frankfurt, Germany: Verlag Herbert Lang, 1974.

Place, Janey. *"Women in Film Noir."* In Kaplan, *Women in Film Noir*, pp. 35–67.

Pratley, Gerald. *The Cinema of John Huston*. New York: A.S. Barnes, 1977.

Renoir, Jean. *My Life and My Films*. New York: Atheneum, 1974.

Ruhm, Herbert, ed. *The Hard-Boiled Detective: Stories from* Black Mask Magazine—*1920–1951*. New York: Vintage, 1977.

Sadoul, Georges. *Chroniques du cinéma français, 1939–1967*. Paris: Union Générale d'Éditions, 1979.

Schumach, Murray. *The Face on the Cutting Room Floor*. New York: William Morrow, 1964.

Shadoian, Jack. *Dreams and Dead Ends: The American Gangster/Crime Film*. Cambridge, Mass.: MIT Press, 1977.

Sherman, Eric, and Martin Rubin. *The Director's Event: Interviews with Five American Film-Makers*. New York: Atheneum, 1970.

Sokel, Walter H. *The Writer in Extremis: Expressionism in Twentieth-Century German Literature*. Stanford, Calif.: Stanford Univ. Press, 1959.

Stanford, Harry. "Joseph Kane." In *Close-Up: The Contract Player*, ed. Jon Tuska, pp. 143–87. Metuchen, N.J.: Scarecrow, 1976.

Symons, Julian. "An Aesthete Discovers the Pulps." In *The World of Raymond Chandler*, ed. Miriam Gross, pp. 19–29. London: Weidenfeld and Nicolson, 1977; reprint, New York: A & W, 1978.

Telotte, J.P. *Voices in the Dark: The Narrative Patterns of Film Noir*. Urbana: Univ. of Illinois Press, 1989.

Todorov, Tzvetan. *Genres in Discourse*. Trans. Catherine Porter. New York: Cambridge Univ. Press, 1990.

Tudor, Andrew. *Theories of Film*. New York: Viking, 1973.

Tuska, Jon. *Dark Cinema: American Film Noir in Cultural Perspective*. Westport, Conn.: Greenwood, 1984.

Walsh, Frank. *Sin and Censorship: The Catholic Church and the Motion Picture Industry*. New Haven, Conn.: Yale Univ. Press, 1996.

Warshow, Robert. *The Immediate Experience*. New York: Atheneum, 1972.

Wellek, René, and Austin Warren. *Theory of Literature*. 3d ed. New York: Harcourt, 1977.

Woolrich, Cornell. *Darkness at Dawn: Early Suspense Classics*. Ed. Francis M. Nevins Jr. New York: Peter Bedrick, 1977.

———— [William Irish, pseud.]. *I Married a Dead Man*. 1948. Reprint, New York: Penguin, 1994.

————. *'Rear Window' and Other Short Stories*. New York: Penguin, 1994.

Zimmer, Jacques, and Chantal de Béchade. *Jean-Pierre Melville*. Paris: Edilig, 1983.

PERIODICALS

Appel, Alfred, Jr. "The Director: Fritz Lang's American Nightmare." *Film Comment* 10, no. 6 (1974): 12–17.

————. "The End of the Road: Dark Cinema and Lolita." *Film Comment* 10, no. 5 (1974): 25–31.

Archer, Eugene. "*Laura.*" *Movie*, no. 2 (1962): 12–13.

Chandler, Raymond. "The Simple Art of Murder." *Atlantic* (*Monthly*), Dec. 1944, pp. 53–59.

Chartier, Jean-Pierre. "Les Américains aussi font des films 'noirs.'" *Revue du Cinéma* 1, no. 2 (1946): 67–70.

Coursen, David. "Closing Down the Open Road: *Detour.*" *Movietone News*, no. 48 (1976): 16–19.

Durgnat, Raymond. "Genre Populism and Social Realism." *Film Comment* 11, no. 4 (1975).

Flinn, Tom. "*The Big Heat* and *The Big Combo*: Rogue Cops & Mink-Coated Girls." *Velvet Light Trap*, no. 11 (winter 1974): 23–28.

Frank, Nino. "Un Nouveau Genre 'policier': L'Aventure criminelle." *L'Écran Français*, Aug. 28, 1946.

Holden, Stephen. "A Brash Outsider inside Hollywood." *New York Times*, Mar. 11, 1994, sec. C.

Jacob, Gilles. "La Tragédie de la rapacité et la poésie de l'echec sont deux thèmes importants de l'univers hustonien." *Raccords*, no. 2 (Mar. 1950): 15–21.

Jensen, Paul. "The Return of Dr. Caligari: Paranoia in Hollywood." *Film Comment* 7, no. 4 (1971–1972): 36–45.

Kemp, Philip. "From the Nightmare Factory: HUAC and the Politics of *Noir.*" *Sight and Sound* 55 (1986): 266–70.

Kerr, Paul. "Out of What Past? Notes on the B *Film Noir.*" *Screen Education*, nos. 32–33 (1979–1980): 45–65.

Leibman, Nina C. "Piercing the Truth: Mildred and Patriarchy." *Literature and Performance* 8, no. 1 (1988): 39–52.

Madden, David. "James M. Cain and the Movies of the Thirties and Forties." *Film Heritage* 2, no. 4 (1967): 9–25.

Miller, Don. "The American B Film: A Fond Appreciation." *Focus on Film*, no. 5 (Nov.–Dec. 1970): 31–48.

Missiaen, Jean-Claude. "A Lesson in Cinema: Interview with Anthony Mann." *Cahiers du Cinéma in English,* no. 12 (Dec. 1967): 45–50.

Obstfeld, Raymond. "Opus in G Minor for Blunt Instrument: The Development of Motive in Detective Fiction." *Armchair Detective* 14 (1981): 9–13.

Perkins, V.F. "The Cinema of Nicholas Ray." *Movie*, no. 9 (1963): 4–10.

Polonsky, Abraham. "How the Blacklist Worked in Hollywood." *Film Culture*, nos. 50–51 (1970): 41–48.

Rich, B. Ruby. "Dumb Lugs and *Femmes Fatales*: *Film Noir* Is Back with a Vengeance, from *The Last Seduction* to *Devil in a Blue Dress,*" *Sight and Sound* 5, no. 11 (1995): 6–10.

Rosenbaum, Jonathan. "Black Window: Cornell Woolrich." *Film Comment* 20, no. 5 (1984): 36–38.

Salt, Barry. "From Caligari to Who?" *Sight and Sound* 48 (1979): 119–23.

Schrader, Paul. "Notes on *Film Noir*." *Film Comment* 8, no. 1 (1972): 8–13.

Shadoian, Jack. "America the Ugly: Phil Karlson's *99 River Street*." *Film Culture*, nos. 53–55 (1972): 286–92.

Silver, Alain. "Old Hollywood: *Kiss Me Deadly*." *Film Comment* 11, no. 2 (1975): 24–30.

Simsolo, Noël. "Notes sur le *film noir*." *Cinéma '77*, no. 223 (July 1977): 23–30.

Siodmak, Robert. "Hoodlums: The Myth . . ." *Films and Filming* 5, no. 9 (1959).

Sobchack, Thomas. "Genre Film: A Classical Experience." *Literature/Film Quarterly* 3 (summer 1975): 196–204.

Taylor, Russell. "Encounter with Siodmak." *Sight and Sound* 28 (1959): 180–82.

Thompson, Richard. "The Flavor of Ketchup: Samuel Fuller Interviewed." *Film Comment* 13, no. 1 (1977): 25–31.

Truffaut, François, and Claude Chabrol. "Entretien avec Jules Dassin." *Cahiers du Cinéma* 8, no. 46 (1955): 3–13.

Walker, Michael. "Hawks and *Film Noir*: *The Big Sleep*." *CineACTION!* nos. 13–14 (1988): 29–39.

Welles, Orson. Letter to the editor. *New Statesman* 55 (1958): 666.

Welsh, James M. "Knockout in Paradise: An Appraisal of *The Set-Up*." *American Classic Screen* 2, no. 6 (1978): 14–16.

Whitney, John S. "A Filmography of *Film Noir*." *Journal of Popular Film* 5 (1976): 321–71.

Wilmington, Mike. "Nicholas Ray: The Years at RKO, Part Two." *Velvet Light Trap*, no. 11 (winter 1974): 35–40.

Wilson, Harry. "The Dark Mirror." *Sequence* 2, no. 6 (1949): 19–22.

DISSERTATION

Porfirio, Robert Gerald. "The Dark Age of American Film: A Study of the American *Film Noir* (1940–1960)." Ph.D. diss., Yale Univ., 1979.

INDEX

Page numbers of illustrations are italicized.

MR 19 '03

DATE DUE